HEY, IRELAND!
ISRAEL'S ON THE LINE

ARE WE PREPARED

FOR A POTENTIAL HOLOCAUST?

AUDREY GRIFFIN

ISBN-13: 978-1-7399098-0-2
Published by Lo Azuvah Publications
Cover artist: Emer Creed

CONTENTS

Acknowledgements

I would like to thank those who have stood by me and have been a support in various ways since I first embarked on this venture almost a decade ago. I am most grateful for the contributions made by the following people:

Catherine Melia for her unwavering commitment to editing the various drafts of the manuscript as it evolved over the years.

Paul and Nuala O'Higgins for their encouragement and enthusiasm.

Ann Glanville who proofread the manuscript in the early days and whose eye for detail was a great help.

The late Bill and Helen Lacy for their keen interest and faithful prayers.

John Gere for his wise counsel and knowledge of Israel.

Husband Tom for his patient love, solid faith and sound advice.

Dad for his steadfast prayers and spiritual mentorship.

Last but not least, the encouragement and moral support of family and faithful friends.

Míle buíochas!

Foreword

This book is a plea to the Irish people to awaken to the truth and examine the broadly held misconceptions surrounding the Middle East conflict. In her erudite depiction of the struggles of the Jewish people, the miraculous United Nations Declaration of 1947 that resulted in Israel again becoming an independent Jewish state and the bonds between Judaism and Christianity, Audrey Griffin's priority is truth, understanding and an end to distortion. Her breadth of knowledge, insight and analysis takes her readers on an original and sometimes entertaining journey of personal enlightenment through the complexities of the tragic and long enduring Israeli-Palestinian conflict and confronts contemporary anti-Semitism. She exposes the wrong path walked over the centuries by Christian churches, their leaders and followers and argues for a deepening of Judeo-Christian relations. "Hey Ireland! Israel's on the Line" is a must read for everyone who values truth and wishes for peace, reconciliation and an end to all conflict between today's Israelis and Palestinians.

Alan Shatter, former Minister for Justice, Equality and Defence

Introduction

Some years ago I attended a Bible college in Jerusalem. Up to that point, I had never had a special interest in Israel – the people or the land. My heart was already receptive to Arabs, since I had previously spent some months helping out in an orphanage in Lebanon. But, regarding the issue of Israel, I was quite ignorant. It wasn't until I spent some time in the Land that my eyes were opened.

Having always had a love for Scripture, I knew the lectures I attended in Jerusalem were in adherence to the Word of God. Thanks to the help of the international lecturers, I no longer see the Bible as a collection of encouraging stories from different times in history. Now I recognise that it is one story, divided into different sections (or books, as the case may be). It is the unique narrative of God's remarkable redemptive plan for mankind.

It was wonderful to befriend at Israel College of the Bible international students and Israelis (Jewish and Arab), all believing in the God of Israel and the Messiah, Jesus. As well as having the option to study Hebrew in the college, a Christian Arab provided Arabic lessons. What a brilliant opportunity this college presented to experience in the Body of Christ a taste of the 'one new man', i.e. Jew and non-Jew united by the Cross of Jesus.[1]

During the ten months I spent that year in Jerusalem, I had opportunities on a daily basis to witness Jews and Arabs interact with one another. I never once saw a Jewish policeman, soldier or security guard treat Arabs any differently to one of their own. As international students and tourists, we were also treated with dignity and respect by the Israelis.

---

[1] See Ephesians 2:14-16 (i.e. chapter 2, verses 14-16).

When I was eight months in the Land, I realised that, although I didn't have any issues with the Jewish people, I didn't yet have a revelation of God's heart for them. So, one day I asked the Lord to give me His heart for the Jews and for the land. About two weeks later it occurred to me that my prayer had been answered. The realisation struck when I was walking down Jaffa Street towards the old walled city of Jerusalem against a stream of Jewish Orthodox families returning from weekly prayer at the Western Wall. This was a familiar sight for me, as I had walked this route many times before. On this particular occasion however, I noticed that my heart was bursting with love for them and I became aware of how endearing they suddenly appeared to me. Let me explain that the black, stark and sombre attire of ultra-Orthodox Jews in no way complements their pale complexions and their serious and guarded manner, and that neither their demeanour nor their appearance could ever be described as appealing or charming. Yet, as I continued walking past them I realised that something very special had happened to me: God had poured His love for His people into my heart – from the secular to the Orthodox, and everyone in between. I had truly received a revelation of the Father's heart for the people and the land, which has become clearer to me in the years following. This does not mean that I think they are perfect; the Jewish people are just as flawed as the rest of the human race. Yet, neither are they the pro-apartheid predators the world typically makes them out to be.

You may wonder why I want the Irish to see a fresh perspective on this issue. For as long as I can remember, I have had a passion for truth and believe in the value of exposing lies and deception. I hate to see people wrongly accused and oppressed. In this book you will discover that anti-Semitism is not a thing of the past. It is alive and kicking. The recent desecration of 10 Jewish graves in Belfast prove this point.[2] I am concerned because the people of

---

[2] The desecration and toppling of 10 Jewish headstones in Belfast's City Cemetery in April 2021 has been strongly condemned by leaders on both sides of the political divide and is currently under investigation by the PSNI, which is treating it as a 'hate crime'.

Ireland seem to have adopted the general European attitude in this regard, while only hearing one side of the story. Whether you have faith in God or not, please allow me to take this opportunity to show you the other side.

It will help to understand the layout of the book. PART ONE provides a general introduction to the subject of Israel. This section focuses mainly on their ancient history and explains in simple terms the purpose of the Jew and the origin of 'Palestine'. It is essential to have some understanding of these rudiments before reading PART TWO, which addresses historic and current political issues relating to Israel. PART THREE provides an in-depth study of Israel's most recent full-scale offensive: the 2014 Gaza conflict. In light of where we now stand on history's timeline and in view of God's prophetic calendar, the reader is asked to evaluate Ireland's current relationship with Israel and carefully consider its future prospects.

Finally, to conclude our introduction: it is a well-established fact that Jesus is Jewish. Are we aware that it wasn't a haphazard decision of the Creator to choose Israel as His birthplace and place of sacrifice? Did you know that Israel is destined to play a major part in 'end times' events, according to hundreds of prophecies from Genesis to the book of Revelation? These are just some of the questions I intend to address, as this is a subject that has become impossible to avoid and one we cannot afford to ignore. Author David Silver says it this way: *'I believe that the truth concerning Israel is the final, and perhaps the most important revelation which God is restoring to the Church since the reformation.'*[3]

Have you heard that Jesus will one day reappear, not as a humble baby, but in majestic glory? Do you know where will that be? The

---

Local Sinn Féin Councillor Steven Corr urged that *'These unbelievable attacks … need to stop.'* See *The Irish Times, Belfast Live,* the *Irish Post,* the *Jerusalem Post,* etc.

[3] David Silver, *A Slow Train Coming: God's Redemption Plan for Israel and the Church* (Haifa, 2007), p. 54.

Old and the New Testament tell us plainly that when He returns, the King of the Jews will set foot on the Mount of Olives in Jerusalem. Therefore, any religious or political leader who demands that the Jewish nation be wiped off the face of the earth is out of touch with Bible prophecy. They are treading on the *territory* of the God of Israel and the place that *occupies* His heart.

Father God, in the name of Jesus, Your Son, and by the power of Your Holy Spirit, we invite You to come and be present with us now. We want to hear Your thoughts on this delicate subject of Israel. We want to know Your truth as conveyed in Your Word. We ask You, Father, to still our hearts and minds as we choose to turn to You for understanding and guidance. Help us, Lord, to submit our will to You. Help us to lay down all prejudice and bias. Forgive us if we have judged Your chosen people out of ignorance. As believers in Jesus – the God of love – and the One who taught us not just to love our neighbour, but our enemies too, we choose right now to reject all forms of prejudice and anti-Semitism. Shine Your light of conviction deep into our spirit and soul. By the power of Your Word, renew our minds, we pray in Jesus' name. Amen.

Part One

Origins And Biblical Foundations

1

Lineage Matters

In his novel, *The Boy in the Striped Pyjamas*, Irish award-winning author John Boyne provides an intuitive insight into the minds of children affected by the Holocaust. Here nine-year-old Bruno, son of a Nazi commandant, asks his older sister why he and his family must be segregated from people in the nearby camp: Auschwitz.[4]

> '"Because they have to be kept together," explained Gretel.
> "With their families, you mean?"
> "Well, yes, with their families. But with their own kind too."
> "What do you mean, their own kind?"
> Gretel sighed and shook her head. "With the other Jews, Bruno ... They can't mix with us."
> "Jews," said Bruno ..."All the people over that side of the fence are Jews?"
> "Yes, that's right," said Gretel.
> "Are we Jews?"
> Gretel opened her mouth wide, as if she'd been slapped in the face. "No, Bruno," she said. "No, we most certainly are not. And you shouldn't even say something like that."
> "But why not? What are we then?"
> "We're ..." began Gretel ... "We're ..." she repeated ..."Well we're not Jews," she said finally.
> "I know we're not," said Bruno in frustration. "I'm asking you, if we're not Jews, what are we instead?"

---

[4] John Boyne, *The Boy in the Striped Pyjamas* (3rd edn, Oxford, 2010), pp. 182–83.

"We're the opposite," said Gretel, answering quickly and sounding a lot more satisfied with this answer. "Yes, that's it. We're the opposite."
"Don't the Jews like the Opposite then?"
"No, it's us who don't like them, stupid."
"Well, why don't we like them?" he asked.
"Because they're Jews," said Gretel.'

JEW AND GENTILE

From a Biblical perspective, there are essentially two people groups in the world, Jew and non-Jew (aka Gentile). A Jew is one who descends from the line of Abraham, through his son Isaac and grandson Jacob.[5] A Gentile is one who originates from anything *other* than that particular ancestry. The reason communities of Jewish people can be found on every continent is because they were exiled long ago from the land of their forefathers. Fed up with their rebellion, the Creator painfully plucked them from the land of Israel and scattered them around the globe. This exile was due to last a long time.

ARABS AND PALESTINIANS

There are over 400 million Arabs in the world, the majority of whom live in the Middle East and North Africa. Arabic is their language, and today Islam is the religion of the majority. So, where does the Palestinian fit into all of this? Those who call themselves Palestinians are non-distinguishable from other Arabs. They possess neither a distinct Palestinian culture nor a Palestinian language. They, like their Arab neighbours, speak Arabic. From the media, we might get the impression that these people have been identified as 'Palestinians' for centuries. In fact up until 1948 it was the Jews of Palestine who were called 'Palestinians'. The following extract explains this critical point:

---

[5] This shall be explained in more detail in chapter 2.

'Throughout the British mandate, the Jews living in Palestine were always carefully referred to as "Palestinian Jews" by the British. This was done in order not to offend the Arabs. The Arabs, who came mainly from Syria, Egypt, Iraq and what is now known as Jordan, scorned the name and were simply referred to as Arabs. After the creation of the State of Israel in 1948, the "Palestinian Jews" became "Israeli Jews" and the name "Palestinian" became almost defunct. A few Arabs did pick up the name "Palestinian" as a way of laying claim to the land, but it was then an unpopular practice.'[6]

It is only since the inception of the Palestinian Liberation Organisation (PLO) in 1964 that the Arabs of the land have been termed 'Palestinian', due to the influence of terrorist leader Yasser Arafat.[7] Thus, the world has been persuaded to believe that the Jews have stolen the land from the 'Palestinians'. This leads us to our next question, which pertains to the dispute over the name of the land: Is it Israel, or should it be called Palestine?

ORIGIN OF THE NAME ISRAEL

The land of Canaan, to which Abraham was called, comprised a number of different people groups. He and his immediate descendants remained as foreigners in the land throughout their lifetime. It was not until hundreds of years after the call (and following the exodus from Egypt) that the time was ripe for his descendants to claim it as their own.[8] The third chapter of Exodus records the various tribes who were occupying the land at the time: *'Now I [God] have come down to deliver them [i.e. the Israelites] from the Egyptians and to bring them up from there to a broad and good land, to a land flowing with milk and honey, to*

---

[6] Ramon Bennett, *When Day and Night Cease* (3rd edn, Jerusalem, 1996), p. 208.
[7] Incidentally, Arafat was born to an Egyptian father and raised in Egypt, not Palestine.
[8] One reason for the 430-year delay was the time required for Jacob's seed to multiply (from twelve sons to a minimum of two million people – enough to fill the land). See Exodus 12:37-38; Numbers 1:45-46.

the country of the Canaanites, the Hittites, the Amorites, the Perizzites, the Hivites and the Jebusites.' Exodus 6 explains that this land was to be their inheritance as promised by God. 'When you enter the land of Canaan, which I give you.'[9] Hence the Israelites took possession of the land[10] as commanded by the Lord. What was once Canaan, and identified by the Israelites as the Promised Land, would now officially become known as the Land of Israel.[11] This would remain the situation until a century after the death and resurrection of the Jewish Messiah, Jesus. And so, for at least 1,100 years the land was called Israel.[12] We are left then with the question: Why did it latterly come to be known as Palestine?

PHILISTINE PERSECUTION

Many of us have heard of the Philistines, the historical enemy of Israel, thanks to the miraculous slaying of their mighty giant, Goliath, by the Israeli shepherd-boy, David. On numerous occasions during Old Testament times, the Philistines stirred up much trouble with Israel. Steve Maltz explains how the Philistines entered the equation: 'These were a seafaring and aggressive people, sailing in from the Mediterranean, who quickly established themselves along the coastal plain and then turned their beady eyes eastwards, toward the land settled by the Israelites.'[13]

In the period leading up to the Christian era, the land of the Israelites came under Roman occupation. Disaster struck when in AD 70 the Romans went on a rampage slaughtering 600,000 Jewish men, women and children in the Jerusalem vicinity and burning the Jewish Temple to the ground.[14] And if things were not

---

[9] Leviticus 14:34.
[10] Psalm 44:3: 'For not by their own sword did they possess the land, neither did their own arm gain deliverance for them; but it was Thy right hand and Thine arm'.
[11] Despite the division of the land into two Jewish kingdoms, God never revoked the name Israel.
[12] Steve Maltz, The Land of Many Names (Reading, 2003), p. 30.
[13] Ibid, p. 28.
[14] This temple, the focal point and liturgical centre of the Jewish faith, was located on

bad enough, a subsequent Roman emperor took the persecution a step further. Tormented by a series of Jewish uprisings and aware of the Philistine's historical antagonism toward Israel, Hadrian in AD 135 banished the Jewish population from Jerusalem and changed the name 'Israel' to *Palæstina*. This was clearly the adapted Roman version of the name Philistine.[15] Even though an attempt was also made to change the name of Israel's capital city, Jerusalem, to Aelia Capitolina, it never stuck. Nonetheless, *Palestine*, the antagonistic adaptation of 'Philistine' remained ... until recent history corrected the misnomer.

STATE OF ISRAEL

When people in this day and age call the land of Israel 'Palestine' they are speaking out of ignorance. In all truth, there is no such place as Palestine anymore. The land in question has been internationally recognised as the State of Israel since 1948, ever since the first proposal for a 'two-state solution' was presented. The Jewish population accepted what was offered to them. The reason why a state of Palestine does not run abreast with it is because the Palestinian Arab leadership rejected it outright. In short, they took the 'all or nothing' route and ended up losing as a result. This will be looked at in greater detail in a later chapter. It is important to realise that attributing the name Palestine to the land today is offensive to the Jewish worldwide community purely because it signifies that they are not entitled to their own land. A consideration of post-colonial Ireland may help us to relate. Whenever people in foreign lands mistakenly say I am from the United Kingdom, I like to bring them up to date – the Republic of Ireland is not part of the UK after all.

---

the Temple Mount in Jerusalem, where the Al Aqsa Mosque now stands. Jewish people continue to gather at the Western Wall to lament the absence of their temple and pray at the ancient holy site.

[15] The name with which we are familiar, Palestine, derives from *Palestina*. Hadrian did this for no other reason than to insult and scourge the Jews.

GOD OF ISRAEL

Are you aware that the Almighty calls Himself the 'God of Israel'? God, who has no beginning or end and lives outside the bounds of time, has attached to His title a people group He created. I find this very significant. One of the earliest examples of God associating Himself with this particular line of people is in the book of Exodus where God challenges Pharaoh to let 'His' people, the Israelites, go. *'I will make a distinction between My people and your people.'*[16] In Exodus 4:22, He calls Israel His *'firstborn son'.* The late Derek Prince (1915–2003), who was a world-renowned Bible teacher and Hebrew and Aramaic scholar, shed some light on another title of the Lord: *'The title of Jesus in eternity is "the lion of the tribe of Judah." Judah is the name from which we get the word Jew. In Hebrew Judah is Yehuda and Jew is Yehudi.'* [17] The New Testament book of Revelation ascribes this glorious title to the One, *'who was and is and is to come'.* God clearly has not given up on the tribe of Judah, so why should we?

GOD OF ABRAHAM, ISAAC AND JACOB

His eternal name He revealed to no other people group than the 'children of Israel.' [18] It was to Israel that God chose to disclose His name, Yahweh (aka 'Jehovah'). *'God said further to Moses, "You tell the Israelites: 'Jehovah, the God of your fathers, the God of Abraham, of Isaac and of Jacob has sent me to you.' This is My name for ever and by this I am to be remembered through all generations."'*[19] God Almighty associates Himself with three human beings of a certain lineage: Abraham, Isaac and Jacob. Were we to ask Him why He has done such a thing, He might say it serves as a reminder to the Jews neither to forget their God nor their identity, so that they can carry out the task to which they were called.

---

[16] Exodus 8:23.
[17] Derek Prince, *Prophetic Guide to the End Times* (Michigan, 2008), p. 119.
[18] When the Bible mentions the 'children of Israel', it is referring to Jacob's descendants. This is because God changed Jacob's name to Israel; see Genesis 32:28.
[19] Exodus 3:15.

Lineage matters. Is it a warning to them not to assimilate into the surrounding nations and cultures? Perhaps it is to show the Gentiles that we ought to be careful how we treat the Jews – God's people. Lineage matters. Maybe it serves to remind the church not to forget her roots. Church of Jesus Christ, please remember your roots are in Judaism. Do not forget to honour your parents. Lineage matters. By associating Himself with the nation which He birthed, I believe this sovereign God is reminding us that He has a perfect plan that is unfolding even now – a plan, which like an endless thread is woven through the fabric of history.

TRINITY

If you are not truly convinced that lineage matters and, if you are inclined to believe that God learned from His mistakes in calling a nation to be His own and pursued a different strategy in the New Testament, then let me share some scriptures with you that may help clarify the matter. In the beginning, God said, *'Let Us make man in Our image, after Our likeness.'*[20] God is speaking in the plural form. The Holy Spirit has been in existence from eternity. We are first introduced to Him in the opening chapter of the Bible, which speaks of the 'Spirit of God' hovering over the waters. Many other verses throughout the Old Testament indicate that the one true God is made up of three distinct persons – Father, Son and Holy Spirit. This explains why, when reading the Old Testament in the Hebrew language, the plural form *Elohim* is used for 'God' instead of the singular form: *El*.

JESUS, SON OF GOD

Jesus Christ is not elected to the Trinity or elevated to the position of 'God' following His successful appearance in the New Testament. He, the Word of God, who has always existed, humbled Himself and forsook His heavenly throne. (*'In the beginning was the Word, and the Word was with God, and the*

---

[20] Genesis 1:26.

Word was God.'[21]) While among His disciples on earth, the Son of God neither concealed His eternal existence nor His identity: *'Now, Father, glorify Me alongside Yourself. Give Me the same glory I had with You before the world existed.'*[22]

In God's plan to redeem mankind, the Jewish Jesus is not a last-minute addition to the script.[23] The Producer had Him in mind from the very beginning to play the lead role. Although we see only subtle appearances of Him in the first act, He is very much present behind the scenes. Indeed, the Old Testament points to the coming Messiah. *('Then, beginning at Moses and through all the prophets He [Jesus] explained to them in all the Scriptures what referred to Himself.'*[24])

NATIVE ISRAELI PRIEST

Allow me to introduce Father Gabriel Nadaf. Here is a non-Jewish native Israeli who differentiates between his roots and those of the Arabs. In a televised interview in 2014, *Breaking Israel News* reporter Josh Reinstein commented: *'Father Nadaf, you always call the local Christian community here Israeli Christians, never Arab Christians, which is what people call them all over the world. They call them the Arab Christian community in Israel'.* Father Nadaf's response explained why he makes this distinction. (It will help to bear in mind that he is not a native English speaker). *'Because the local Christian here in Israel has been for 2,000 years, before the Arabs [came to] this land. And ... Jesus Christ [spoke] Hebrew, not speak Arabic.'*[25] If nothing else, it is clear in the eyes of this native Israeli priest that lineage matters.[26]

---

[21] John 1:1; See also Philippians 2:6-7.

[22] John 17:5; CJB.

[23] Revelation 13:8; KJB: *'... the Lamb [Jesus – Lamb of God] slain from the foundation of the world'.*

[24] Luke 24:27.

[25] *Israel Now News*: Ask the Source; August, 2014.

[26] If only Pope Francis had invited Fr Nadaf to the Vatican, instead of the terror-supporting Palestinian Authority leader Mahmoud Abbas, then he might not have chosen to publicly recognise the statehood of Palestine.

ROYAL LINEAGE

Every person on earth today is either a Gentile or is of Jewish descent. That is not to say that one is superior, or more highly favoured. In the words of Irish authors Paul and Nuala O'Higgins: *'[God's] promise is to bless the nations and His salvation is for Jew and Gentile without distinction ... Though salvation is from the Jews, it is for all.'* [27] Salvation can be found in Jesus Christ alone and is for all who will receive it. However, it is important to understand that Jesus is not of Gentile lineage.

It is no accident or oversight that the Son of God enters history as a Jew. His ancestry was not randomly chosen. He was destined to be of the line of King David[28] and a descendant of Abraham, Isaac and Jacob. The genealogy in the opening verses of the New Testament remind us of the importance of such a selection: *'Jesus Christ, son of David, son of Abraham.'* [29] So attentive to detail is God that, the Messiah is born just at the right time in order for the population census to direct Joseph and Mary to Bethlehem and in order for the star to guide the wise men from the East. It is certainly no coincidence that the King of the Jews (who becomes the Saviour of the world) is born in Israel. We will explore the reasons for this a little further down the line. But for now, it will suffice to bear in mind: Lineage matters.

---

[27] Paul & Nuala O'Higgins, *In Israel Today with Yeshua. A Believer's Guidebook to Israel* (4th edn, Florida, 2004), p. 28.
[28] Luke 2:4 says: *'He was of the house and lineage of David.'*
[29] See Matthew 1:1-16.

2

'It's For You!'

TELECOMMUNICATIONS

In the 1980s British Telecom (BT) produced a series of TV advertisements with a catchy slogan. One ad depicts the climax of the movie the *'Hunchback of Notre Dame'*. Quasimodo is captured high up in the cathedral tower taunted by the menacing mob below, when all of a sudden he hears a ringing sound. But these are no church chimes. An outstretched arm produces a phone, as the mob shouts in jest, *'It's for you-hoo!'* The Hunchback is relieved to hear his darling Esmerelda on the other end of the line. Another ad captures a frustrated Robin Hood, who with bow and arrow has unsuccessfully been trying to shoot a letter through the castle window of his beloved Maid Marian. Suddenly, an extended arm with a phone appears, along with the familiar, *'It's for you-hoo!'* A third ad features a tribe of Indians fighting against the cavalry, who are momentarily interrupted by that same extended arm ...

ABRAHAM'S CALLING

The Bible teaches that Abram was born in Ur of the Chaldees (located in modern-day Iraq). He wasn't a Jew, as there was no such thing at the time. He was, however, a man of great faith. Out of the blue, Abram got a call from God: *'The Lord said to Abram, "As for you, leave your land, your relatives and your father's household for a land which I will show you."'*[30] Abram forsook all

---

[30] Genesis 12:1. Before God changed his name to Abraham, he was called *Abram*.

15

comforts and security and taking his wife Sarah, nephew Lot, and a few servants set out for this distant land of Canaan. The not-so-young Abram would never again set foot on the soil of his ancestors. To a childless man of seventy-five, the Lord made an amazing promise. He vowed to give him a thriving progeny: *'I will make you into a great nation. I will bless you and make your name famous and you shall be a blessing.'* [31] Abram's offspring would multiply copiously.

ABRAHAM'S DESCENDANTS

'I will bless those who bless you and upon him who insults you I will put my curse. Also in you all the families of the earth shall be blessed.' [32] Because we know that Abraham in his lifetime went no further than the land of Canaan and had no means of blessing the whole earth, it is clear that God was referring to his collective descendants throughout the ages. It is still relevant that those who fail to bless the nation of Israel will miss out on a blessing; equally, those who mistreat Israel in any way can expect a Divine response. Additionally, all the families of the earth (every tribe and nation) would be blessed through the offspring of Abraham, namely Jesus the Messiah. Here we see that the Gospel (aka Good News) was alluded to in God's address to Abraham, about 2,000 years before Christ was born. New Testament writers recognise this: *'in anticipation that God would justify the Gentiles through faith, the Scripture foretold the good news to Abraham in the promise, "In you will all the nations be blessed."'* [33] Hence, with the call of Abram, God introduced His global redemption plan.

COVENANT-KEEPER

In times of old when a person 'gave his word' it was taken seriously. Nowadays, breaking a promise is as easy as crossing

---

[31] Ibid, verse 2.
[32] Ibid, verse 3.
[33] Galatians 3:8; see also Acts 3:25–6.

your fingers. *'The Eternal One of Israel,'* on the other hand, *'will not lie ... because he isn't a mere human being subject to changing his mind.'*[34] The Creator of the universe does not operate according to the laws of our fallen human nature. Hence, when He attaches the word 'eternal' to a promise we ought to take note.

In the Bible the word covenant is used. A covenant is more than a promise. One might say that it is a binding agreement between two parties, usually initiated by the stronger party. With that in mind, let's return to the call of Abram, focusing specifically on a covenant God made with him. Abram was already a pilgrim in the land of Canaan for almost a quarter of a century; he was ninety-nine years of age (and yet without the heir of promise) when the Lord appeared to him, saying: *'I am God Almighty ... I will make My covenant between Me and you and I will in a most unusual way multiply you ... Your name shall no longer be Abram but your name shall become Abraham, because I have designated you a father of many nations.'*[35]

ETERNAL COVENANT

What were the terms of this particular contract? To begin with, God specified the duration of the covenant. *'I will establish My covenant between Me and you and your descendants in their successive generations for an everlasting covenant, to be your God and your offspring's after you.'*[36] The covenant would have no end. It would not finish in Abraham's lifetime, nor in that of his descendants yet to be born. It is a covenant that no one could break. If it could be broken God, who lives outside the boundaries of time and knows the end from the beginning, would never have called it 'everlasting'. And what is the covenant in question? It is the vow to be their God for all time.

Another term of the contract relates to property. *'To you and to*

---

[34] 1 Samuel 15:29; CJB.
[35] Genesis 17:1-5.
[36] Ibid, 17: 7.

your descendants after you I will give the country to which you have migrated – the whole Canaanite country – for an everlasting possession.' [37] Once again, there can be no ambiguity about the duration of his descendants' claim to the land. For all time God has granted the specific land in question to the sons of Abraham. But, to which line of sons was it promised? To those who descended from his wife, Sarah. *'But My covenant I will establish with Isaac, whom Sarah will bear you this season next year.'* [38] A little later, God re-establishes His covenant with Abraham through his son, Isaac and subsequently through his grandson, Jacob. I believe He did this in order to eradicate any possible confusion regarding the heir of promise.

COVENANT SIGN

In His covenant dealings with man, the Lord often either *gave* a covenant sign or *required* one from the other party. For example, in His covenant with Noah, God gave the sign of the rainbow. This would serve to remind the Creator of His promise to never again submerge the earth in water. In the case of the Abrahamic Covenant, a sign would be required from Abraham's descendants, whereby every male child would be circumcised on the eighth day. *'God said to Abraham, "You must keep My covenant, you and your descendants after you in their respective generations and this is My covenant ... Every male of you shall be circumcised; you must circumcise the flesh of your foreskin; it shall be for a covenant sign between Me and you."'* [39] Thus circumcision was proof of the existence of the covenant. In obedience, the descendants of Abraham, Isaac and Jacob around the world today continue to carry out circumcision.

---

[37] Ibid, verse 8.
[38] Ibid, verse 21.
[39] Ibid, 17:9-11.

SEALING THE COVENANT

Before envelopes were introduced, letters were sealed by an impression made in hot wax. The function of the seal was not only to bind but to authenticate the document. (In the Book of Esther, the king's signet ring was used to substantiate the royal decree.) In the Genesis account, God informed Abraham that a blood sacrifice was required in order to 'seal the deal': *"'Get me a three-year-old heifer, a three-year-old she-goat, a three-year-old ram, a turtledove and a young pigeon." All these he [Abraham] got himself and cut them into halves, then laid the halves opposite each other.'* [40] Soon after, Abraham was overcome by a deep sleep. It was during this curious sleep of Abraham's that the Lord completed the ceremonial act. *'When the sun had set and dense darkness had come, there appeared a smoking oven and a burning torch passing between those pieces.'* [41] The 'burning torch' alludes to God. He is the One who passed between the sacrificial offerings. Incidentally, the coming Messiah is also described in later times by one of the prophets as a *burning torch.*[42] As Jesus came as a burning torch to endorse the Abrahamic Covenant – the initial covenant that spoke of God's plan to redeem mankind – He would come again in the future as a burning torch to ratify the New Covenant.

UNCONDITIONAL COVENANT

That God alone validated the contract was not the usual practice of the day. Traditionally, both parties were required to pass between the sacrificial offerings. What was the significance of this unorthodox ritual? God was highlighting that the covenant was 'unconditional'. When a covenant is conditional, certain conditions have to be met in order for the covenant to remain valid. An unconditional covenant has no terms of agreement that can warrant it dissolvable. Whoever is the recipient of the

---

[40] Ibid, 15:9-10.
[41] Ibid, 15:17.
[42] See Isaiah 62:1. Note that *Yeshua* (Hebrew for Jesus) means *salvation.*

covenant – in this case Abraham and his descendants through Isaac and Jacob – could do nothing whatsoever that would cause the Lord to terminate it. This is one reason why it is termed a covenant of grace. However much they break God's laws the covenant will remain. That is not to say that the Almighty will not punish Abraham's descendants for rebellion. That He does. Even so, the covenant made with the nation remains unconditional and forever binding.

RUTH'S CALLING

What, you may ask, has a Gentile lady from the land of Moab (modern-day Jordan) got to do with this? To begin with, Ruth is no insignificant character in Scripture. Let's review her biography to see what we can glean from it. Following the death of her husband and two sons in the land of Moab, Naomi (Ruth's mother-in-law) set out to return to her home in Bethlehem. Although encouraged to go home to her parents and remarry, Ruth was determined not to abandon Naomi and insisted on offering the remainder of her life in service to her. She put the needs of her grieving, Jewish mother-in-law before her own and said, *'Wherever you go, there I will go; wherever you lodge I will lodge. Your people are my people, and your God is my God; wherever you die I will die, and there I shall be buried. Thus may God do to me and worse if anything but death separates you and me.'* [43] For her faithfulness Ruth received ample blessings. Not only did the God of Israel provide work and food for this stranger in a foreign land, but He orchestrated for her to capture the affection of a kind, prominent Jewish man called Boaz. The late David Pawson, a prolific writer, explained the significance of this God-ordained union: *'Ruth was one of the earliest Gentiles to embrace the God of Israel. She is a picture of all believers who are in the royal line, brothers of Jesus through faith in him ... If the Church is like Ruth, Boaz is like Christ – the kinsman redeemer. The Church has been brought into the line of the Old Testament people*

---

[43] Ruth 1:16-17.

of God.'[44]

Ruth's testimony is recorded in the annals of Jewish history. Not only did she become great-grandmother of King David, but she also became ancestor to the King of the Jews, Jesus Christ. This was no accident or coincidence; the Moabitess was answering the call. *'Ruth's right choice in joining with Naomi and returning to be part of her people was part of God's right choice, for he had chosen her to be part of the royal line.'* [45] The Body of Christ would do well to remember that we, like Ruth, are the ones who have been grafted into the family of the Jewish Messiah.[46]

GENTILE FRIEND

The name 'Ruth' derives from an ancient Hebrew word meaning 'friend'. How apt is that? She is *a friend who sticks closer than a sister* you might say. Ruth is a Gentile who bound her whole uncertain future to a descendant of Abraham, Isaac and Jacob. This required faith. She even adopted Naomi's God as her own and wished to be buried not at home in Jordan, but in the land of Israel. What lesson can be learnt from the life of such an honourable lady? Fellow Gentile believers and men and women of Ireland, Israel needs friends. She is alone in the world, bereft of much of her family, surrounded by foreigners in far-away places. She is desperate for support and Gentiles whom she can call *friends.*

RIGHTEOUS GENTILES

'A new command I give you: Love one another. As I have loved you, so you must love one another.' [47] The type of love that Jesus promotes is an all-inclusive love. The God of Israel is looking for believers in His Son to show compassion to His people. Jewish

---

[44] David Pawson, *Unlocking the Bible. A unique overview of the whole Bible* (London, 2007 edn), p. 264.
[45] Ibid, p. 260.
[46] See Romans 11:1–20.
[47] John 13:34; NIV, 1984.

people have a term they use for those from the nations who have empathised and suffered on their behalf. These they call 'Righteous Gentiles'. Ruth could easily be considered one. She, a Gentile, stepped out in faith and bound her life and service to an Israeli. Let those of us who have bound our life to the Jewish Jesus love and serve His brothers and sisters in Israel and in all the countries where they have been dispersed.

Hey Ireland, 'It's for you!' Ruth's on the line.

It appears she's recruiting.

Will you answer the call?

3

Stepping Out Of Line

Run with the herd, follow suit and stand in line like everyone else. This is what society expects of us. By setting the children of Israel apart, God was deliberately calling them to step *out* of line. They would be noticeably different, as they conformed to His Kingdom standards. Alternatively, 'stepping out of line' has a negative connotation. More often than not, it is associated with misbehaving, and entails crossing a boundary. Yet, without a boundary, it's impossible to step out of line. In this chapter we will question the need for boundaries and see the relevance of both interpretations of the idiom. We'll begin by asking: What was the purpose of being set apart?

SIN CAUSES SEPARATION

To understand the purpose of the call, we need to revisit the Garden of Eden. God never intended for mankind to lose intimate fellowship with Him. Humans were not supposed to separate themselves from God through sin. A serious consequence was that they bought into the lie that there are many gods (such as the sun, kings, etc.). The tribes and nations became warped by putting their trust in these non-existent gods. To set mankind straight, God would select a people group to represent Him on the earth; these ambassadors would be the voice and the visible expression of the invisible Godhead. In other words, their calling was prophetic (in the directional sense) in nature and required of them to shine a spotlight on the Creator, on what He says to be true, and to redirect the worshipful gaze of humanity back to Him the one, true God.

UNDESERVING

But, who would go for Him? He wouldn't choose a popular bunch, as the focus was supposed to be on Him. The job required not a self-sufficient, but a God-dependant people: *'It was not because you were greater in numbers than any other nation that the Lord ... chose you; for you were the least of all peoples. No, it was because the Lord loved you.'* [48] Even if others reject and scorn His people, His love toward them is eternal. God professes to love them *'with an everlasting love.'* [49] At the same time, He is not afraid to point out Israel's stubbornness: *'It is not because of any merit you may possess that the Lord your God will be granting you this good land, for you are a stiff-necked people ... from the day you came out from ... Egypt until your arrival here, you have been rebellious against the Lord.'* [50]

PERSONAL TRAINER

God raised up this people to be His own, a *'people I formed for Myself'* [51]; He would be their personal trainer. Their mission was to educate the surrounding nations that turning to idols is deeply offensive to the Creator, who says: *'You shall have no other gods before Me.'* [52] They were to exemplify the integrity set out in the Creator's manual [53]: *'You shall not behave ... as they do in the land of Canaan where I am taking you ... You will practice My regulations ... I am the Lord your God. Therefore keep My law and My ordinances; whoever practices them enjoys life through them.'* [54] This was to be an exemplary family for the whole world to imitate.

---

[48] Deuteronomy 7:7, 8.
[49] Jeremiah 31:3.
[50] Deuteronomy 9:6, 7.
[51] Isaiah 43:21a.
[52] Exodus 20:3; NIV 1984.
[53] See the Ten Commandments in Exodus 20 and Deuteronomy 5.
[54] Leviticus 18:3–5.

PROPHETS OF THE ONE TRUE GOD

This prophetic nation would impart His laws to mankind, in order that all would know when they have sinned.[55] They would be holy – separated from the sin of the world – as He is (*'For you are a holy people, set apart to the Lord your God.'*[56]). They would lead the nations not by subjugating, but by serving them.[57] These servants would bring glory to Him.[58] And, the whole world would come to know Yahweh, Creator God, through them.[59] Although that was the plan, the majority of Israelites missed the whole point of it. They failed to recognise the goal of their calling, and the purpose of the Law.

LAW IS GOOD

The mere mention of 'the law' can sometimes evoke a negative response. Might this be because we expect our law enforcers to be perfect? Judges and Gardaí are bound to disappoint us some of the time because imperfect people cannot enforce the law perfectly. When people speak of God's Law, they are usually referring to the instructions of God imparted to Israel through the prophet Moses.[60] Regarding it, the New Testament informs us that the Law is of the Spirit; the Law is just and good.[61] No wonder Jesus said He did not come to abolish the Law, but to fulfil it. Thus, when God prescribed His instructions for mankind, He was doing something good. To say the least, without God's law of gravity and without His laws governing the sun, moon and stars mankind could simply not exist. Similarly, the instructions He gave regarding our conduct are for our good and protection. Try to imagine life without it, a world

---

[55] Romans 7:7: *'Were it not for the Law, we should not have known sin.'*
[56] Deuteronomy 7:6; see also 2 Corinthians 6:17 AMP; Isaiah 52:11.
[57] Isaiah 43:10: *'"You are My witnesses," says the Lord, "and My servant whom I have chosen."'*
[58] Ibid 43:21, NIV 1984: *'...that they may proclaim My praise.'*
[59] Ibid 49:6: *'I will make you a light to the nations that My salvation may reach to the end of the earth.'*
[60] The other important aspect of the Law (the sacrificial system) will be dealt with in the next chapter.
[61] See Romans 7.

where anything coveted was stolen – without shame or condemnation; where anyone who caused offence was assassinated – without legal conviction or any consciousness of guilt. That kind of world doesn't bear thinking about.

FUNCTIONS OF THE LAW

Sin, like cancer, will not disappear of its own accord. Untreated, it will multiply and destroy. This cancer has been growing since mankind first rebelled against God. So here we are now in the twenty-first century influenced and affected by the sins of our ancestors, while at the same time grappling with our own sin nature. Had God never introduced the Law, we probably wouldn't have a clue what is right and wrong and wouldn't have a proper grasp of the principles of life. Other functions of the Law are: to enable us to see that sin harms us and those around us; to introduce punishment, both as a deterrent, and to reinforce that sin ultimately results in separation, pain and torment; and to bring awareness of our need to seek forgiveness and reconciliation.

Heavenly Father is pure and sin cannot enter His presence. Are you aware that, not a single person who has ever walked the face of the earth (save Jesus) has kept all of the Ten Commandments without fail? The Bible clearly says that all have sinned: *'There is none righteous; not even one ... All have strayed ... There is none doing right, not even one ... For all have sinned.'* [62] Enabling us to see that every one of us is a sinner, who has fallen short of God's standard of righteousness, dispels the popular myth that all mankind will get to heaven.

WHAT THE LAW WAS NOT

Knowing the right thing to do and doing it, however, are two very different things. How frustrating it is not to be able to do what we know is right. The Law was never meant to deal with our sin

---

[62] Ibid 3:10, 12, 23.

nature and eradicate the curse of sin. *'The law ... can never, by the same sacrifices repeated endlessly year after year, make perfect those who draw near to worship.'*[63] It serves to inform us of the Creator's standards, but has no power in itself to enable us to obey.[64] God never once expected anyone in all of history to attain righteousness by means of legalistic observance of His commands. That was not the goal of the Law.

FAILURE TO RECOGNISE THE GOAL

In the oft-recited prayer of Israel, the *Sh'ma,* the Creator tells His people exactly what He expects of them. *'Hear, O Israel, the Lord our God is one Lord, and you shall love the Lord your God with all your heart, with all your soul, and with all your strength.'*[65] They were called to live their lives passionately loving the one true God. Out of pure love comes the desire to be obedient to the One we love. Otherwise, we obey out of a sense of duty. It's no wonder, when asked by the teacher of the Law which was the greatest commandment, that Jesus gave the following answer: *'You shall love the Lord your God with your whole heart, with your whole soul, and with your whole mind. This is the great and chief commandment. The second is like it, "You shall love your neighbour as yourself." On these two commandments the whole Law and the Prophets depend.'*[66] Had we lived in a perfect world, the Jewish people would have recognised the true purpose of the Law. Instead, they failed to see that *'love is the fulfilment of the law.'*[67] After all, He is the God of love, not the God of law.

LAW AND ORDER

Knowing how much they would frustrate Him, do you ever wonder why God chose Israel in the first place? I'm inclined to

---

[63] Hebrews 10:1; NIV 1984.
[64] Romans 8:3; CJB: The Law, *'lacked the power to make the old nature cooperate.'*
[65] Deuteronomy 6:5. See also Deut. 11:13, 22.
[66] Matthew 22:37–40.
[67] Romans 13:10; NIV 1984.

think that He did so in order to show them that they were every bit as much in need of a Saviour as anyone else. The fact that they were the chosen ones would not give them an automatic ticket to heaven. They, too, were cursed with an inherited sin nature, and doomed by their own sinful actions. Also, the descendants of Abraham stepped out of line by giving their heart to law and order, instead of giving it to the God of law and order Himself. By doing so, they brought themselves under a curse. *'For everyone who depends on legalistic observance of Torah commands lives under a curse, since it is written, "Cursed is everyone who does not keep on doing everything written in the ... Torah."'*[68] *Torah* is the Hebrew word for teaching or instruction, or what we Gentiles would call *Law*. Torah was supposed to direct the gaze of faithful, loving 'children' to the coming Messiah. Instead the Law had become a stumbling block for these people. By putting their trust in the Law and not in God Himself, they had come under the judgement of the Law; the fruit of judgement is punishment and death.[69] Instead of being servants of the one true God, the children of Israel had made themselves slaves of the Law. All who failed to recognise its goal were imprisoned in that system to which they had subjected themselves.[70]

FOLLOWING IN THEIR FOOTSTEPS

Lest we are tempted to think this is a failure peculiar to Jewish people, and use the above to endorse the argument that God has given up on them, we might ask ourselves if the Gentile world has succumbed to this temptation also. St Paul, the emissary to the Gentiles, warned believers in the Messiah not to return to the Law, and would not have cautioned them unless it was an issue at the time. If we were to be honest with ourselves, we would confess that Ireland has seen her fair share of legalism over the years,

---

[68] Galatians 3:10; Deuteronomy 27:26; CJB.

[69] Romans 7:10; CJB: *'the commandment that was intended to bring me life was found to be bringing me death.'*

[70] Galatians 3:23; NIV, 1984: *'Before this faith came, we were held prisoners by the law, locked up until faith should be revealed.'*

where many (myself included) believed that self-initiated and self-enabled righteous works could earn God's approval and favour. Scripture says that all our righteous works are 'as filthy rags.'[71] This means that religious activities that are not God-enabled (by the power of His Holy Spirit) are fruitless. In contrast to faith-activated works which resemble gold and silver and cannot be consumed by fire, religious works are like wood, hay and stubble that will burn in the Day of Judgement.[72] Religious behaviour never has and never will free anyone from sin; it is an inadequate sacrifice which has never pleased God. The enemy of our souls, Satan, has deceived us into believing the lie that we can reach heaven's standard of perfection by our own doing and in our own strength.

PROPER ORDER

Now that we partly know the purpose of the call of Israel and the reason God gave us the Law through these imperfect, beloved people, we are beginning to see that the Almighty was working out a plan – a perfect plan – from the very beginning. They would shine like beacons in the world from a strategic geographic position. *'God was planting a people at a crossroads where they could be a model of the kingdom of heaven on earth.'*[73] These prophets of God, the descendants of Abraham, through Isaac and Jacob, would convict the world of sin and encourage it to turn in repentance to the one true God. But, bringing consciousness of sin, on the one hand, and the act of absolving it, on the other, are two different things entirely. The price of sin would have to be paid ...

---

[71] Isaiah 64:6.
[72] See 1 Corinthians 3:12, 13.
[73] Pawson, *Unlocking the Bible*, p. 9.

4

Intersection

'Stand at the crossroads and look;

ask about the ancient paths, "Which one is the good way?"

Take it, and you will find rest for your souls.' [74]

By cutting across the timeline of history, with the death of Jesus, the Creator was marking the ultimate sign of redemption. Those born in the pre-Christian era were to look forward with anticipation to this definitive moment, while those born after the event were forever to look back to it. By calling His covenant people to step out of line and separate themselves, they would embark on a journey, leading to the *crossroad*. There was only ever one route to this vital intersection – the narrow road of 'faith', which few would find.

'HALL OF FAITH'

Salvation was obtainable for those living in pre-Christian times, by means of faith. Quoting an Old Testament prophet, St Paul explains: *'[The] Good News tells us how God makes us right in his sight. This is accomplished from start to finish by faith. As the Scriptures say, "It is through faith that a righteous person has life."'* [75] In Hebrews 11, we discover that a number of Old Testament characters will be waiting to greet us at the pearly

---

[74] Jeremiah 6:16; CJB.
[75] Romans 1:17; NLT, 2007.

gates.[76] This chapter is often referred to as the 'Hall of Faith'. It is interesting that it is not called the 'Corridor of Law'. That would suggest they had achieved salvation by their own merit, which was clearly not the case.

FATHER ABRAHAM

We should not be surprised to see Abraham among these devoted heroes. Because of his faith, Abraham obeyed God and immigrated to the distant land of Canaan in which he would live out the rest of his days as a nomad.[77] He believed the promise that he and his elderly wife would produce a child. *'Abraham believed God, and it was accounted to him for righteousness.'*[78] By his trust in God, Abraham was approved as righteous. Note that the book of Romans is quoting Genesis, proving that the doctrine of 'righteousness by faith' is not a New Testament concept. It was there from the beginning.

MOSES' FAITH

Despite the fact that he was the one to whom the Law was imparted, Moses recognised that *faith*, not good works, would lead him down the road to redemption. The desire to obey stemmed from this foundation of faith. Hebrews 11:26 specifically attributes Moses' obedience to his belief in the coming Christ. By trusting, it says, *'He had come to regard abuse suffered on behalf of the [coming] Messiah as greater riches than the treasures of Egypt.'* Because of his faith, Moses was willing to suffer.

BLOOD SACRIFICE

On Mount Sinai, the Lord instructed Moses that forgiveness could only be obtained through blood sacrifice. *'According to the Law*

---

[76] Among whom are Enoch, Noah, Sarah and Rahab; see Hebrews 11:15.
[77] See Hebrews 11:8–9.
[78] Romans 4:3; Genesis 15:6. If someone is 'righteous' he has been made right with God.

almost everything is purified by blood, and without bloodshedding there is no forgiveness.'[79] This brings us to a second problem which required God's attention. The first was the need for prophets. The second relates to the punishment aspect of the Law. The Lord knew that we would be doomed unless conclusive action was taken to get us out of the cycle of sin.

PRIESTS AND THE TABERNACLE

Priests were required to represent the people, and stand in the gap between a holy God and sinful man. From divine blueprints, a tabernacle was erected.[80] There, the (animal) blood sacrifice was offered by the priests on behalf of the sins of individuals and of the nation. Thus, the sacrificial system was established, and the concept of atonement was introduced. To 'atone for' in Hebrew is the verb, *Kaphar*. This means to 'cover over', like placing a lid on something.[81] From the Hebrew perspective, atonement implies an offence being covered over, as if it had never happened.

A FORESHADOW

But, why would God establish the system when He knows that the blood of animals is, *'powerless to take away sins'*?[82] It could not perfect the person: *'offerings ... cannot make the worshipper's conscience perfect.'[83]* What was the point of a sacrificial system that failed to deal with the sin nature? Here's a clue: *'The law is only a shadow of the good things that are coming – not the realities themselves.'[84]* As the purpose of the Commandments was to foreshadow the blessing of the New Covenant, so was the

---

[79] Hebrews 9:22.

[80] This special tent, the Tabernacle, was a mobile temple of worship. King Solomon would eventually replace the mobile Tabernacle with the Temple building in Jerusalem (located on the Temple Mount).

[81] *Kaphar*: the noun used in the Hebrew Scriptures for the lid of the Ark of the Covenant – the Mercy Seat.

[82] Hebrews 10:4.

[83] Ibid 9:9.

[84] Ibid 10:1; NIV 1984.

purpose of the sacrificial system.[85] Thus, off in the distant future the price of sin would be paid once and for all by means of a blood sacrifice.

THE FINAL HIGH PRIEST

'He had to be made like His brothers in every respect in order to become a merciful and faithful High Priest ... for the atonement of the people's sins.'[86] Jesus, Son of God, forsook His heavenly throne and became the High Priest, who uniquely offered His own life as a sacrifice for sin. *'He is Himself an atoning sacrifice for our sins, and not for ours only but also for the whole world.'*[87] Thankfully, not only St John and his believing Jewish friends, but also Gentiles are offered this free gift of forgiveness.[88]

FLAWLESS SUBSTITUTE

We know that the sacrificial offering had to be without blemish. There has only ever been one person who lived a life completely free of sin and without blemish: Jesus Christ. He, the spotless Lamb of God, offered Himself as a substitute for us. I like Charles Spurgeon's description of this divine act of substitution, *'You stand before God as if you were Christ, because Christ stood before God as if he were you ... Christ standing for men and bearing the thunderbolts of the divine opposition to all sin ... Man standing in Christ's place, and receiving the sunlight of divine favour.'*[89] Each and every one of us deserved to die for our personal sin and rebellion. But, the sinless One took our place in God's court of Law and took upon Himself the punishment we deserved. He paid the penalty of the Law, so that we would not have to. In fact, Jesus'

---

[85] The Old Covenant foreshadowed the Kingdom life which was made available by the New Covenant.
[86] Hebrews 2:17.
[87] 1 John 2:2.
[88] *'Or is He God of the Jews only? Is He not also the God of the Gentiles? He is the Gentiles' God as well.'* Romans 3:29 (written by the Jewish St Paul).
[89] See charlesspurgeon.org sermon: 'Justification by Faith'.

final utterance on the Cross, 'It is finished' (from the Greek transliteration: 'Tetelestai'[90]) can mean 'Paid in full'.

THE CURSE IS BROKEN

Yeshua (Hebrew for Jesus) became the curse, which had separated mankind from the Father. By dying, He broke the curse, setting free all who put their trust in Him. *'Christ has ransomed us from the curse of the Law inasmuch as He became a curse for us ... in order that in Christ Jesus the blessing of Abraham might be realized for the nations and that we through faith might receive the promise of the Spirit.'*[91] This one-time sacrifice fulfils the Old Covenant legal requirements, and ratifies the New. The 'blessing of Abraham' is such that through Abraham's offspring *'all the nations [will] be blessed.'*[92] The Jewish Messiah becomes the Saviour of mankind.

SCIENTIFIC DISSECTION

Here below is some scientific evidence that Jesus was truly the prophesied Messiah. In his book, *Science Speaks*, Professor Peter Stoner dissects the facts regarding the Messiah, and proves Jesus was who He claimed to be. Messianic Jew[93], Don Goldstein summarises Stoner's findings, as follows:

> *'The purpose of the study was to determine the odds of one man in history fulfilling all the prophecies recorded in the Scriptures [i.e. Old Testament] that point to the Jewish Messiah. There are over 300 Messianic prophecies in the Scriptures ... eight prophecies were chosen that were totally*

---

[90] The Greek word, Τετέλεσται, translates 'It is finished'. Some scholars claim that, during New Testament times, it was written on receipts to indicate that a bill was paid in full.

[91] Galatians 3:13–14.

[92] Genesis 12:3.

[93] A Messianic Jew is a believer in Jesus who is of Jewish lineage.

beyond the human control of Yeshua:

1. *His place of birth (Micah 5:2) ... [i.e. Bethlehem]*

2. *Time of birth (Daniel 9:25) ...*

3. *Manner of birth (Isaiah 7:14) ... [i.e. Immanuel – 'God with us' – born of a virgin]*

4. *Betrayal (Zechariah 11:12–13) ... [i.e. for 30 pieces of silver]*

5. *Manner of death (Psalm 22:16–18). Note the detail, down to the gambling for His robe.*

6. *Piercing of hands, feet and side (Zechariah 12:10)*

7. *People mocking (Psalm 22:7, 8)*

8. *Burial (Isaiah 53:9)*

The compound probability of just these eight prophecies being fulfilled is 1 in 100,000,000,000,000,000 (1 in 10 to the 17th power) ... Yeshua fulfilled them all! ... Yeshua fulfilled over 300 prophecies ... It would take more faith to deceive yourself that Yeshua is NOT the Messiah, than to accept the FACT that He is!'[94]

Do you find it interesting that this same Messiah explained to a Jewish ruler of His day, Nicodemus, that a person must be 'born from above,' or born again?[95] Let's explore the meaning of this.

BORN AGAIN

A person who is born again has chosen to place his trust in Jesus as Saviour and Master of his life. The physical body has not been born again – one is not exempt from the physical signs and features of ageing. It is the human spirit – which had been dead because of sin – that is revived and brought into restored fellowship and a living

---

[94] Goldstein, Don, *I Have a Friend Who's Jewish, Do You?* (Florida, 1986), pp. 30–31.

[95] See the Gospel of John, Chapter 3.

relationship with God. Water baptism is an outward expression of what has already happened internally for the born-again believer. Baptism is essentially a public demonstration that one has died to their old life (symbolised by being submerged) and is now raised to new life in Christ (symbolised by re-emerging from the water). It is a powerful proclamation to the spiritual realm that their life is no longer their own; they now belong to God.

FREE WILL

Unlike the spirit, the soul (the mind, will and emotions) is not the part of us that is 'born again' at the Cross junction. A gradual and ongoing transformation occurs as we spend time in the cleansing presence of Jesus, the Healer. We don't need to search long in the Scriptures for a good role model in this regard: Mary, who was the sister of Lazarus and Martha, was publicly honoured by the Lord for her exemplary worship.[96] Believers also regularly 'wash the mind' in the Word of God. The Bible is powerful in its ability to cleanse and free the mind from that which binds it. Jesus once prayed to the Father: *'Sanctify them by the truth. Your word is truth.'*[97] The need to daily surrender our will is vital. The free will that God bestowed on man back in the beginning has not been taken away. We can still act in sinful and selfish ways, or we can choose to act in obedience to the will of God. The good news is that when we choose to surrender to His will, He equips us with the grace and strength to accomplish it. This brings us to an indispensable element of salvation.

THE MESSIAH'S PROMISED BLESSING

Old Testament prophets spoke of a day when the Suffering Servant[98] would die for the sins of the people and rise to life, in order to make them righteous. Paul's letter to the Hebrews,

---

[96] See Luke 10:38–42 and John 12:1–3.
[97] John 17:17.
[98] See Isaiah 53; Psalm 22.

however, informs us that pre-Christian era believers were lacking something. *'And all these, having gained approval through their faith, did not receive what was promised.'[99]* The gift they lacked could only be bestowed *after* the death and resurrection of the Messiah, because it was only the risen and glorified Jesus who could impart it. This promised blessing for 'New Covenant' believers was the impartation of the Holy Spirit. On the day Jesus was resurrected He appeared to His disciples and 'breathed on them', and by so doing bequeathed His Spirit to them (see John 20:22[100]).

SPIRIT-FILLED: TO BE HUMBLE AND CHRIST-LIKE

Although the Spirit of God had 'fallen' momentarily on *certain* people in Old Testament times, now He would 'fill' forever *all* disciples of this Messiah. A new era had dawned. With the Spirit of God residing within, God's nature is imparted to the believer, enabling him to live the Kingdom life. The fruits of the Spirit (e.g. love, joy and peace) can overflow from him and produce much good. This blessing was foretold by the prophets of Israel. *'See, the days are coming, says the Lord, when I will make a new covenant with the house of Israel ... not like the covenant that I made with their fathers in the day that I took them ... out of the land of Egypt ... But this is the covenant ... I will put My law in their inward parts, and upon their hearts will I write it.'[101]* The prophet Ezekiel also spoke of the coming New Covenant well in advance of its appearance: *'I [the Lord] will purify you. A new heart, too, I will give you ... I will put My Spirit within you ... and you shall observe My ordinances and do them.'[102]*

---

[99] Hebrews 11:39; NASB.

[100] Hebrews 11:40 says: *'God had provided something better for us, so that apart from us they would not be made perfect.'* Old Testament believers can now partake in this blessing also (even though they existed before the appearance of the Messiah), because both Christians and pre-Christian era believers in the Messiah are united in one body (Christ is the Head and believers are the body).

[101] Jeremiah 31:31–33.

[102] Ezekiel 36:25–27.

SPIRIT-EMPOWERED: EQUIPPED FOR WORK

Later on, the Spirit of God was given for a different purpose. Prior to His ascension the Lord gave the following instruction to His followers: *'Do not leave Jerusalem but await what the Father promised ... after a few days you will be baptized with the Holy Spirit.'*[103] True to His word, on the day of Pentecost[104] the Spirit of the Messiah, descended on the disciples gathered in the upper room. They were already born again, since the Resurrection they had the Spirit of God living in them. But now Yeshua's followers received the baptism of the Holy Spirit: *'suddenly there came a roaring from heaven like ... a mighty wind... And they were all filled with the Holy Spirit and began to speak in foreign languages as the Spirit granted them expression.'*[105]

This baptism of the Holy Spirit would enable the disciples to continue the work of Jesus. Now they were equipped for the Great Commission: to bring the Gospel to the ends of the earth. They would speak with the power and authority of the Messiah, and perform the miraculous. Prophecy, speaking in other tongues, healing, the casting out of demons, and more besides would be gifts with which the Spirit of Jesus would empower them. As the O'Higgins' have expressed in their clear and concise booklet on the subject: *'The first giving of the Holy Spirit reproduces the character of Christ in us (the fruit of the Spirit), and the second produces in us a share in the ministry ... of Jesus.'*[106]

CROSSPOINT

Let's sum up the content of this pivotal chapter. The 'Cross' might metaphorically mean the time when history's two eras, BC and AD, met: that collision of our fallen world with the Kingdom of

---

[103] Acts 1:4–5.

[104] Pentecost took place fifty days after the resurrection, and ten following Jesus' ascension into heaven.

[105] See Acts 2:1–4.

[106] Paul & Nuala O'Higgins, *Have You Received the Holy Spirit? Receiving the Double Gift of the Holy Spirit* (3rd edn., Florida, 2013), p. 16.

God. At the Cross, the Old and New Covenant merge; Jew and Gentile meet. Faith in God, and not 'righteous' works, leads each of these groups to that junction – for the salvation of their souls and the joy of 'Kingdom living' on earth. The purpose of the Hebrew animal sacrifices was to point to the future sacrifice of the innocent Messiah.

A free gift is offered at the Cross. As with any gift we have a choice to receive it or not. Goldstein makes a sobering point about those who refuse the gift: *'Understand that if you don't choose God's camp, you are drafted into Satan's camp by default.'*[107] The sentiment is not His own; Jesus Himself made this point very clearly when He said: *'Whoever is not with me is against me.'*[108] For those who choose life, there is no more 'going around in circles'. At the Cross junction it is finished. The old life makes its onerous journey uphill to the cross. Then as the burden of sin is cast away, new life begins. It's downhill from there.

WHEN TWO PATHS INTERSECT

'You must know ... it was all for you.'[109] Is there a lover who could exceed the heartfelt confession of the dashing Mr Darcy? Jane Austin enthusiasts will agree that there are few stories as romantic as *Pride and Prejudice*, in which the admirer confidentially pays a substantial sum to a manipulative enemy in order to save the family of his beloved from disgrace. Others may argue that there is hardly a story that captures the splendour of divine grace as well as Victor Hugo's *Les Miserables*. This is a tale that honours the value of 'going the extra mile', at great cost to oneself.

As intriguing as these fictional stories may be, could they really compare to God's love letter to His precious created ones? God loves us so much that He allowed Gentile Roman soldiers to

---

[107] Goldstein, *Friend who's Jewish*, p. 34.
[108] Matthew 12:30; ESV.
[109] Screenplay: *Pride and Prejudice* (Universal Studios, Working Title Films and StudioCanal, 2005).

torture and execute His Son. He permitted His own people to scorn and condemn Him even while He was paying the price for their redemption.

SYMMETRY

Yet, it's not true to say that Jesus was a victim. He deliberately laid down His life as a sacrifice for the salvation of mankind. Have you ever pondered Jesus' occupation while He walked the earth? He was not a farmer or a fisherman. Up to the age of thirty Jesus was a carpenter, and thereby constantly reminded of the prophecies of suffering that awaited Him. The wooden cross of Calvary was His destiny after all. Did His future sacrifice cross His mind each time he drove a nail into a plank of wood?

MEET ME AT THE CROSSROADS

There's no denying it, the motive of the Bridegroom was selfless. Out of undying love for His Bride,[110] He gave up His life. Our Creator did it all for love and restored fellowship with His beloved creatures. Jesus' outstretched arms on the cross of Calvary are open to embrace each and every one who will respond. But like any formal invitation of significance, a response is required. The 'wedding supper of the Lamb'[111] is scheduled and we are all invited!

RSVP

---

[110] The 'Bride of Christ' is a Biblical symbol of the true followers of Jesus Christ.
[111] See Revelation 19:9.

Part Two

Geography, Modern History And Politics

5

Whose Line Is It Anyway?

'Location! Location! Location!' Will we ever forget the national mantra of the 'boom years'? Who would have predicted that the Celtic Tiger (mid-1990s to 2007) would have so quickly retreated into oblivion and triggered a new Irish diaspora, with emigration levels spiking? I wonder if those disillusioned jobseekers were received warmly in the lands to which they flocked? It was not so long ago, after all, that Irish emigrants (in post-war years) were confronted with racial intolerance abroad. Signs displayed on business windows: 'No Irish wanted' left a bitter aftertaste for the struggling Irish labourer.

EPICENTRE

'Israel, therefore, was at the crossroads of the world, with trade routes arriving from all directions and Megiddo [the plain of Armageddon] the place where they all met.'[112] Have you ever pondered the strategic placing of Israel on the map? Cushioned (or rather perhaps, squeezed) between the continents of Asia, Africa and Europe, it is a major historic intersection. 'Thus says the Lord God: This is Jerusalem, which I have set in the centre of the nations with other countries around her.'[113] The location was not of Israel's choosing. The opportunity was never presented to study the property market and decide where best to invest. No, it was God's decision to place her there.

---

[112] Pawson, *Unlocking the Bible*, p. 6.
[113] Ezekiel 5:5.

Like some Irish folk, many Jews have known the hardship of being uprooted. They too have faced discrimination in foreign lands. Tattooed on the memory of the Jewish community is: 'Jüden verboten!' the Nazi sign which was posted in public places, meaning 'Jews are forbidden!'[114] Is this to be their eternal portion in life?

While Ireland's economy had taken steps towards recovery (pre-Covid-19), she was still far from being *ar mhuin na muice,*[115] or on the tiger's back, for that matter. Our floundering nation is in need of the King of this jungle to come and deliver her. Israel too needs to see the Lion roar on her behalf. Has God changed His mind about the land deal and adopted a new name, Palestine? Would the *Lion of Judah* forsake His own? Would He leave her alone in the wilds to fend for herself?

HIS-STORY

The Bible helps us to understand the current geo-political situation in the Middle East and discern the right path to follow. Something which is difficult to dispute and found in this historic bestseller is the following: *'He has cast the lot for them; His hand has apportioned* the land *for them by a line. They shall possess it for ever and shall dwell in it from generation to generation.'*[116] For those who are not convinced, here's another quote from the timeless classic, *'"So I will plant them on their land, and they shall not be plucked up again from their land which I have given them," says the Lord.'*[117] If the Author of Life and the One who 'knows the end from the beginning' has decreed such a thing for Israel, who is the author of controversy?

---

[114] The caption of a contemporary article reads: 'Istanbul Store Bans Entry to "Jew Dogs"' (September 2014). There is photographic evidence of the mobile phone shop – which is located in an area where there are a number of Jewish-owned stores – with a sign forbidding entrance to Jews hung on its door.
[115] Translation: 'On the pig's back'.
[116] Isaiah 34:17.
[117] Amos 9:15.

HISTORY SPEAKS

While few would deny that the people of Israel were exiled from the land (roughly a century after the Messiah's resurrection), most are not aware that there has always been a remnant of Jewish people living there since then. Here's a synopsis of the many powers that occupied Israel throughout the centuries. The land went from Roman occupation in the early Christian era to Persian, then Byzantine and Muslim control in the seventh century; followed by the so-called 'Christian' Crusaders at the turn of the first millennium. Shortly thereafter, the Arab Saladin invaded and occupied the land until eventually the European Crusaders had the upper hand again. These were followed by the Mongols of Asia and then by the Egyptian Mamluks who took over for 300 years. In the sixteenth century the Turkish Ottoman Empire took control of the land until the League of Nations stepped in after the First World War, and brought 'Palestine' under the governance of the British Mandate in 1920.[118]

AWAITING RESULTS

Meanwhile, the majority of Israelis were scattered in the nations. Can we Irish possibly imagine what it would be like to wait almost two millennia to see a promise of God fulfilled on behalf of our nation? That for which they ceaselessly prayed finally came to pass. That which was prophesied by their ancestors thousands of years before was now being fulfilled before their eyes. God chose a particular long-awaited moment in history; then He repositioned His people in the land. Indeed, out of the ashes of the Holocaust this feeble nation rose and the way was paved for them to return to their ancient homeland. It fell into place all of a sudden. *'Who ever heard of such a thing? Who ever saw its like? Shall a land be brought forth in a single day? Shall a nation be born in a moment? Yet Zion had hardly travailed, when she gave*

---

[118] For a more in-depth study, I recommend Steve Maltz's book: *The Land of Many Names.*

birth to her children.[119]

TURN A BLIND EYE

That a resolution would be passed in 1947 in the United Nations in favour of the establishment of a Jewish State is a modern-day miracle – especially when less than a decade before the nations of the world had deafened their ears to the plight of the Jew. Shiploads seeking refuge beyond the shores of Europe had been refused entry and sent back to face ominous prospects. It is a shame to confess that Ireland went with the flow of the times; we failed to stand and have our collective voice heard when it was desperately needed. In 1938, Ireland was among the thirty-two representative nations of the Evian Conference in France who unanimously voted against receiving the hounded asylum seekers.

IRISH HISTORY

Although Ray Rivlin's, *Jewish Ireland*, details kindnesses shown to the Jewish community, she also gives account of times in Irish history when we mistreated the minority group in question. From the following extract we will see that our government was neither innocent nor ignorant:

'In 1936, the Department of Justice stated, "... concerning the number of alien Jews who became established in this country ... the Minister (for External Affairs) will not look with favour on any policy which might lead to an increase in that number." In 1938, when ... Germany's triumphant entry into Austria, rendered 120,000 Austrian Jews stateless, the Irish Government made entry into Ireland for holders of German or Austrian passports ... available only to applicants "not of Jewish or partly Jewish origin."'

---

[119] Isaiah 66:8.

To our shame, the story goes from bad to worse:

> *'In 1946, when a London Jewish Society bought a refuge at Clonlyn Castle in Delvin, Co. Westmeath, to house 100 Jewish war orphans aged from seven to sixteen, Gerry Boland TD ... and Minister for Justice, refused to admit them on the grounds that, "it has always been the policy of the Minister for Justice to restrict the admission of Jewish aliens for the reason that any substantial increase in our Jewish population might give rise to an anti-Semitic problem."'*

It is obvious that *'an anti-Semitic problem'* already existed in our little nation even prior to independence from the British, to which the following comment of Sinn Féin founder Arthur Griffith (1871–1922) will attest: *'I have in former years often declared that the Three Evil Influences of the century were the Pirate, the Freemason, and the Jew.'* Boland's unyielding and heartless response led to the intervention of the Chief Rabbi of Palestine. *'It took a personal visit from Rabbi Herzog, then Chief Rabbi of Palestine, to persuade Gerry Boland to let the Clonlyn Castle children enter Ireland and even then their stay was limited to a year.'*[120]

It was not enough that Taoiseach Eamonn de Valera ignored various diplomatic requests to intervene in the Jewish crisis, but he also offered our condolences to the German diplomat, Eduard Hempel, upon news of Hitler's demise. Might I remark that as a Christian nation we bear the guilt of refusing to help Yeshua's blood brothers. To whom in our scriptures, if not to us Gentiles, does God address the following: *'Comfort ye, comfort ye My people, says your God?'*[121] The 'people' here with whom He identifies are none other than the children of Israel; throughout the Scriptures He calls them 'My people.'

---

[120] Ray Rivlin, *Jewish Ireland. A Social History* (2nd edn, Dublin, 2011), p. 41–43.
[121] Isaiah 40:1.

THE QURAN SPEAKS

The majority of Arabs (including Palestinians) are Muslim. Despite the Islamists' claim to Israel and the holy city of Jerusalem their 'holy book', the Quran, says otherwise. University lecturer and student of Middle Eastern affairs, Nissim Dana, shares the following points of interest in an article headlined: *Even the Koran claims Israel belongs to the Jews*:

> '[In the Quran] Israel is mentioned eight times ... and there is not a single mention that it belongs to Arabs or Muslims ... Koran 7:7, where G-d [God] Himself bequeaths the Land of Israel to the Jews ... the fifth chapter of the Islamic holy text whereby Mohammed says on his deathbed that returning to the Land of Israel is impossible in and of itself, because G-d placed in Moses' mouth the declaration that the Land of Israel belongs to the Jewish people.'[122]

While far too many Muslims continue in their determination to exact from the Jew the land of Israel, are we Irish still convinced we should support them? Must we also turn a blind eye?

THE GOOD BOOK

Inspired by the Spirit of God the Bible, from cover to cover, mentions Jerusalem over 800 times. Ultimately, the God of Abraham, Isaac and Jacob is the One who has the last say about His city of Zion (Jerusalem), *'But Judah shall be inhabited forever and Jerusalem from generation to generation ... I am the Lord, dwelling in Zion.'*[123] God may not operate according to our schedule but His timing is perfect. In *Unlocking the Bible* Pawson explains that over 80 per cent of Bible predictions have already been fulfilled with absolute precision. *'There are 735 separate*

---

[122] *JNN* editors, 12 February 2014, alluding to *Arutz-7* article.
[123] Joel 3:20-21.

events predicted in the Bible. Some are predicted only once or twice ... Of those 735 events, 593 (81 per cent) have already happened. The Bible has been 100 per cent accurate so far. The remaining 19 per cent of its predictions have yet to be fulfilled, but we can be sure that they will be.' [124]

THE TIDE TURNS

'God is in control and will bring things to the ending He intends. History is indeed "his story."' [125] The nations that defy His plans will experience something akin to the crushing waves of the Red Sea which engulfed Pharaoh's army. *'For I am the Lord your God, who stirs up the sea that its billows roar ... saying to Zion, "You are My people!"'* [126] With God having stated His destiny for Israel it's really not advisable to hinder her flow. As certain as the Lord will judge individuals He will judge nations at the close of the age. The following sentiment is repeated in many of the prophetic books of the Bible: *'In that day I shall seek to exterminate all the nations that come up against Jerusalem.'* [127] It is obvious that day has not yet arrived as there are a number of nations still shaking the fist at Israel.

FULFILLED PROPHECY

As soon as the land was back in the hands of its God-appointed stewards last century, her God-ordained name was restored. The following portion of Israel's Declaration of Independence attributes weight to an historic European event, *'In the year 5657 (1897), at the summons of ... Theodor Herzl, the First Zionist Congress convened and proclaimed the right of the Jewish people to national rebirth in its own country.'* [128] What is perhaps most

---

[124] Pawson, *Unlocking the Bible*, p. 618.

[125] Ibid, p. 240.

[126] Isaiah 51:15.

[127] Zechariah 12:9.

[128] Yanky Fachler, *God's Little Errand Boys. Christian clergymen who helped the Jews come home* (Dundalk, 2011), p. 148.

interesting about Theodor Herzl, the father of modern (political) Zionism, is the entry he made in his diary after the convention. He boldly declared that his dream would be fulfilled if not in five years, certainly fifty. Little did he know, his words were prophetic. In 1947, exactly fifty years later, the United Nations General Assembly voted in favour of a Jewish State. Malcolm Hedding highlights the significance of this remarkable timing: *'In Scripture the 50th year is always the year of Jubilee which requires that all property be turned over to the original owner! In 1948, a goodly portion of Palestine reverted back to Jewish control – the original owners.'*[129]

GEOGRAPHICAL POINT

Let us consider the significance of the setting. It is as if before time began God targeted the prime location for His redemption plan. *'I am giving thee Canaan, the land, your inheritance bounded by line, though you are insignificant now, very few and mere pilgrims therein.'*[130] He strategically marked out Israel's territories and borders. When the time was ripe the Son stepped down from His heavenly throne and humbly crossed over into that part of our primitive world: Israel.[131]

Moreover, in the heart of the land was the chosen location of God's headquarters here on earth. *'Jerusalem, the city where I Myself chose to put My name.'*[132] Indeed it was just outside the walls of the ancient city of King David (in Israel, the commercial 'crossroads' of the ancient world) that the Son of God paid the price in full to redeem mankind from the power of sin and death.

---

[129] Malcolm Hedding, *Understanding Israel* (2nd edn, Oklahoma, 2002), p. 28.
[130] 1 Chronicles 16:18-19.
[131] In Matthew 2:19–21, you will notice that when an angel appeared to Joseph in a dream, he was instructed to return with Mary and the baby Jesus to the *land of Israel.*
[132] 1 Kings 11:36; see also 14:21.

THE ARAB WORLD

Since the main voice of opposition to the existence of a Jewish State is Arab, it is necessary to explore the dimensions of the Arab world. Where does it begin and where does it end? The Arab League, founded in 1945, stretches from North West Africa across the Middle East. Although, 'Palestine' is not recognised internationally as an official state, it was declared a member of the Arab league in 1964, bringing the total number of members to twenty-two. That is no insignificant number, when you take into account that there are less than 200 official countries in the world. According to the BBC, the Arab League covers an area of over 13 million km^2, that's 5.2 million square miles.[133] This equals no less than 9 per cent of the planet's land area.

ISLAM'S INFLUENCE

These statistics do not take into account the other nations influenced by the dominant religion of the Arab world: Islam. Many miles away in the Far East, Indonesia boasts a Muslim population of 220 million, which amounts to at least 87 per cent of its total population. The country with the largest population of Muslims in the world is in fact Indonesia. Apart from all the other obvious nations with a high Muslim density such as Afghanistan (99% Muslim), Azerbaijan (93%), Iran (99.4%), Kazakhstan (70%), Kyrgyzstan (75%), Malaysia (61%), Pakistan (96%), Tajikistan (90%), Turkmenistan (89%) and Uzbekistan (88%), there are for sure ten African countries with a strong Muslim contingent (which are not official members of the Arab League).[134]

According to one report, there are no less than fifty-two countries where at least half of the population practise Islam. In other words, more than a quarter of the world's countries have a population that is at least 50 per cent Muslim. These statistics

---

[133] BBC Profile: Arab League, 5 February 2015. <http://www.bbc.com/news/world-middle-east-15747941> (9 August 2016).
[134] The statistics in this section can be found in the 2014 Demographic Profile of indexmundi.com.

should be a cause of international concern (especially since Islam does not hide the fact that it intends to conquer the world). On the other hand, how many countries are the Jews known to have conquered? None. In how many instances have they sought to convert a nation to Judaism? None. Indeed, how many countries do they even seek to call their own? Not twenty-two; not even two, just one: the one allocated to them a long time ago.

ISRAEL'S DIMENSIONS

One would think Israel ought to be a sizeable piece of land that their Arab neighbours covet. Many people are not aware of the physical dimensions of Israel. Actually, you can barely spot it on the globe. Including Judea, Samaria and the Golan Heights, Israel has a total area of 17,273 sq. miles. That's a tiny portion compared to the substantial landmass of the Arab League (5.2 *million* sq. miles, which excludes the other thirty, or so, nations with a strong Muslim population).

To see it in comparable terms: if one could remove the provinces of Leinster, Connaught and Ulster from our island that's how 'big', or rather 'small', we're talking. Israel is roughly the size of Munster.[135] It is said that it could fit into Ireland three times. Knowing that, how would we feel if a cluster of close countries made no secret of their intentions to wipe out Ireland? We need to see things in perspective. As Ireland is the only official homeland of the Irish, Israel is the only official homeland of the Jew. The Arab, on the other hand, could settle in a number of different countries in which the Arab culture and language are established – 22 at the very least. Let's be reasonable, why ever would a sliver of land only 290 miles long[136] and between 9 and 85 miles wide[137] be the envy of the vastly powerful Arab world? Take away from the Jewish nation the only place they can officially and truly call home and what have they left? Where in the world can they turn?

---

[135] Our southern province is 24,675km²; Israel is 27,799km².
[136] I.e. 470 km long.
[137] I.e. 135 km at its widest point.

JESUS' LAST WORDS

Samaria and Judea are the biblical and historical names of the two areas north and south of Jerusalem – names that have not become redundant and are still in common use among Jews and Christians. The area is probably the second most contested place on earth, after Jerusalem. The following report attests to this, and makes one wonder why the obsession with tiny Israel: *'There are some 200 nations in the world … If Israel did not exist, the UN might not have much to do. Last year the General Assembly adopted 25 resolutions against particular countries – 21 were against Israel.'*[138] Additionally, for the Lord Jesus to have mentioned this little trio – the hotspot of Israel and of the whole world – in His final discourse deserves some attention. *'You will be My witnesses both in Jerusalem and in all Judea and Samaria and to the remotest end of the earth.'*[139] This took place forty days after He was resurrected from the dead and immediately before being assumed into heaven. These were Jesus' *very last words* on earth. I sincerely doubt that the final statement of a Rabbi, whose unique wisdom and authority were held in esteem, was purely random.

WEST BANK

In the same spirit as the persecuting Romans who attempted to rename the Jewish capital of Jerusalem in the first century, contemporary persecutors of Israel have succeeded in renaming Judea and Samaria. It's a shame that most people you meet will not bat an eyelid at the mention of these historic names; they probably won't even know what you are talking about. Thanks to the influence of propaganda (and that same old evil spirit of anti-Semitism) the mere mention of the 'West Bank' will often spark a charged reaction. If people knew the reality of what takes place there, they would see no reason to be angry with Israel.

---

[138] *JNN* editors, 27 June 2014, alluding to a *National Review* article.
[139] Acts 1:8.

PARTITIONING

To divide and conquer is an age-old war strategy. For a number of decades, demands have been made by the Palestinian Authority (PA) and applauded by short-sighted world leaders to partition the land of Israel. While it may appear to be the obvious solution to an impossible situation, its end is not peace but destruction. 'Land for peace' is a myth. Dividing up the land leaves Israel extremely vulnerable to attack. The issue is not about her unwillingness to yield. Israel has done that on a number of occasions and still suffers as a result.[140] Furthermore God, who has drawn up the map and carefully marked the boundaries, condemns the partitioning of the Holy Land, as the late Derek Prince noted:

> "'They have divided up My land" [Joel 3:3] ... *In modern political language, dividing up is partitioning. In 1920 or thereabouts, the League of Nations assigned to Britain a mandate for the land of Israel, both sides of the Jordan [river]. The terms of the mandate was to provide a national home for the Jewish people. In 1922, with a stroke of his pen, Winston Churchill signed away 76 per cent of that land to an Arab nation ... now called Jordan, and in that territory no Jew is permitted to live. So they divided up the land – 76 per cent to 24 per cent ... In 1947 the United Nations, the successor to the League of Nations, arranged a scheme to divide up the land so that out of the remaining 24 per cent Israel would get maybe 10 per cent and 14 per cent would go to the Arabs. What are they guilty of? Dividing up God's land.'[141]*

---

[140] The issue of Disengagement will be addressed in Chapter 8.
[141] Prince, *End Times*, pp. 116–17.

WHOSE LINE IS IT ANYWAY?

TEACHER KNOWS BEST

A lady I know once had a bumper sticker which read: 'My Boss is a Jewish Carpenter'. Contrary to the beliefs of some, Jesus is not just a friend; He's the Headmaster. *'If you love me, keep my commands.'*[142] Two key components of the Cross of Redemption are love and obedience – the extravagant, self-sacrificing love of God for mankind, and the total obedience of the Son to the Father's will. Jesus expects the same from us. One without the other is incomplete. *'Our over-emphasis on love has led us away from standing for the truth. Love without truth is like a body without bones, and truth without love is like bones without a body.'*[143]

THE LION KING

Didn't the late CS Lewis do a wonderful job of depicting the King of creation? Humbly and voluntarily Aslan, the lion king, gave up his life for the sake of his friends and by so doing set creation free from the curse of the evil one.[144] Out of a seemingly tragic ending hope arose and Aslan had the last word. The message here is never to underestimate the tenacity of the Lion King. Just because we haven't heard Him in a while doesn't mean He can't still roar!

ENTITLEMENTS

As King of the universe, God has every right to intervene on behalf of His people. What He has done in times past He has every intention to do in times to come. *'The sun and the moon are darkened ... For the Lord roars from Zion, and from Jerusalem He utters His voice. The heavens and the earth are shaken; but the Lord is a refuge for His people and a stronghold for the sons of Israel.'*[145] In no uncertain terms God makes the message known to

---

[142] John 14:15; NIV.
[143] Johannes Facius, *As in the Days of Noah* (Kent, 1997), p. 40.
[144] See Lewis' *The Lion, the Witch and the Wardrobe*.
[145] Joel 3:15-16.

Israel that the Land is not hers, but His. While referring to Scripture, Steve Maltz explains, *'God holds the title deeds to the land and the Jews are the only tenants in the contract: "because the land is mine and you are but aliens and my tenants" (Leviticus 25:23)'.*[146] Indeed, Israel is on the line and the line is God's – the land belongs to *Him*. If we respect the Lion King, we will respect His decision to bestow the land on whomever He pleases.

> *'He granted their land as a possession,*
>
> *for His covenant love is everlasting;*
>
> *as a possession to Israel, His servant,*
>
> *for His covenant love is everlasting.'* [147]

---

[146] Maltz, *Many Names*, p. 15.
[147] Psalm 136:21-22

6

Age-Old Lines And Wrinkles

'Wonderful is the planet Haniyeh and his people are living on, disconnected from the Palestinian people.'

Ismail Haniyeh is the disputed prime minister of the Hamas government in Gaza. 'His people' are his Hamas associates. The above was tweeted on 5 June 2016 by a resident of the Gaza Strip called Hussein.[148] Since then the Hamas leader, who is currently taking time out to do a world tour, has been designated a 'global terrorist' by the USA.[149] In this chapter we will take a close-up look at those who govern the Palestinian territories, their precursors and allies. If we are willing to be honest, we will see how the regime is not only deceiving the world, but is also weighing heavily on its own people. The time has surely come to peel off the masks. Let us begin with what many negligently call the 'moderate faction': Fatah.

THE FATAH FAÇADE

Fatah is the Arabic word for conquest. It is a secularist group which was co-founded by the infamous Yasser Arafat in the late 1950s. The Fatah party currently governs Palestinian Authority

---

[148] Maayan Groisman, 'Gazans slam Hamas leader Haniyeh for painting life in Gaza as "wonderful"', *Jerusalem Post*, 5 June 2016. <https://www.jpost.com/Middle-East/Gazans-slam-Hamas-leader-Haniyeh-for-painting-life-in-Gaza-as-wonderful-455959> (7 June 2016).
[149] *JNN*, 19 February 2018, alluding to articles in *Algemeiner* and *INN*.

territories in the West Bank and East Jerusalem. Much of the world considers Fatah to be the moderate faction of Palestinian politics, yet its terror campaign against Israel began in 1964 (three years *before* the so-called Israeli 'occupation' of Jerusalem, Judea & Samaria and Gaza – the excuse ironically given by supporters of the carnage).[150] These violent attacks against the Jewish populace have continued right through to the present day under the ongoing leadership of Mahmoud Abbas. The following article extract highlights the deception at work in the organisation: *'Abbas' political adviser Nimer Hammad denounced recent violence in a statement broadcasted on official PA TV … However, on the same day, another Abbas adviser, Sultan Abu Al-Einein, wrote on Facebook, encouraging more violence by praising the terrorist murderers who carried out the recent attacks.'*[151] For the sake of its much-needed international sympathisers and supporters, Fatah presents a professional and gracious public image to masquerade its copious corruption and dare I say genocidal agenda. If you think I am exaggerating, please read on. In 2016 Fatah published an official list of accomplishments which, according to *Israel Now News*, *'includes the claim that its operatives have murdered 11,000 Israelis'*. What is not surprising is the exaggerated figure; what is shocking is the fact that this is considered an honourable achievement. Also noteworthy is the lack of any mention of peace endorsement: *'not even one peace-seeking or co-existence promoting effort was included in the list.'*[152]

On International Women's Day in March of that same year, Fatah chose to honour its female terrorists. Some of these violent women have been responsible for the slaying of Israelis of all ages and walks of life during the ongoing 'Al-Quds Intifada' (also called the 'knife intifada'), which is being goaded and hailed by the PA. *'From 13 September 2015 to 26 February 2016, 33 people [i.e. Israelis and tourists] were killed, and 359 people were injured by*

---

[150] In a later chapter we will take a closer look at the facts surrounding the Six-Day War of 1967 and the liberation of these territories.

[151] *JNN*, 12 November 2014, citing an *INN* report.

[152] *Israel Now News*, Daystar TV, viewed 14 August 2016.

Palestinian terrorists. The attacks included 192 stabbings, 75 shootings and 39 vehicular attacks.'[153] It was a shocking day for Ireland on 21 February 2004 when a Dublin bus accidentally lost control on Wellington quay, mounted the pavement, and ploughed into a queue of people at a bus-stop. Five were killed and sixteen injured in the carnage.[154] Could you picture how devastated and terrorised we would be as a nation if we were faced with thirty-nine incidences of drivers *deliberately* ramming into people on the footpath with the intention of killing and maiming as many as possible (and all of these taking place within a mere 23-week period)?

ABBAS' PROFILE

Fatah head Mahmoud Abbas was elected President of the Palestinian Authority in 2005. It was to be a four-year term. Following in the footsteps of his forerunner Yasser Arafat, none of the successive presidential elections have taken place and Abbas is still in office. For the last sixteen years he has been the official leader of the Palestinian people – whether they like it or not. It has been reported that one of his aims is to destroy the rival faction: Hamas. Within the last decade Abbas has had a $13 million palace built for himself. Among the multitudes of disadvantaged Palestinians who live in the region I'm sure there is a sizeable number who would like to know from whence the building funds have come. Meanwhile, his regular appeal to the nations for monetary aid continues. (In case you are wondering, the State of Israel holds a general election every four years and was recently, not unlike Ireland, in stalemate for months after two democratically elected coalitions failed to form a government.)

His connections with the former Soviet Union are worth noting. Mahmoud Abbas, who hails from the Galilee region in Israel, was

---

[153] *JNN* editors, 1 March 2016, alluding to an *INN* article.
[154] Charlie Mallon, 'Five dead in worst tragedy in the history of Dublin Bus', Independent. i.e., 22 February 2004. <https://www.independent.ie/irish-news/five-dead-in-worst-tragedy-in-the-history-of-dublin-bus-26218114.html> (17 July 2020).

awarded his PhD by the University of Moscow in 1982. His doctoral thesis, which features elements of Holocaust denial,[155] *'concludes that the World Zionist Organization, not the Nazis, was responsible for the destruction of European Jewry.'*[156] Hard evidence has been retrieved from Soviet-era archives which state that *'Abbas, Mahmoud, born 1935 in Palestine, member of the central committee of Fatah and the PLO'* was an *'agent of the KGB'* in Syria during the 1980s.[157]

Just a couple of examples of his more recent activities should shed light on the type of character we are dealing with and the kind of people with whom he associates. A headline from 2014 reads: *Abbas' Fatah calls for 'Day of Rage' Terrorism.*[158] This came just a month after he had the audacity to accuse Israel of genocide, which is akin to North Korea's Kim Yong-un accusing South Korea of crimes against humanity. It is illogical and absurd. The following year, in a ceremony broadcast on official PA TV, the self-proclaimed 'President of Palestine' awarded the 'military Star of Honour' to the female terrorist Fatima Barnawi for planting a bomb in a cinema in the 1960s.[159] It should not be surprising that a contingent of lawmakers deemed it necessary to send a letter to the PA urging that its political and religious leaders cease provoking terror. Here is a short excerpt from the missive which was signed by no less than 369 bipartisan members of the American congress and addressed on 3 November 2015 to the Palestinian chief Mahmoud Abbas:

---

[155] Wikipedia, July 2014. <https://en.wikipedia.org/wiki/The_Other_Side:_The_Secret_Relationship_Between_Nazism_and_Zionism> (17 July 2020).

[156] David Bedein, 'Hitler's ally, Abbas's hero, Netanyahu's response', *Times of Israel*, 7 October 2013. <https://blogs.timesofisrael.com/netanyahu-answers-abbass-gowing-praise-of-hitlers-ally> (2 July 2020).

[157] Jeffrey Heller, 'Palestinian leader Abbas was KGB spy in 1980s: Israeli researchers', *Reuters*, 8 September 2016. <https://www.reuters.com/article/us-israel-palestinians-abbas/palestinian-leader-abbas-was-kgb-spy-in-1980s-israeli-researchers-idUSKCN11E1U0> (2 July 2020).

[158] *JNN*, 3 November 2014, alluding to *Arutz-7* article.

[159] *JNN*, 8 June 2015, alluding to an article in *Arutz-7*.

'Statements made by you, other political figures, clerics and official PA media have undoubtedly served to inflame the current situation. False claims about changing the status quo on the Temple Mount or accusations of Israel executing an attacker – when, in fact, he is being treated in an Israeli hospital – only encourage more acts of terror. The abhorrent and deadly rhetoric – including calls for knife attacks on Israelis – must stop.'[160]

This is not the first and will certainly not be the last time Israeli medical professionals have administered medical care to wounded Palestinian terrorists. On 4 January 2013, Abbas gave a televised address to thousands of Gazans gathered for a Fatah rally in the Strip. During his speech he profusely lauded the late Grand Mufti of Jerusalem Hajj Amin al-Husseini and encouraged his fellow Palestinians to emulate the notorious figure whom he called his 'hero'.[161] A study of the Mufti's profile will underscore the message Abbas is sending and that to which he personally aspires.

DARK CIRCLES

The Grand Mufti of Jerusalem and president of the Supreme Muslim Council Hajj Amin al-Husseini (1897–1974) was the most prominent and powerful Arab official under the British Mandate in Palestine. His popularity spread further afield during the 1920s and 30s when he travelled throughout the Arab world drawing the attention of his brethren to his Palestinian agenda and fomenting hatred against the Jews of British Palestine.

He convened pan-Islamic conferences which gained him further favour and prestige among his co-religionists. Wanted by the British for spearheading violent attacks in the Holy Land, the Mufti

---

[160] See <https://boyle.house.gov/media-center/in-the-news/369-house-members-urge-end-palestinian-authority-incitement> (3 July 2020).

[161] *JNN*, 9 January 2013, alluding to articles in *MEMRI* and *Israel Today*.

could not attend the 1937 conference in Syria, of which he was elected 'honorary president'. 'A Proclamation of the Grand Mufti to the Islamic World' was read on his behalf to the 400 assembled delegates, in which he drew a parallel between Arab and German treatment of Jewish people who, in his own words, *'are driven off like mangy dogs'.*[162] Quoting the Qur'an (Sura 4:51–52) he said: *'whomever Allah curses, you will find no helper for him,'* before drawing the following conclusion: *'And it can be seen how this curse has come true. The Jews are scattered homeless across the entire world'.* With nothing but contempt for the predicament of the refugees of his day he goaded: *'Do not rest until your land is free of the Jews.'*[163] Not only was his speech printed and distributed across the Arab world, but the following year, *'in 1938 the Nazis published a German translation in Berlin'.*[164]

By that time, al-Husseini had fled Palestine. While in Iraq, his involvement with a pro-Nazi faction sparked riots in which 179 Jewish residents of Baghdad were murdered.[165] With the British on his tail again he took flight and set his sights on the Fatherland. The Grand Mufti arrived in Berlin on 6 November 1941. But he was no stranger to the Nazis.

'As early as 1933, right after Hitler became chancellor of Germany, al-Husseini reached out to the German consul in Jerusalem, assuring him that, "the Muslims inside and outside Palestine welcomed the new regime of Germany and hoped for the extension of the fascist, anti-democratic governmental system to other countries."'[166]

---

[162] Joseph S. Spoerl, *Palestinians, Arabs and the Holocaust*, in JSTOR.org, p. 17. <https://www.jstor.org/stable/44289822?seq=7#metadata_info_tab_contents> (1 July 2020).
[163] Ibid, pp. 17–18.
[164] Ibid, p. 18.
[165] Ibid, p. 19.
[166] Ibid.

Indeed, the German Reich had supplied him with funds and weapons to aid him in the 1936–39 Arab Revolt in Palestine. By March 1941 he was recognised by Nazi strategists as being the key to the Arab world.[167]

MUFTI-HITLER PACT

The Grand Mufti attended a meeting with Adolf Hitler on 28 November 1941. According to the official record of the dialogue, he told the totalitarian dictator that because of their shared enemies (i.e. the English, the Jews and the Communists) he considered Germans and Arabs to be *'natural friends.'*[168] Aware of Hitler's aspirations to extend the Reich beyond the boundaries of Europe the Middle Eastern leader guaranteed the allegiance of his people who were, *'prepared to cooperate with Germany with all their hearts.'*[169] His appeal to the Nazi regime was that it help liberate the Arab lands which were then either under the British or the French Mandate. He then made reference to an official letter he had received from Berlin which clarified that Germany, *'recognized the aspirations to independence and freedom of the Arabs, just as she supported the elimination of the Jewish national home.'*[170] (It is interesting to note that even before the nations of the modern world acknowledged the existence of a Jewish homeland, the Nazis did.)

On his part, Hitler made a *'confidential declaration'*[171] that as soon as his forces reached the Middle East he would personally, *'give the Arab world the assurance that its hour of liberation had arrived. Germany's objective would then be solely the destruction of the Jewish element residing in the Arab sphere under the*

---

[167] Ibid, p. 20.

[168] *Documents on German Foreign Policy 1918-1945,* Series D, Vol XIII, London, 1964, cited in *Times of Israel,* 21 October 2015, Full official record: What the mufti said to Hitler. <https://www.timesofisrael.com/full-official-record-what-the-mufti-said-to-hitler/> (1 July 2020).].

[169] Ibid.

[170] Ibid.

[171] Ibid.

protection of British power.'[172] In the meantime, he informed his guest that, *'Germany was resolved, step by step, to ask one European nation after the other to solve its Jewish problem.'*[173] Is it possible that the German dictator was spurred to action by this encouraging encounter and the promised allegiance of the powerful Arab world? Or is it simply a coincidence that promptly after the meeting with the Grand Mufti, the Führer ordered Heydrich of the Reich Security Head Office to organise a meeting to take place within ten days in order to settle the, *'final solution of the Jewish question?'*[174] (Due to the unexpected attack on Pearl Harbour, however, the conference which was to be held on 9 December was postponed for three weeks and took place in January 1942.) At this, the infamous Wannsee Conference, it took fifteen German government officials less than two hours to agree unanimously that the annihilation of the Jewish population of Europe would be accomplished using poison gas. As Holocaust historian Christopher R. Browning has noted: *'In March 1942 every major Jewish community [in Europe] was still intact, and 80% of those European Jews who would be murdered in the Holocaust were still alive. By February 1943, just under one year later, 80% of those European Jews were already dead.'*[175]

DEEP LINES

Transcripts from US government archives expose the Mufti's deep involvement in devising pro-Nazi propaganda. *'An enormous body'* of these virulent messages which he together with other Islamic expatriates disseminated were, *'based almost entirely on ... the Qur'an... and sayings of Muhammad'*[176] and were received in printed form and over the airwaves by Arab audiences across the Middle East and North Africa. Some of this propaganda, as

---

[172] Ibid.

[173] Ibid.

[174] Spoerl, *Holocaust*, p. 20.

[175] Christopher R. Browning cited in *Holocaust Memorial Day 2013* printed by Holocaust Education Trust Ireland, Dublin 2013.

[176] Spoerl, *Holocaust*, p. 22.

philosophy professor Joseph Spoerl points out, was nothing other than, *'incitement to genocide'*. Here is an example of just that: *'Kill the Jews wherever you find them. This pleases God, history and religion.'*[177]

The Grand Mufti appears to have befriended certain top SS officials, who were won over by his charisma and charm. *'In his memoirs, he admits that his friend Heinrich Himmler had told him in the summer of 1943 that the Nazis already had liquidated some three million Jews.'*[178] Publicly hailing the annihilation, the Nazi propagandist al-Husseini told his own Palestinian people: *'History will record this action as one of the wisest steps ever taken.'*[179] Senior witnesses for the prosecution at the Nuremburg trials not only corroborated his close ties with Hitler's learned and intelligent sadistic henchmen but made other accusations of a far more serious nature. The following is an excerpt from the affidavit of one of those witnesses: an SS subordinate of Eichmann's, Dieter Wisliceny.

> *'The Mufti was* one of the initiators *of the systematic extermination of European Jewry for the Germans and had been the* permanent collaborator and advisor *of Eichmann and Himmler in the execution of the plan ... He had* repeatedly suggested *to the various authorities with whom he had been in contact, above all before Hitler, Ribbentrop and Himmler, the extermination of European Jewry. He considered this as a comfortable solution of the Palestinian problem.'*[180] [Emphasis added.]

This testimony implicates the Grand Mufti for the influential role he played in motivating the Nazi leadership to implement the 'final solution' A.S.A.P. 'Cleansing' Europe of its Jewish population

---

[177] Ibid
[178] Ibid, p. 23.
[179] Ibid, p. 22.
[180] Bedein, 'Hitler's ally'.

was a *'comfortable solution'* in his eyes, as it would hugely diminish the number of Jewish immigrants in Palestine. The SS Haupsturmfuhrer Wisliceny continued to expose al-Husseini's culpability as follows: *'In his messages broadcast from Berlin, he surpassed us in anti-Jewish attacks. He was one of Eichmann's best friends and had constantly incited him to accelerate the extermination measures.'*[181]

When given the opportunity to intervene on behalf of child victims of the Holocaust, the Mufti responded with complete callousness of heart. The British and Germans had agreed upon a deal in May 1943 to, *'allow 4,000 Jewish children to enter Palestine in exchange for 20,000 German prisoners of war,'* yet the Grand Mufti prohibited it, thereby condoning the execution of these children.[182] Books, essays and articles are replete with lengthy indictments against Hajj Amin al-Husseini. This was the man – the 'hero' – who has been championed by Mahmoud Abbas; this was the leader – one of the founding fathers of radical Islam – whom the head of the PA in his 2013 speech described as a 'martyr' and 'pioneer'. As Spoerl has accurately discerned: *'This is akin to a German chancellor in 2013 praising Adolf Hitler as a "martyr" and "pioneer."'*[183]

SKIN DEEP

Before we close the lid of the Grand Mufti's coffin, it is worth noting that he groomed a young Egyptian to carry his baton to the next generation of Palestinian Arabs. That young man was the late Yasser Arafat (1929–2004). According to Arafat's younger brother and sister: *'the Mufti performed the role of a surrogate father figure and mentor to the young Arafat.'*[184] The notorious radical leader who headed Fatah and later became Chairman of the

---

[181] Ibid.
[182] Ben Cohen, 'The Mufti and the Holocaust, Revisited', *The Algemeiner*, 23 October 2015. < https://www.algemeiner.com/2015/10/23/the-mufti-and-the-holocaust-revisited/> (3 July 2020).
[183] Spoerl, *Holocaust*, p. 28.
[184] Bedein, 'Hitler's Ally'.

Palestine Liberation Organisation (PLO) evidently lived up to the expectations of his predecessor, as he spent most of his life fomenting violent attacks against Israelis. It appears that Mahmoud Abbas was not the first Palestinian President to have had close connections with the USSR's infamous secret police; Arafat was a *'KGB-backed terrorist'*. These are the words of a former Romanian intelligence officer, Ion Mihai Pacepa, who defected to the USA. A telling article which he wrote for the Wall Street Journal in 2002 proves this point, while at the same time exposing Arafat's merciless mantra and its serious implications.

> *'When I first met Arafat, I was stunned by the ideological similarity between him and his KGB mentor. Arafat's broken record was that American "imperial Zionism" was the "rabid dog of the world," and there was only one way to deal with a rabid dog: "Kill it!" In the years when Gen. Sakharovsky was the chief Soviet intelligence adviser in Romania, he used to preach in his soft, melodious voice that "the bourgeoisie" was the "rabid dog of imperialism," adding that there was "just one way to deal with a rabid dog: Shoot it!" He was responsible for killing 50,000 Romanians.'*[185]

There came a day when Arafat strategically transformed his international image from one of violent antagonist and instigator of terrorist acts to the new tame and peace-seeking leader of the Palestinians. Among the likely reasons he changed tack were that PLO funds were running low (after the collapse of its major financer: the Soviet Union) and securing a peace deal would guarantee financial aid from the West; his popularity was fading among his own people who were growing tired of his tyranny and colossal corruption and of his failure to procure for them an

---

[185] I.M. Pacepa, 'The Arafat I knew', *Wall Street Journal*, 12 January 2002. <https://webhome.weizmann.ac.il/home/comartin/israel/pacepa-wsj.html> (29 July 2020).

independent state.[186] Sitting down to peace talks worked very much in his favour. In a nutshell, the 1993 Oslo Peace Accords laid the groundwork for the Palestinians to self-govern the Gaza Strip and eventually most of the West Bank. Thus the establishment of a Palestinian state with East Jerusalem as its capital was there for the taking.

All that was required of the Palestinian leadership was that it renounce the jihadist element of the PLO covenant which calls for the destruction of the Jewish State; accept the creation of an interim government: the Palestinian Authority to replace the PLO (which would have its terror status revoked);[187] and recognise Israel's statehood. Arafat accepted these preconditions, signed the deal and began the incremental take-over of the West Bank. For this historic decision he and his Israeli counterpart[188] shared the 1994 Nobel Peace Prize. There was great elation in much of Israel as peace and security finally appeared to be within their grasp. Sadly, that joy would be short-lived.

Terror attacks against the Jewish populace increased both in intensity and ferocity at that time and it soon became clear that the leader of the PLO had no intention of living up to his promises. Here is an extract from a speech made by Arafat to Arab diplomats in Sweden in 1996 which was leaked to the press: *The PLO plans to eliminate the State of Israel and establish a purely Palestinian State.'* Far from peace-seeking, the statement reveals both his duplicity and his goal which was to ethnically cleanse the land of its Jewish residents. He continued, *'We will make life unbearable for Jews ... have no use for Jews; they are and remain Jews. We now need all the help we can get from you in our battle for a united Palestine under total Arab-Muslim domination.'*[189]

---

[186] Jewish Virtual Library, 'Yasser Arafat 1929 – 2004'.
<https://www.jewishvirtuallibrary.org/yasser-arafat> (29 July 2020).
[187] JNN, 29 April 2016, alluding to an Israel National News report.
[188] Both President Shimon Peres and PM Yitzhak Rabin shared the award with Yasser Arafat.
[189] C. Thomas, 'US deluding itself about Arafat's intent', *Washington Times*, 1 March 1996, cited in Ben-Dror Yemini, *Industry of Lies*, ISGAP, 2017, p. 227.

Such disparagement proves Arafat's true feelings on the subject of Israel, and exposes his callous deceit and deep insincerity which he hid behind a broad smile on the world stage.

CLEANSING PROPERTIES

There was much enthusiasm among many prominent Arab leaders, including the Saudi Arabian king and the Egyptian president, in the year 2000 when President Clinton unveiled his peace proposal at Camp David. Making their feelings known to the Palestinian leader, the Saudi Arabian Ambassador to the US Bin Sultan warned: *'If we lose this opportunity, it is not going to be a tragedy. It is going to be a crime.'*[190] Contrary to the warnings, Yasser Arafat turned down the Camp David proposal, as verified by Bill Clinton, and stepped up the terrorism. The subsequent atrocities of the five-year so-called 'uprising' would shatter his veneer in the eyes of many. This, the 'Second Intifada', prominently featured suicide bombers who made global headlines for causing a bloodbath by blowing up buses, bustling markets and busy restaurants in the cities and towns of Israel.[191]

The following statistics make it clear which side was deliberately targeting civilians: *'the Second Intifada which had begun within weeks of the failure of the Camp David Summit was raging and intensifying. Thousands of Israelis and Palestinians were killed. 1,137 Israelis died between 2000-2005, 78 per cent of them civilians, while only a third of Palestinian deaths were uninvolved civilians.'*[192] Had Arafat not violated the Oslo agreement and had he accepted the highly advantageous Camp David offer, the Palestinian State would be on the map and both sides could have had the opportunity to live peaceably and progressively. Instead, as Israeli Prime Minister Ariel Sharon remarked:

---

[190] Yemini, *Industry of Lies*, p. 231.
[191] Further details of which will be considered in a later chapter.
[192] Yemini, *Industry of Lies*, p. 231.

'Israel is in a war, a war against terror. This is a war that was forced on us. It is not a war that we decided to embark upon ... This terror is operated, directed and initiated by one man – Palestinian Authority Chairman Yasser Arafat ... Arafat heads a coalition of terror ... All those who were raised on the values of freedom and democracy, must know that Arafat is an obstacle to peace in the Middle East.'[193]

As a mark of respect for the genuine noble recipients of the prestigious award and on behalf of future laureates, ought not the Nobel peace prize have been retracted from the late Yasser Arafat? Even posthumously?

SOLUTIONS

Arafat's successor, the current Palestinian leader also *claims* to favour the 'two states for two peoples' solution, one for the Palestinians alongside another for the Israelis; yet this completely contradicts his actions. Abbas' true colours came to the fore while speaking at a Fatah conference in 2009 where he made the following uncompromising statement: *'There must be absolute opposition, from which there is no withdrawal, to recognizing Israel as a "Jewish State".'[194]* The PA's ambassador to Tehran in 2014 unashamedly expressed, *'The Zionist regime is an aggressive, cancerous growth that must be eliminated sooner or later,'[195]* thereby disclosing that they have no intention of living side-by-side with Israel. Let there be no confusion regarding the 'Zionist regime'; in the eyes of Abbas' Palestinian government as also in the eyes of jihadists in the region, it simply means the Jewish nation. This explains what Abbas meant when on 2 March 2012 he admitted that his Fatah party and the overt terrorist organisation Hamas share the same ideology[196] and again on 9 July 2014 when

---

[193] https://www.jewishvirtuallibrary.org/operation-defensive-shield> (13 August 2020).
[194] Yemini, *Industry of Lies*, p. 240.
[195] *JNN*, 29 December 2014, citing the *Jerusalem Post*.
[196] Spoerl, *Holocaust*, p. 32.

he affirmed that the goal of both parties is the same. This message was clearly conveyed on the official Fatah Facebook page which featured photos of terrorists from the military wings of Fatah, Hamas and Islamic Jihad, above the slogan *'Brothers in arms: one God, one homeland, one enemy, one goal.'*[197]

Mahmoud Abbas has rejected each and every peace deal to date, beginning with the very appealing Olmert proposal in 2008: that Israel withdraw from a staggering 93 per cent of the disputed territories (meaning, the West Bank and East Jerusalem); John Kerry's plan in 2014; and President Trump's 'Deal of the Century' in 2020. Conversely, on each of these occasions – and indeed every time a formal two-state solution was brought to the negotiating table – Israel actually yielded and accepted the deal, despite the huge sacrifices it would entail on every level: community, social, economic, political and, most vital of all, security.

HAMAS FOUNDATION

'The Palestinian group that most clearly reflects the world-view of Haj Amin Al-Husseini is Hamas, the name taken in 1987 by the Palestinian branch of the Muslim Brotherhood. Haj Amin belonged to the Brotherhood and actively supported it throughout his life.'[198] Labelled a terrorist organisation by the European Union,[199] Hamas is one of a network of Islamic jihadist groups. Issued in 1988, the *Covenant of Hamas* not only elevates the anti-Semitic, conspiracy-rooted *Protocols of the Elders of Zion* publication, but calls for Jihad[200] in Israel,[201] and rejects all possibilities of a peace settlement.[202] In the preamble it states: *'Israel will exist and will continue to exist until Islam will obliterate it.'*[203] Incitement to

---

[197] *JNN*, 10 July 2014, alluding to articles in the *Gatestone Institute* and *INN*.

[198] Spoerl, *Holocaust*, p.29.

[199] To their shame, this label has been retracted.

[200] Jihad is an Islamic word meaning 'holy war'.

[201] Covenant of Hamas, Article 15, cited on Irish Christian Friends of Israel flyer, August 2014.

[202] Ibid, Art. 13.

[203] Ibid, preamble.

violence against Jews, is a priority on the agenda which, citing the Hadith[204], Article 7 states: *'The Day of Judgment will not come about until Moslems fight Jews and kill them. Then, the Jews will hide behind rocks and trees, and the rocks and trees will cry out: "O Moslem, there is a Jew hiding behind me, come and kill him."'[205]* Anyone who offers moral support to Hamas aligns himself with the covenant and condones the murder of innocent men, women and children. I recommend you keep an eye out for political figures on the world platform who prop up Hamas. Anti-terrorism 'watchdog', *Palestinian Media Watch*, in 2014 quoted Hamas PM, Ismail Haniyeh. Referring to Israel as the enemy, he proudly declared: *'We love death like our enemies love life! We love Martyrdom, the way in which Hamas leaders died.'*[206] Please do not gloss over Haniyeh's admission that Israel 'loves life', which implies the honouring and the preservation thereof; and would you not agree that this statement as a whole, made by a government head, is politically *incorrect*?

PROMINENT FEATURES

A consideration of how Palestinian children are esteemed in the eyes of their own leaders and how they are thus treated is worth our attention. Social media posts and TV clips make for a quick and easy evaluation in this regard. In autumn 2015 on Fatah's official Facebook page an image was posted of the front cover of a Nazi children's book from the 1930s; needless to say it featured an anti-Semitic caricature of a Jew.[207] In much of the world today an image of this kind is shown with the purpose of exposing the evils of anti-Semitic propaganda; this is evidently not the case among the PA's lawmakers and educators whose motive is to encourage further hate crimes. It is no secret that Fatah is guilty of inciting its people to hatred and violence on social networking

---

[204] According to Britannica.com, Hadith is the *'record of the traditions or sayings of the prophet Muhammad'*; it is second in importance to the Quran.
[205] Ibid, Art. 7.
[206] *JNN* editors, 31 July 2014.
[207] *JNN*, 30 October 2015, alluding to an article in *Arutz-7*.

sites, and encourages parents to raise their children for terror: *'According to Palestinian Media Watch (PMW), a prominent [Facebook] post reads, "Teach your children to love the soil. Teach them there is a seed in the soil and if you water it with blood, it will sprout a revolution." The statement is accompanied by an armed man standing over a large crowd with a rifle, under the Palestinian Arab flag.'[208]* Such exploitation of young and developing minds and hearts is criminal. It is a violation of the basic need for safety and security that is inherent in every child – an abuse of their right to freedom from terror.

Hamas' official television network Al-Aqsa TV last year aired a music video titled 'Death to Israel' which contained the following lyrics: *'Strap on an explosive belt ... O martyrdom seeker, respond to Al-Aqsa's call ... Send them to hell ... Let fire burn them, turn them into body parts, roast them.'[209]* Is it any wonder that there are so many warped and violent adolescent Palestinians when they are being cruelly brainwashed in this way? It is as equally tragic as it is horrific that a nineteen-year-old should be so deceived that he would blow himself up and take as many Jewish people as possible with him. This is what Abu Srour from Bethlehem did after boarding a Jerusalem bus in April 2016.[210] A BBC Two documentary film titled *One Day in Gaza* featured a twenty-four-year-old Gazan man, Bader Saleh, who described the effect the ongoing border riots had on him: *'The revolutionary songs, they excite you, they encourage you to rip a Jew's head off.'[211]* Even the horribly biased United Nations has spoken out (albeit rather feebly) against such incitement; an August 2019 report on the Palestinians by the UN Committee on the

---

[208] *JNN*, 8 February 2014, citing *INN*.

[209] *Jerusalem Post*, 7 March 2019, Sara Rubenstein: 'Al-Aqsa TV: Death to Israel, turn them into body parts, roast them.' < https://www.jpost.com/arab-israeli-conflict/al-aqsa-tv-death-to-israel-turn-them-into-body-parts-roast-them-582692> (18 August 2020).

[210] *JNN*, 22 April 2016, alluding to an article in Ynet.

[211] *Conservative Friends of Israel*, 17 May 2019, 'BBC documentary confirms Hamas role in Gaza border protests'. <https://cfoi.co.uk/bbc-documentary-confirms-hamas-role-in-gaza-border-protests/> (18 August 2020).

Elimination of Racial Discrimination (CERD) logged its concerns about, *'Hate speech in media outlets, social media, public officials' statements, and school curricula and textbooks which fuel hatred and may incite violence against Israelis, which at times also fuels anti-Semitism.'*[212]

Without question, the systematic indoctrination of parent and child is incredibly destructive to society as a whole. Yet the PA Minister for Education Sabri Saidam who in the presence of a young girl, Sidra Al-Shawamreh, during a television broadcast in March 2019 illustrated that all Israel is 'Palestine'. A song was frequently played on PA TV and radio in the summer of 2018 which encouraged pregnant women to dedicate their unborn child to martyrdom. Here are a couple of lines from the song which have been translated from Arabic by Palestinian Media Watch (PMW): *'Palestine is etched on the heart of the foetus, a proud Martyr in his mother's womb.'*[213] Nowhere in Israel, as in any other democratic state, will you find such brainwashing propaganda dominating the airwaves; neither is there a political agenda to control and exploit the family unit.

BLEMISH FREE

There is no doubt about it, life in Palestinian neighbourhoods is tough. Non-compliant residents of the Gaza Strip are routinely beaten by Hamas. Yet this despotic abuse of authority is not solely confined to the coastal enclave, the PA also rules with an iron fist. In a comprehensive report titled: 'Two Authorities, One Way, Zero Dissent' *Human Rights Watch* published their disturbing findings following two years of researching human rights violations in Palestinian territories. *'The West Bank and the Gaza Strip ... authorities have established machineries of repression to crush*

---

[212] *JNN*, 3 September 2019, 'A United Nations' first on behalf of Israel.'

[213] *Breitbart*, 7 July 2018, Breitbart Jerusalem 'PA TV to pregnant Palestinians: 'Your baby is a martyr for Palestine.' <https://www.breitbart.com/middle-east/2018/07/07/pa-tv-to-pregnant-palestinians-your-baby-a-martyr-for-palestine/> (11 July 2018).

dissent, including through the use of torture.'[214] Forget the right to freedom of speech: criticism of the powers that be, however peaceably expressed by journalists, demonstrators or social media users, has resulted in *'scores of arbitrary arrests'* in recent years.[215]

Conscientious objectors and non-conformists must not only face harsh punitive measures inflicted by the governing authorities but are often shunned by the community. On 1 July 2016 a Palestinian man was the first to arrive at the scene of a terror attack in which a car moving at speed was targeted by snipers, killing the middle-aged rabbi who was driving and injuring his wife and one of his daughters. He tended to the needs of Rabbi Michael Mark's family as best he could by releasing them from the overturned vehicle and shielding them from non-sympathetic and aggressive Palestinian passengers in passing vehicles. *'People in the dozens of cars that passed by threatened him and demanded that he refuse to help Jews.'*[216] It is quite shocking that rather than receive recognition for this humanitarian act, Abbas' Palestinian Authority fired him from his post in the public sector. Furthermore, a relative of the 'good Samaritan' told Israel Hayom news, *'since it became clear that he was the first to arrive at the scene of the attack and that he helped the victims, he and his family have been subjected to a smear campaign and received threats.'*[217] To the contrary, Israel, (the supposed enemy) has offered him an Israeli work permit. On his Facebook page the director of the Hebron Regional Council, Yochai Damari, wrote: *'It is our duty as a Jewish nation to show gratitude toward people who behave like upstanding human beings. Specifically at a time like this, it is important … to send a clear message that normal and positive behaviour like this will result in a*

---

[214] *Human Rights Watch*, 23 October 2018, 'Two Authorities, One Way, Zero Dissent'. <https://www.hrw.org/report/2018/10/23/two-authorities-one-way-zero-dissent/arbitrary-arrest-and-torture-under> (20 August 2020).
[215] Ibid.
[216] Israel Hayom, 9 August 2016, 'PA fires Palestinian who helped Jewish terror victims'. < https://www.jns.org/pa-fires-palestinian-who-helped-jewish-terror-victims/> (21 August 2020).
[217] Ibid.

normal and positive reward from us.'[218]

TIRED AND DRY

One could not help but feel sympathy and compassion for these oppressed Palestinian men, women and children, many of whom are sick and tired of being overlooked, maltreated and exploited by their own leaders. The Hamas government places more importance on striking Israel and pounding its civilians than looking after its own neglected people. According to Israeli and Palestinian estimates, approximately 20 per cent of Gaza's annual budget – a whopping $100 million – is spent on the preparation and execution of attacks against the Jewish nation.[219] Ismail Haniyeh's $4 million home covers an area of 27,000 square feet and overlooks the beautiful Mediterranean Sea. The affluence enjoyed by his henchmen is sure to disillusion and embitter any honest and hardworking Palestinian: *'hundreds of the terror group's bosses have become millionnaires by commanding a shadowy smuggling industry and depriving their own people of the chance to prosper.'*[220] To enjoy having access to 24–7 electricity from Gaza's sole power plant one must be a Hamas leader; the rest of the populace tolerates a mere four-hours supply a-day.[221] While the two million citizens of Gaza are subjected to substandard and insufficient medical services, wounded ISIS fighters from the Sinai Peninsula have been receiving medical treatment in Gaza hospitals.[222] The United Nations Relief and Works Agency (UNRWA) which is based in the Strip and employs

---

[218] Ibid.

[219] *Tablet*, February 2018, Liel Leibovitz 'The New York Times is puzzled: Who's responsible for the mess in Gaza?'
<https://www.tabletmag.com/sections/news/articles/the-new-york-times-is-puzzled-whos-responsible-for-the-mess-in-gaza> (21 August 2020).

[220] Ibid.

[221] Arutz-7, 15 February 2018, 'Gaza's only power plant shut down over fuel shortage'.
< https://www.israelnationalnews.com/News/News.aspx/241988> (14 August 2020).

[222] *J Post*, 8 February 2016, 'ISIS operatives in Sinai are receiving medical treatment at Hamas hospitals in Gaza'. <https://www.jpost.com/middle-east/isis-operatives-in-sinai-are-receiving-medical-treatment-at-hamas-hospitals-in-gaza-444233> (14 August 2020).

hundreds of Palestinian teachers, healthcare and social service workers has complained of staff resignations due to threats from local jihadist groups.[223]

Child labour is not a foreign concept in the Strip. Exactly how many children are recruited by the regime God only knows. One thing is certain, Hamas cares little for the dangers faced by the youths it exploits. A 2012 report written for the Institute of Palestine Studies and confirmed by Hamas officials reveals that more than 160 children lost their lives digging terror tunnels from Gaza into Israel.[224] I doubt the Hamas chief would somehow be foolish enough to brag of the numbers of child fatalities that have occurred since then. Writing for the *Washington Post*, Jennifer Rubin comments: *'Hamas is responsible not only for the deaths of the children sent to dig tunnels, but also those who could have been healed and educated if the cement from Israel had been used for schools, clinics and housing rather than to create a subterranean military apparatus.'*[225] Contrary to false reports circulated by much of mainstream media Israel which, by the way considers child labour an outrage, has been and continues to be very generous in its humanitarian outreach to the exploited citizens of Gaza. In the words of Mosab Hassan Yousef, a prominent Hamas dissenter who for fear of his life now lives in the USA: *'Israel helps the Palestinian people more than anyone else.'*[226]

A group of international NGOs came together in February 2020 to raise public awareness surrounding Palestinian child soldiers. Their service on the battlefield side-by-side with adult militants

[223] *CNN*, 2 October 2018, Oren Liebermann, 'UNRWA pulls some staff from Gaza amid threats'. <https://edition.cnn.com/2018/10/02/middleeast/unrwa-gaza-intl/index.html> (17 August 2020).

[224] *Tablet*, 25 July 2014, Meir Freimann, 'Hamas killed 160 Palestinian children to build tunnels'. <https://www.tabletmag.com/sections/news/articles/hamas-killed-160-palestinian-children-to-build-terror-tunnels> (17 August 2020).

[225] *Washington Post*, 31 July 2014, Jennifer Rubin, 'If liberal elites really cared about Gazan children ...' <https://www.washingtonpost.com/blogs/right-turn/wp/2014/07/31/if-liberal-elites-really-cared-about-gazan-children/> (17 August 2020).

[226] *JNN* editors, 24 November 2012, alluding to an article from *INN*.

and terrorists can start as young as nine-years-of-age. In its petition to the nations the coalition of NGOs wrote that Palestinian children have for decades,

> *'Fulfilled the role of combatants, human shields, rioters, labourers ... and even suicide bombers. As a result, their childhoods have been cut short by death, severe injury, or imprisonment. The global community's unwillingness to address the issue has emboldened organizations such as Hamas, Fatah, Palestinian Islamic Jihad and PFLP in their exploitation of children as war resources.'*[227]

The legal system in Palestinian territories is not a place to which females who wish to be treated equally can turn for safety or justice. According to *Reuters* the penal code, *'dates to the 1960s and has been criticized for inadequate protection for women.'*[228] In such a society family honour is sacrosanct and the discovery – perceived or actual – that a girl or woman has been 'sexually immoral' can warrant the taking of life. Lenient penalties, at best, are administered to the perpetrators, who are usually relatives of the victims. Between January and September 2019 at least 18 women were slain by family members, prompting hundreds of Palestinian women to take to the streets of Ramallah in the West Bank in protest against the 'honour killings' and demanding protection from their government. A 30-year-old activist from Jerusalem, Amal Khayat declared: *'I'm here to say enough is enough. We've lost enough women. Enough victims have died, have been killed, have been tortured, raped, harassed, and still*

---

[227] *J Post*, 12 February 2020, Donna Rachel Edmunds, 'NGOs call for public support in ending use of Palestinian child soldiers'. <https://www.jpost.com/arab-israeli-conflict/ngos-call-for-public-support-in-ending-use-of-palestinian-child-soldiers-617332> (2 September 2020).
[228] *Reuters*, 4 September 2019, Ali Sawafta, 'Palestinian women demand legal protection after suspected 'honor killing'. <https://www.reuters.com/article/us-palestinians-women-killings/palestinian-women-demand-legal-protection-after-suspected-honor-killing-idUSKCN1VP2AW> (31 August 2020).

there's no justice.'[229]

When one considers the amount of human rights abuses inflicted upon the Palestinian people by their own governments, it is not surprising that there has been growing social unrest. Fed-up with President Abbas, crowds of protestors are demanding the ballot vote and new leadership. In September 2019, a Lebanese Christian, Jonathon Elkhoury, who now resides happily in Israel tweeted the following message: *'Looking at Israel having its 22 [general] elections the Palestinians are sick of Mahmoud Abbas and Hamas dictatorship for the last 14 years.'[230]* Elections which were scheduled for 2012 in Gaza never materialised. *'We want to live'* was the slogan chanted by hundreds of activists in the towns and villages of Gaza during a three-day protest against tax hikes in March 2019. According to the official PA news agency Wafa, demonstrators who had set tyres alight were met with excess force and assaulted by Hamas gunmen who used, *'live ammunition and clubs.'[231]* Later in the year hundreds took to the streets in Fatah and Hamas-ruled territories, appalled and outraged by the self-immolation of a homeless 28-year-old demonstrator from the Strip, Yahyah Karajeh, who was refused an audience with the Hamas chief and could no longer face living on the streets with his brother.[232]

HEZBOLLAH'S TONE

The headline of a 2020 *Arab News* report reads 'New government shows Hezbollah "takeover of Lebanon is complete"'. Of its twenty newly appointed ministers, *'the majority'*, according to the Saudi daily, *'belong to Hezbollah and its allies.'[233]* This is not

---

[229] Ibid.

[230] *JNN*, 18 September 2019, citing a report on *Breaking Israel News*.

[231] *JNN*, 20 March 2019, alluding to a report in *INN*.

[232] *J Post*, 10 November 2019, Khaled Abu Toameh, 'Gaza orphan's self-immolation sparks outcry on social media'. <https://www.jpost.com/israel-news/gaza-orphans-self-immolation-sparks-outcry-on-social-media-607408> (2 September 2020).

[233] *Arab News*, 22 January 2020, Najia Houssari & Randa Takieddine, 'New government shows Hezbollah "takeover of Lebanon is complete".'

considered good news either for Lebanon or for Saudi Arabia and other Sunni Muslim states in the region, a number of which have classified Hezbollah as a terror organisation, as have the UK, Germany, Canada and the USA. The Shi'ite political movement and its guerrilla army was founded and continues to be funded by the Iranian regime.[234]

A glance at a quotation from Hezbollah's long-established leader Hassan Nasrallah will suffice to illustrate the threat Israel constantly faces on her northern border. *'If all Jews gather in Israel, it will save us the problem of chasing them around the world* [i.e. to destroy them].'[235] Nasrallah is fearless and brazen regarding his wicked agenda. Before a crowd of tens of thousands of Hezbollah supporters in 2012 he made a vow to the prophet Mohammad: *'God's prophet, we will sacrifice ourselves, our blood, our families and our money for your honour.'[236]* According to a 2016 report, Hezbollah's arsenal contains no fewer than 150,000 rockets, which apparently exceeds the amount most countries possess.[237] This includes a large number of long-range missiles, capable of reaching the southern cities of Israel, along with some precision missiles which it has recently acquired from Iran. In the words of a Hezbollah veteran operative, Haj Mohammed, *'the game has changed entirely'* since the last war with Israel in 2006, *'This time … we'll make it rain missiles with pinpoint accuracy.'[238]*

Despite the presence of the United Nations Interim Force in Lebanon (UNIFIL) to oversee its 'blue line' border with Israel, the area is a beehive of terrorist ingenuity. Hezbollah's extensive

---

<https://www.arabnews.com/node/1616716/middle-east> (27 August 2020).

[234] *Reuters*, 4 August 2020, compiled by Beirut bureau, 'Background on Lebanon's Hezbollah'.
<https://www.reuters.com/article/us-lebanon-tribunal-hariri-hezbollah-fac/background-on-lebanons-hezbollah-idUSKCN2500LF> (27 August 2020).

[235] *JNN* editors, 4 March 2015, alluding to a *Jerusalem Post* article.

[236] Ibid, 19 September 2012, alluding to a *Ynet* article.

[237] Ibid, 24 October 2018, alluding to an *Arutz-7* article.

[238] *The Atlantic*, 22 July 2018, David Kenner, 'Why Israel fears Iran's presence in Syria.' <https://www.theatlantic.com/international/archive/2018/07/hezbollah-iran-new-weapons-israel/565796/> (27 August 2020).

subterranean infrastructure in south Lebanon which was discovered by Israel was confirmed by the international peacekeeping body to be a *'violation of resolution 1701.'[239]* This UN resolution calls for the disarmament of all Lebanese guerrilla forces and prohibits them from entering within roughly 20 kilometres of the blue line, from which they had previously carried out terror attacks on Israel. Thus when the Israel Defence Force (IDF) undertook Operation Northern Shield in 2018 to neutralize the terror tunnels that ran underground from towns in South Lebanon to settlements in northern Israel her actions were met with approval, most notably by Britain, Germany, Russia and the USA.[240] Moreover, when a large tour of UN diplomats were given the opportunity to examine the tunnels, Panama's Ambassador Melitón Arrocha Ruíz commended Israel's endeavour and promised, *'We will pass on what we saw and convey how Israel is thriving, open and democratic and that we all certainly share similar rule of law values.'[241]*

It is no secret that the Lebanese terror group has close ties with Syria's authoritarian President Bashar al-Assad and has supported the cruel regime during its ongoing civil war. Affected by the immense influx of refugees into Europe – a tragic feature of the Syrian conflict – and by the trail of terror unleashed by undercover ISIS operatives in their midst, in May 2019 the European Parliament wrote: *'Hezbollah's growing arsenal and entanglement in regional conflicts severely destabilizes certain countries and the wider Middle East. It is high time to acknowledge that Islamist inspired terrorism is not only a threat to the Middle East, but is also the top threat to Europe's security.'[242]* Nasrallah's far-reaching terror tentacles are not going unnoticed. Meanwhile in Ireland intense lobbying was underway to pass into law a bill which sought to criminalise the sale of produce originating

---

[239] *JNN*, 29 April 2019, citing an article from *INN*.

[240] *JNN*, 7 December 2018, alluding to articles in *Ha'aretz*, *Times of Israel* and *INN*.

[241] *JNN*, 7 February 2019, citing an article from *Ynet*.

[242] *Jerusalem Post*, 1 April 2019, Benjamin Weinthal, 'EU parliament politicians call for a full ban of Hezbollah'. <https://www.jpost.com/middle-east/eu-parliament-politicians-call-for-a-full-ban-of-hezbollah-543447> (28 August 2020).

from Israel's disputed territories. In response to this, PM Benjamin Netanyahu remarked, *'Instead of Ireland condemning Syria for slaughtering hundreds of thousands of civilians, Turkey for the occupation of northern Cyprus and the terrorist organisations for murdering thousands of Israelis, it attacks Israel, the only democracy in the Middle East. What a disgrace.'*[243] I may be proud to be Irish but in this case, and with a heavy heart, I cannot but agree with the Israeli Premier; it is a disgrace.

Hezbollah may be the largest terror organisation in Lebanon, but it is not the only one; Fatah also has a presence in the country and is equally eager to take advantage of vulnerable and deceived civilians. On its Facebook page on 3 September 2012 a photograph was posted of a mother attaching a suicide belt to her young child. Included in the accompanying text was the following: *'The homeland needs you, son. Go and blow up the sons of Zion.'*[244]

REFLECTIONS

Perhaps while in an Irish city or in one of our universities you noticed a group of activists wearing PLO scarves and handing out literature bearing the campaign slogan: *'From the river to the sea Palestine will be free.'* And perhaps it evoked compassion and a common longing for justice. It is good if your conscience was awakened to the hardships faced by the oppressed Palestinian people; not to care is callous and inhumane. I have two concerns, however. The first is that the blame is almost always directed at those who are not responsible for the suffering and who on the contrary endeavour to alleviate it, namely Israel, while the true tyrants are living a life of luxury which is steeped in corruption and comes at the expense of the serenity, safety and sanity of their own people. Secondly, the above slogan which has become the mantra of demonstrators at pro-Palestinian rallies sounds innocent and

---

[243] *JNN*, 28 January 2019, citing an article from *Koenig*.
[244] *Palestinian Media Watch (PMW)*, 3 September 2012, 'Mother places suicide belt on child, on Facebook page for Fatah in Lebanon'. <https://palwatch.org/page/4077> (28 August 2020).

honourable (who in their right mind doesn't support freedom?) yet one must be willing to ask what is truly being conveyed when Palestinian leaders declare: 'From the river to the sea.' The river represents the Jordan River, which is Israel's eastern border and the sea denotes her coastal border in the west, the Mediterranean Sea. At best, this may appear to be a call for ethnic cleansing – the expulsion of every Jew from the land. From the facts, statistics and citations relayed in this chapter, however, it should be obvious to the reader that this chant is far more sinister in nature and demands the absolute elimination, indeed the annihilation of the Jewish nation. Don't be fooled: this is unquestionably an exhortation to support genocide. Every compassionate yet ill-informed human rights activist ought to know this.

As for me, I am genuinely pro-Palestinian, and pro-Israeli. Each needs a safe place to call home; each deserves to live as much as the other. The ones whose testimony my conscience will not allow me to condone are the jihadists and most especially the wicked behaviour of their leaders, the majority of whom are themselves terrorists. Thankfully, there are a number of Palestinians who are turning to the light and facing the true facts.

Ramallah-born Sandra Solomon is the niece of one of the founders of Fatah and a prominent leader during the height of the suicide bombings in Israel, Saher Habash. She explains that she and her peers were raised to, *'hate the Jews, hail Hitler and praise the Holocaust.'*[245] After becoming a believer in Jesus Christ her perspective on Israel changed. Now living in Canada she speaks out against the anti-Semitic narrative which is prevalent in her native land and claims, *'They blame Jews for everything. They rejoice in the killing of Jews. There is no respect, no love, no peace, just anger and hatred.'*[246]

It is tragic that the hate speech and incitement to violence wielded

---

[245] *Israel Today*, 30 October 2016, 'Palestinian Woman Becomes Christian, Defends Israel'.
<https://www.israeltoday.co.il/read/palestinian-woman-becomes-christian-defends-israel/> (3 September 2020).
[246] Ibid.

by the PA and Hamas leadership is producing the desired effect; a travesty that thousands of Palestinian people, infected by poisonous lies, have effectively become puppets on a string, wreaking havoc on behalf of these autocratic regimes. You can be sure that neither Mahmoud Abbas, Ismail Haniyeh nor any other top Fatah or Hamas leader will endure interrogation or face incrimination for the vile assaults inflicted by their militant minions. They won't serve a prison sentence for the fatal stabbing of a 13-year-old Jewish girl in her bedroom[247] nor for the father murdered in front of his wife and children, who were also injured in the brutal attack.[248] Both of which occurred during a horrific week of terror in July 2016. Although clearly guilty of provocation, the Palestinian chiefs will not be the ones who are brought to justice for the 2,370 terror attacks in Judea and Samaria in 2019;[249] their dictatorship shields them at home and their cunning façade protects them abroad. Through their lies and propaganda these despots have captivated the global audience. This leads us to the subject of our next chapter: the influence and biases of the worldwide media. But by way of conclusion allow me to draw your attention to an incredibly laudable and illuminating statement: *'I want to be clear: if they make the decision to stop digging tunnels, smuggling arms and firing rockets at us, we will be the first investors in the rehabilitation of the Gaza Strip. We will be the first to invest in a maritime trading port, airport and an industrial zone.'*[250] This avowal was made in late 2016 by the then Israeli Minister of Defence, Avigdor Lieberman, who concluded by declaring, *'Gaza could one day be the new Hong Kong or Singapore.'*

---

[247] *J Post*, 30 June 2016, Tovah Lavaroff, 'Kiryat Arba attack: Palestinian terrorist stabs teen girl to death in bedroom'. < https://www.jpost.com/Arab-Israeli-Conflict/Initial-report-Suspected-terror-shooting-in-Kiryat-Arba-2-wounded-459126> (30 June 2016).

[248] *JNN*, 2 July 2016, alluding to an article in the *Jerusalem Post*.

[249] *VFI News*, 10 January 2020, 'Statistics: Terrorist hits in Israel during 2019.'

[250] *i24 News*, 24 October 2016, 'Lieberman tells Palestinian media next war with Hamas "will be their last."' <https://www.i24news.tv/en/news/israel/diplomacy-defense/128427-161024-lieberman-tell-palestinian-media-next-war-with-gaza-will-be-the-last> (30 October 2016).

7

Hook, Line And Sinker

Living in a 'microwave society' has its advantages. On the one hand, it's a relief not to slave over a clothes' washing board, or to wait for the fire to painstakingly boil a pot of water. At the 'flick of a switch', the home can be heated in minutes; clothes washed and dried; and individual 'instant' dinners served up. On the other hand, the disadvantages of 'hi-tech' living should not be ignored.

TECHNOLOGY INTRIGUE

The pace at which life is accelerating is disquieting. We are left without a minute's peace, under the growing pressure to be electronically available 24/7. The average person is besotted, hook, line and sinker with Web communications while paradoxically, communication person-to-person diminishes. It's one thing to be able to Whatsapp or Zoom call family and friends in our global village and quite another to be regularly out of physical or emotional reach because we're electronically preoccupied.

FAR FROM THE MADDING CROWD

Perhaps much of the ignorance regarding Israel pertains to the fact that modern man is bombarded with distractions. Writing for *Ireland's Own*, Patrick O'Sullivan says, *'there must be many more restless minds now than ever for we live in an age that smothers us with noise on every side.*[251] In His great wisdom, Jesus often

---

[251] Patrick O'Sullivan, 'Heaven's Whisper', *Ireland's Own*, 28 June 2013.

retreated to an isolated place. With His soul subdued and spirit attentive, He engaged with His heavenly Father. If, as the days grow darker, I fail to manage my time effectively, will I be able to recognise the voice of God above all the clamour?

MAKING HEADLINES

Before Nigeria's Boko Haram and the Islamic State (ISIS) began to make world headlines, most people were not aware of the daily martyrdoms of Christian individuals and villages, taking place in as many as sixty countries worldwide. Does it shock you that there have been more Christians martyred for their faith in the twentieth century than in the previous 1,800 years combined? Equally, just because the media is not inclined to give it coverage, please don't assume that Jewish people no longer face racial discrimination.

INTERNATIONAL PRESS

A fundamental objective of journalism is the prompt delivery of news. During the 2014 Gaza conflict, *CBC* published articles which they later revised. In defence of their actions, the ombudsman remarked: *'In a breaking news story, the facts ... are not always apparent at the outset, and that is why stories are amended ... In a war situation it is even more ... difficult to get the facts.'*[252] That may be so but it does not excuse reporters for making assumptions. In this case, the Israel Defence Force was later found *not* to be responsible for the bombing of the Gaza power plant. Yet, the damage to Israel's reputation was already done.

Journalist Matti Friedman associates the current predicament of the Jew with the psychological condition of the world:

> *'Having rehabilitated themselves against considerable odds in a minute corner of the earth, the descendants of*

---

[252] *CBC* Ombudsman's review, September 2014.

powerless people who were pushed out of Europe and the Islamic Middle East, have become what their grandparents were – the pool into which the world spits. The Jews of Israel are the screen onto which it has become socially acceptable to project the things you hate about yourself and your own country.'[253]

Friedman blames reporters for facilitating anti-Semitic bias: *'The tool through which this psychological projection is executed is the international press.'*[254]

OLD NEWS

Before we consider anti-Semitism in Ireland today, may we reflect on how it was handled by the media in the past? Neither the *Freeman's Journal* nor the *Evening Telegraph* responded favourably to anti-Semitic comments in letters from their readers in 1886. In contrast with the Jewish community, which they described as 'hardworking and inoffensive', the *Freeman's Journal* labelled the intolerant Irish writers as 'a set of ruffians' and 'hare-brained fanatics'. To its credit, the *Evening Telegraph* proudly published the following, 'Ireland stands alone among nations in freedom from the odium of having ... persecuted the Jews.'[255] It would be heartening if the same could be said of our nation today.

IRELAND'S LINES OF COMMUNICATION

In 2011 an article was posted on *Broadsheet.ie* titled, *'Ireland "Most Hostile Country in Europe" Towards Israel?'*[256] Meanwhile, a Jewish man who resides here was verbally assailed by a stranger who barked: 'Hitler should have finished you off!'

---

[253] Matti Friedman article in *The Tablet*, cited in *Toronto Star*, 26 August 2014.
[254] Ibid.
[255] Rivlin, *Jewish Ireland*, p. 37.
[256] See the complete article in Appendix 1.

It is troubling that the Irish have become desensitised to anti-Zionist attitudes. Thus, the candour expressed by journalist Chris Jackson, in his condemnation of the racist graffiti on a derelict financial building was refreshing. On almost all levels of the eight-storey Dublin city tower, blood-red anti-Semitic incitements were daubed, such as: *'JEWISH FINANCIAL GLOBAL TERRORISM'* and *'ZIONIST ENGINEERED GLOBAL FINANCIAL HOLOCAUST.'* Jackson's article[257] not only pinpointed the motive but stressed the grave implications of allowing these mindsets to go unchecked: *'The form of anti-Semitism exhibited ... is not a new phenomenon ... [it] is increasingly prevalent, in large part due to ... political and economic uncertainty ... As history attests such scapegoating ... in the past has led to mass exodus or execution. It is imperative that such attitudes are arrested before they have a chance to percolate and pervade the population.'*

In the words of eighteenth-century Irish politician Edmund Burke, *'All that is necessary for the triumph of evil is that good men do nothing.'* We must not underestimate the power of persuasion and the influence of the media – be it journalism, vandalism, or other.

VILE VILIFICATION

Israel is often accused of committing war crimes. Are they being maligned or is there truth to the allegations? An informative *YouTube* presentation titled *Who Else is being Injured by the Vilification of Israel?* details United Nations' investigations into three allegations, as recorded below:

> *'EXAMPLE #1:*
>
> *In April 2002, after Israel was struck with a wave of suicide bombing attacks, Israeli troops entered the Jenin Refugee Camp in the West Bank ... Palestinian leaders accused Israel of carrying out a massacre ... The UN took the Palestinian*

---

[257] Chris Jackson, 'Graffiti that can't be ignored', *Sunday Independent*, June 2013, p.12.

leaders at their word. Secretary-General Kofi Anan spoke about "grave violations" by the IDF, and dispatched UN investigators. Yet, after the damage caused to Israel's reputation, the UN investigation concluded that the accusations were false. There was never a massacre in Jenin.

"UN says no massacre in Jenin. [Headline]

"A United Nations investigation has rejected claims that hundreds of Palestinian civilians were killed in Israel's attack on the Palestinian refugee camp in Jenin." (BBC News World Edition, Thursday, 1 Aug 2002.)

EXAMPLE #2:

In December 2008, after constant Palestinian rocket fire on Israel the Israel Defence Forces entered Gaza in an attempt to protect its southern cities. Palestinians accused Israel of deliberately targeting civilians. A fact-finding team appointed by the UN Human Rights Council and headed by Justice Richard Goldstone initially accepted the Palestinian accusations. However, Justice Goldstone later retracted the main claim against Israel: "Civilians were not intentionally targeted as a matter of policy." (The Washington Post, 1 Apr 2011)

EXAMPLE #3:

In May 2010, the Israeli Navy stopped a flotilla of six ships on their way to Gaza. Israel was accused of imposing an illegal naval blockade and denying civilians access to food and humanitarian aid. UN Secretary General Ban Ki-moon empowered the Palmer Commission to investigate the claims. The Palmer Report concluded that the blockade was legal under international law and that there was no humanitarian crisis in Gaza. Moreover, Israel did not block humanitarian aid from entering Gaza by land. In the month prior to the flotilla alone, over 17,000 tons of aid entered Gaza. The markets of Gaza were in fact full of fresh produce *[dated photographic evidence added].*

... The Palestinians' fabrications against Israel ... [are] aimed at discrediting and delegitimizing the State of Israel. However, hijacking the agenda of the United Nations by Palestinians comes with a price. As early as November 2006, the UN Secretary General, Kofi Anan, criticized the UN Human Rights Council: "Since the beginning of their work, they have focused almost entirely on Israel, and there are other crisis situations, like Sudan, where they have not been able to say a word."'

THE DECEIVED ARE DANGEROUS

To what does the vilification of Israel lead, if not to isolation from the international community, sanctions and anti-Semitic outbursts? Bolivia – situated thousands of miles from Israel – not only experienced an increase in anti-Semitism in 2014 (which included the bombing of a Jewish cemetery), but the government decided to brand Israel a 'terrorist state'! The saddest part of all is that these people think they are standing for justice and equality. Who is going to tell them that they are being dreadfully deceived?

Vilification is not a new mode of attack. A poster was publicly displayed in the mid-1950's, which read:

'WARNING!

The JEWS started the War – Jewish people cannot be trusted.

They must not occupy any responsible position or Public Offices ...

THROUGH THIS PARASITIC RACE THE WORLD HAS BEEN CONTINUALLY INVOLVED IN WAR, REBELLION AND MISERY (HITLER WAS RIGHT)

DON'T HARM THEM BUT MAKE IT THAT THEIR LIFE HERE COMPELS THEM TO RETURN TO ISRAEL.

Now that the Jews have Israel drive them back to Israel and do not allow them to have any control in our affairs ...

Notice the harsh and divisive tone, not to mention the classic provocative lexicon of Jew-haters. In the last line, the accusers recognise the Statehood of Israel. Could you hazard a guess in which country this was being circulated? Perhaps the concluding petition will help:

'Irishmen play your part in boycotting these Human Leeches from OUR SOIL.

IRELAND FOR CHRISTIANS ONLY'[258]

ISRAEL: A DEMOCRACY

Have you ever heard an Irish journalist acknowledge that Israel is a modern democratic state? If not, why not? Communist leader Vladimir Lenin once said: *'A lie told often enough becomes the truth.'* Believe me when I say, it is simply not true that the Jews won't allow the Arabs to live in peace with them. 2019 statistics reveal that there are now close to 1.907 million Israeli Arabs, which amounts to 21 per cent of the population of the State of Israel.[259] *'They [Arab citizens of Israel] have precisely the same privileges as resident Jews including the right to work, education, health care, and other benefits provided by the Israeli government, and yet not one Israeli will be welcome to live in a future Palestinian state.'*[260]

It is little wonder that in the days following the release of the 2020 Peace Deal proposal thousands of Arab citizens of Israel took to the streets in protest. Why? They understand that they would experience nothing of democracy if they were to live under the

---

[258] Rivlin, *Jewish Ireland*, p. 51. This poster was circulating in Dublin in 1956.
[259] JNN News, 1 October 2019.
[260] JNN editors, 16 December 2013.

sovereignty of a Palestinian state.[261] Academic researcher and journalist Ben-Dror Yemini,[262] highlights that 65 per cent of Israeli Arabs are 'proud to be Israeli'.[263] In fact, a 2018 poll reveals that as much as 71 per cent of Palestinians would not have an issue with working in Israel or in an Israeli settlement.[264]

As the only functioning democracy in the Middle East, Israel bestows *full* democratic rights on all of its citizens – Jew, Arab and otherwise – including freedom of speech. The PA leadership does not want you to know this. Where the Arabs are suffering injustice is within the territories of the Palestinian Authority, not Israel. This is the misconception surrounding the issue that has been swallowed like a whale. In contrast to the Israeli democracy, *'the Palestinians do not have a functioning parliament or a free media under the PA in the West Bank or under Hamas in the Gaza Strip.'*[265] These are the words of an Israeli Arab reporter. Hamas dissenter, Mosab Hassan Yousef agrees and moreover remarks: *'The Jewish nation is the true democracy in the ocean of darkness.'*[266] Let's not brush over the fact that these words are coming from the mouths of two Arabs – the latter of whom is from the heart of the West Bank.

It wasn't until the inception of the Jewish State in 1948 that people of all religions were finally allowed to freely practice their faith in the land of Israel. *'In Israel freedom of worship is one of our core values and is guaranteed under the law.'*[267] Conversely, in Muslim states in which Sharia Law is administered, infidels (i.e. non-compliant citizens) are at the very least imprisoned, if not

---

[261] *JNN*, 25 February 2020, alluding to an article from the *Gatestone Institute*.

[262] Ben-Dror Yemini writes for *Ynet* news; he has had numerous personal meetings with former PLO chief Yasser Arafat; Yemini published an intriguing fact-filled book in 2019, *Industry of Lies*, on the Israel/Palestine issue.

[263] Zoom meeting, 23 April 2020, guest speaker: Ben-Dror Yemini.

[264] Poll conducted by the *Jerusalem Media and Communication Centre* and released 7 August 2018.

[265] Khaled Abu Toameh, 'What are Palestinians Doing with U.S. Money?' *Gatestone Institute*, 19 August 2015.

[266] *JNN*, 24 May 2016, alluding to a *Jerusalem Post* conference, citing speaker Mosab Hassan Yousef.

[267] *JNN* editors, 19 June 2015, quoting Israeli Prime Minister Benjamin Netanyahu.

tortured and even executed. On that note, the question begs to be asked of PA Chairperson Mahmoud Abbas, what has become of the Christian population of Bethlehem which has plunged from 80 per cent in 1995 (when Israel handed the town over to the Palestinian Authority) to 20 per cent in 2018,[268] and if they have left the town of their own volition, why were they not content to stay? Also, how does Hamas leader Ismail Haniyeh account for the dramatic drop in the number of Christians in Gaza from 3,500 (prior to the their violent take-over of the Strip in 2007) to approximately 500 today?[269] On the other side of the fence, as it were, 2017 saw a 2.2 per cent increase in the Christian population of Israel, which currently stands at roughly 175,000, 77.7 per cent of whom are Arab Christians.[270]

In its annual survey of 167 democracies in 2018 the *Economist Intelligence Unit*, whose headquarters are in London, ranked Israel in 30th place.[271] As one commentator remarked, that is a healthy democracy. The administration of the State of Israel is shared by Jewish and non-Jewish members of parliament (MKs), regardless of their political persuasion. In fact, some Arab MKs have been known to demonstrate allegiance to terrorist organisations. In February 2016 three Arab members of the Israeli government, Jamal Zahalka, Haneen Zoabi and Basel Ghattas, met with families of terrorists and honoured the 'Palestinian martyrs' with a moment of silence.[272] For this provocative act of disloyalty and duplicity and for their apparent disdain for the men, women and children murdered at the hands of these terrorists they were suspended from the parliament for between two and four months per individual.

In 2018, Israel sent its first Christian Arab envoy to work.[273] The

---

[268] *JNN*, 28 December 2018, alluding to a *Times of Israel* article.
[269] *VFI News*, 24 December 2019.
[270] *JNN*, 28 December 2018, alluding to an article in *Israel Today*.
[271] *JNN*, 28 December 2018, alluding to an article from *Bloomberg*.
[272] *Times of Israel*, 8 February 2016, 'Knesset suspends Arab MKs for meeting Palestinian terrorists' families'. <https://www.timesofisrael.com/knesset-bans-arab-mks-for-meeting-palestinian-attackers-families/> (10 February 2016).
[273] *JNN*, 19 November 2018, alluding to an article in the *Jerusalem Post*.

judge who sent former President of Israel Moshe Katsav to prison for seven years was Justice George Kara, an Arab Israeli. The 30,000-member strong Israeli police force is comprised of Jews and non-Jews; Muslim Jamal Hachrush who is second in command of the entire force was promoted to Assistant Chief of Police in 2016.[274] Similarly, Jews, Arabs, Druze and Christians make up the Israel Defence Force (IDF). Multi-national doctors and surgeons work together in the same Israeli hospitals; the General Director of the Ziv Medical Centre in the north of Israel, for example, is Dr Salman Zarka, from the Druze community which is an Arab sect. The chairman of Israel's oldest and second largest banking corporation, *Leumi* Bank, is Israeli Arab Dr Samer Haj Yehia.[275] In 2013, the title *Miss Israel* was bestowed on Ethiopian immigrant Yityish Aynaw. In the words of former MP and President of the ACDP Party in South Africa, Rev Kenneth Meshoe, '*The very idea that Israel is an apartheid state cheapens the word apartheid – it is an insult to every South African who endured the inhumanity and pain of it.*' You will see both Jewish and Arab players on the Israeli national football team ... These are some of the many facts that disprove allegations of apartheid in the land of Israel. The following testimony should help to reinforce the argument.

IDF MAJOR ALAA WAHIB

'*There's only one country in the Middle East that could produce a soldier like me.*' These are the words of Alaa Wahib, an Arab major in the Israel Defence Force. In early 2016, he visited universities in the UK which were celebrating 'Israeli Apartheid Week' to share his views on the country which he is '*proud to call home*'. Here, as follows, is an article he wrote:

'*I am an Israeli, an Arab, and the highest ranked Muslim in the IDF. Is Israel inherently racist, an apartheid state? Well,*

---

[274] *JNN*, 15 April 2016, alluding to an article in the *Jerusalem Post*.
[275] Zoom meeting, 23 April 2020, guest speaker: Ben-Dror Yemini.

do you think that such a country would tolerate a person like myself getting to the position I am today? ... Twenty per cent of Israelis are non-Jewish, have full rights, and are represented throughout society ... Would a truly racist state allow me to play such an integral role in our nation's defences? ... I do not serve in the army to kill people – I serve in it to save people. When Hamas fires rockets, or Fatah encourages stabbings, we are here to protect the lives of all Israeli citizens, Jewish and non-Jewish.

The town I grew up in did not recognize the right of Israel to exist as a Jewish state ... I was raised to believe the worst things about Jews, and, had I not eventually met and worked alongside them, I might still believe those things today.' [276]

Emphatically and unapologetically, Major Wahib declares Israel *'sure as hell isn't an apartheid state'.*

DEVIOUS DELEGITIMIZATION

One definition for 'delegitimization' reads: 'To diminish or destroy the legitimacy, prestige or authority of.' Through the use of slander and propaganda the instigators of this evil mission tear down the validity and credibility of the nation of Israel. And, it's working. If it were not, then the BDS (Boycott, Divestment and Sanctions) movement wouldn't exist. Founded in 2005, this divisive association is sadly gaining momentum. It targets no other nation but Israel – not Iran or North Korea or any other fascist regime, but Israel. Many people who consider themselves human rights activists promote this popular cultural, academic and economic boycott. I'll bet they are not familiar with the writings of Israeli Arab journalist Khaled Abu Toameh, who regularly exposes the devious agenda of the Palestinian Authority. Here's one such comment he made: *'In addition to inciting its people against Israel on a daily basis, the Palestinian Authority leadership has been*

---

[276] Published in *www.jewishnews.co.uk* on 5 March 2016.

using these [Western aid] funds to wage a massive campaign in the international community with the purpose of isolating and delegitimizing Israel and turning it into a pariah state.'[277]

BDS EFFECTS

One must ask, how effective is the BDS movement?[278] Not only Jewish, but thousands of Palestinian farmers in the settlements are taking the knock of these sanctions and disinvestment. An article in the *Daily Alert* online newsletter, titled *EU Directive on Labelling Products Would Harm 20,000 Palestinian Families*, emphasises these concerns. Israel's then deputy foreign minister Zeev Elkin informed Elmar Brok, who was the chairman of the European Parliament Foreign Affairs Committee at the time: *'"You are trying to hurt Israeli enterprises that already exist and provide a respectable livelihood for tens of thousands of Palestinian families," Elkin told Brok. "This is simply bizarre."'*[279] Elkin further explained how a reduction in exports to EU states could cause agricultural and manufacturing businesses in settlements to close down, leaving many of those same Palestinians without a job. Regarding the current Covid-19 pandemic, it is hypocritical that the leader and Co-founder of the BDS movement Omar Barghouti would publicly endorse the use of an Israeli vaccine. *'If you use medical equipment from Israel – not a problem. Cooperating with Israel against the virus – to begin with, we do not consider it normalisation.'*[280] I can only imagine that it must have been an awkward and embarrassing statement for Barghouti to make. It certainly should have been!

---

[277] Toameh, 'What are Palestinians Doing...?'
[278] See in Appendix 2 a letter published in the *Irish Times* by former Israeli Ambassador to Ireland Boaz Modai.
[279] *Ha'aretz* quote in *Daily Alert* online newsletter.
[280] *VFI News*, 10 April 2020.

PALESTINIAN NEWS

Palestinian newspapers have, on occasion, been known to share the truth concerning Israel. In a 2014 article in *Al-Hayat*, Israeli employers of Palestinians are praised for their high level of employment ethics: *'Whenever Palestinian workers have the opportunity to work for Israeli employers, they are quick to quit their jobs with their Palestinian employers – for reasons having to do with salaries and other rights. The Israeli work conditions are very good, and include transportation, medical insurance and pensions. These things do not exist with Palestinian employers.'*[281] Surely, it is plain to see that the culprit of Palestinian poverty is not Israel, but the governing body of the Palestinians – the Palestinian Authority.

PALESTINIAN PREFERENCE

Statistics show that Palestinians are highly satisfied with Israeli produce, as revealed in the following news report:

'SURVEY: PALESTINIANS PREFER ISRAELI PRODUCTS: ... A recent survey by the Palestinian Authority's Consumer Protection Authority revealed Palestinian Arabs are major consumers of Israeli products ... 70% of the Palestinian Authority's imports come from Israel. Israel does not restrict imports to the Palestinian-controlled areas, and Israeli goods sold there must compete with those imported from Europe and other Arab states. The reason Israeli products are doing so well is simply because Palestinian Arabs prefer them, according to several Palestinian merchants.'[282]

A FEW GOOD MEN

It's good to know that men of valour still exist. These are the daring few who are willing and *can* handle the truth. I was once

---

[281] *JNN*, 27 September 2014, alluding to *PMW*.
[282] *JNN*, 26 February 2014, alluding to *Israel Today*.

introduced to the founder of 'Irish4Israel', Barry Williams, who shared how the non-religious group came about. Back in 2008, Barry, fuelled with political fervour set out for the place he called 'Palestine'. The young Irishman had been well informed of the outrageous injustice and apartheid taking place. It may come as a shock (it certainly did to him) that he returned from Israel with a completely fresh perspective.

> *'I talked to Israelis and they said they really wanted peace. I knew they were genuine. Then I went to Bethlehem, and while standing outside a coffee shop I saw all these posters of men with the Al Aqsa mosque behind them. I asked some kids what were those posters about, and they said, "Oh they are Shaheeds: the martyrs." These posters were only around the corner from a mega tourist destination, yet the Palestinians unashamedly supported these suicide bombers and terrorists.'*

Had he never taken the time to see for himself what was really going on, I shudder to think that today Barry Williams might be heading an anti-Israel group in our nation.

IRISH4ISRAEL

Barry explains how the movement came about: *'When I came home, [Operation] Cast Lead started and I saw a lot of hysteria and hatred towards Israel. And it was then I started to speak out passionately.'* Between the years 2010 (when 'Irish4Israel' was established) and 2018[283] Barry Williams and his associates did tremendous work lobbying TDs and informing the public, often via social media networking, about the reality of life in the land of Israel. And in case you are inclined to doubt Barry's perspective, it might help to know that other Irish men and women who

---

[283] In 2018 Barry passed on the baton to the courageous Jackie Goodall, who is heading what is now called the *Ireland Israel Alliance*.

traversed the Holy Land returned with similar testimonies of conversion.

FILMMAKER: NICKY LARKIN

How inspiring are their testimonies when artists are unashamed to voice the unpopular? With the intention of producing a controversial film on the inhumane treatment of the Palestinian people at the mercy of the infamous Jews, filmmaker Nicky Larkin and his team set out to spend an equal amount of time in both Israeli and Palestinian territories over a seven-week period. Yet, he witnessed the unexpected and had such a change of heart that he now challenges all 'armchair sermonisers' to go and see the reality for themselves. The following extract is from an article he wrote for the *Sunday Independent* in March 2012:

> '*My peers expected me to come back with an attack on Israel ... An Irish artist is supposed to sign boycotts, wear a PLO scarf, and remonstrate loudly about the Occupation. But it's not just artists who are supposed to hate Israel. Being anti-Israel is supposed to be part of our Irish identity, the same way we are supposed to resent the English. But hating Israel is not part of my personal national identity. Neither is hating the English.*'

The full article, titled *Israel is a refuge, but a refuge under siege*, can be found in Appendix 3. For all Irish supporters of the whole 'Palestine' agenda, it may well be an eye-opener.

ACTOR: RORY COWAN

Rory played the character of Rory Brown in *Mrs Brown's Boys*. He proudly confesses that he has been spending his holidays in Israel for the last thirty-odd years. Had he not been reared in a family that championed justice, then we might question his reasoning.

Rory admits that not only were his parents actively involved as trade unionists,[284] but his grandfather, a TD and solicitor was *'always involved in fighting for people's rights; and if people were discriminated against he would take their cause'*. With an inherited passion for justice, Rory could never have revisited the State of Israel if he had smelled a whiff of inequity.

> *'My parents never tolerated an inkling of discrimination or prejudice in our house ... I grew up knowing prejudice and discrimination was wrong. It was bred into me. And if I had gone to Israel in 1981 and I had seen anything like prejudice or discrimination I would never have gone back, but I never did. So I keep going back all the time. It's a wonderful country with wonderful people.'*

To reiterate the point, he says: *'If I saw any example of discrimination, never mind ethnic cleansing or genocide, or all the other false accusations that are thrown about, I wouldn't have gone back. But I do go back, and I look forward to going back every year ... I've been there, and I know what they're saying is not true. None of it is true.'*

Rory compares the bully tactics of Israel boycotters to that of the Nazi storm troopers. Indeed, were they not guilty of dissuading the public from supporting Jewish businesses? Were they not also actively involved in banning Jewish students and lecturers from university campuses? *'I can't see any difference between the tactics of these Israel-boycotters and the Nazi brown shirts; I really can't. I could never support them and I would never support a cultural boycott of Israel.'* Despite the risk taken for speaking out, Rory continues: *'Well nobody wants negative publicity, but I don't care now because I have to do what I think is right. And I support Israel. I stand with Israel, and I'm not ashamed to say it.'*

Men and women of Ireland, can you handle the truth? And if so,

---

[284] At the time of this speech Rory's 80-year-old mother was still actively involved.

are you willing to pay the price? It will require sacrifice, but the rewards will be redeemed in times to come. Alternatively, if you are buying the lie, that will also come at a price, but like the credit card analogy: You won't feel the pinch until further down the line.

THE HON MR JUSTICE RICHARD HUMPHREYS

There are many more heroic men and women who may not be of celebrity status, but are making great efforts to redeem the truth regarding Israel – the people and the land. May I simply mention former legal adviser to the Labour Party, Mr Justice Richard Humphreys, whose pro-Israel rally speech, titled *Israel's Right to Defend itself must be Respected* can be found in Appendix 4.

HALF-PALESTINIAN PASTOR

Despite growing up in the Middle East with a Palestinian mother and Egyptian father, J.D. Farag has not supported either the Palestine Liberation Organisation (PLO), or the Palestinian Authority (PA) that it produced; neither does he agree with establishing a Palestinian state. On the contrary, this candid pastor goes to great lengths to inform the Church of the importance and place of Israel in end-times prophecies. Speaking in August 2014 of the war that was then taking place between Israel and Gaza terrorists, Farag asserted: *'It's really a satanic propaganda war that the world is waging against Israel vis-à-vis the current war that Hamas is waging against Israel.'*[285]

ISRAELI ARAB JOURNALIST

'The investment in Palestinian democracy and peace with Israel has been a complete failure because of the refusal of the US Administration to hold the Palestinian Authority fully accountable.'[286] These were the condemning words of Khaled Abu

---

[285] *YouTube*: 'Mid-East Prophecy Update,' 3 August 2014.
[286] Toameh, 'What are Palestinians Doing...?'

Toameh in 2015. Instead of going with the flow of political correctness and blaming Israel, this Israeli Arab accused western powers of not placing stipulations on colossal donations made to the Palestinian Authority. *'Palestinian economic analysts estimate that the PA has received a total of $25 billion in financial aid from the USA and other countries during the past two decades.'*[287]

The bulk of those donations (which have also come out of the pockets of European taxpayers) has not been used to improve the Palestinian economy, or to dissolve the refugee status of its people (which has actually been encouraged to fester for generations). In the same report Toameh explained that the main benefactors of these funds have been *'Yasser Arafat ... and his cronies.'* There is little doubt in my mind that he would include PA Chairman Mahmoud Abbas among those 'cronies' when one considers the lavish presidential palace he built for himself (presumably from PLO funds). By the way, this is the same chairman whose term officially ended in 2009 (yet who still governs) and likes to call himself 'president' of Palestine.[288] Toameh, who writes for the *Jerusalem Post* and the *Gatestone Institute,* draws attention to the corruption and deception at work in the Palestinian Authority (which he deems more *'ruthless and repressive'* than its counterpart: Hamas). *'The PA took the billions of dollars and continues to operate as a corrupt and undemocratic regime. Democracy is the last thing the Palestinians expect to see from the PA or Hamas.'*[289]

'ANTI-ZIONISM IS THE NEW ANTI-SEMITISM'

Please don't be fooled by terminology. Anti-Semitism is alive and *kicking* today; it is simply appearing under a different guise. In a BBC Newsnight interview former Chief Rabbi of the Commonwealth, Lord Jonathon Sacks, shared a disturbing observation:

---

[287] Ibid.
[288] See 'Abbas Builds Himself a $13 million Royal Palace' article by *JNN* editors, 28 August 2015 (alluding to *Arutz-7*).
[289] Toameh, 'What are Palestinians Doing...?'

'Anti-Semitism is so socially unacceptable that it can only survive the way a virus survives, which is by mutating. In the Middle Ages Jews were hated for their religion. In the nineteenth and twentieth centuries you weren't allowed to hate anyone for their religion, because this is post-Enlightenment Europe. So, they were hated for their race. Today, you can't hate anyone for their race, so you hate them for their nation state. And that is why anti-Zionism is the new anti-Semitism.'[290]

A resolution was passed in the French parliament in December 2019 to label anti-Zionism as anti-Semitism. The centrist party lawmaker who proposed the motion, Sylvain Maillard of LREM, explained that in France today *'Dirty Zionist ... means dirty Jew.'*[291] Dr Martin Luther King Jr once remarked: *'When people criticise Zionists, they mean Jews. You're talking anti-Semitism.'*[292] Yet another formidable leader, the late John F. Kennedy, made the following profound statement: *'The great enemy of the truth is very often not the lie – deliberate, contrived and dishonest – but the myth, persistent, persuasive, and unrealistic. Belief in myths allows the comfort of opinion without the discomfort of thought.'* Clearly, little thought is given to the myth of apartheid in the Holy Land. The 'anti-Zionist' may be hailed a human rights activist, but in reality has been hoodwinked by a spirit of anti-Semitism. Perhaps there is truth in what Adolf Hitler had to say about deception: *'The great masses of the people will more easily fall victims to a big lie than to a small one.'* Well at the moment, the nations are 'swallowing a whale' while Israel's legitimacy dangles dangerously on the line.

---

[290] Posted on the *Breaking Israel News* website on the annual commemoration day of the liberation of Auschwitz concentration camp, 27 January 2019. <https://www.breakingisraelnews.com/120954/lord-jonathon-sacks-anti-zionism-is-the-new-anti-semitism/>(29 January 2019).

[291] *VFI News*, 13 December 2019, alluding to an article in the *Jerusalem Post*.

[292] Cited by Ireland-Israel Friendship League, 'Arab-Israeli Conflict: Primer to understanding the truth beyond the myths', 2015 publication.

8

Jacob's In The Line-Up ... Again!

'I've been in prison for fifteen years for something I didn't do; for something I didn't know anything about. I'm a totally innocent man. I watched my father die in a British prison for something he didn't do.'

Who could forget the haunting words of Gerry Conlon, wrongfully convicted of the Guildford bombing? Paddy Hill, of the 'Birmingham Six', was incarcerated for sixteen years. Upon his release, he vehemently accused the British judicial system of using them as 'political scapegoats.' Sadly, these Irishmen have known the bitter pain of being hauled in as the 'usual suspects'.

FIND THE SCAPEGOAT

In our fallen human nature there is a tendency to hold somebody else accountable when things go wrong. After a few turbulent years of going under, the European economy appeared to have its head above water again and to have survived the recession. Then Coronavirus entered the equation – the full fiscal effects of which are yet to unfold. History clearly records the direct correlation between frantic, panicking communities and the seeking out of a scapegoat to carry the blame. What might begin with whispered insinuations would soon turn to widespread boycotts, then to expulsion and ultimately to violence.[293]

---

[293] A poll conducted in Europe in 2009 by the Anti-Defamation League found that 31% of

HISTORY REPEATS

The concept of history repeating itself inspired the writings of two German philosophers of the nineteenth century, Friedrich Nietzsche and Heinrich Heine (the latter of Jewish descent). What eerily echoes through the corridors of history is an insight that can be found in one of Heine's plays, *Almansor*, *'Das war ein Vorspiel nur, dort wo man Bücher verbrennt, verbrennt man auch am Ende Menschen'* which translates: *'That was but a prelude; where they burn books, they will ultimately burn people also.'*[294] These disturbing words were written over a century before the infamous Nazi book-burnings of Berlin, 1933, sadly among which were the works of this intuitive man. Heine's remarkable foresight can be witnessed in his 1834 publication: *History of Religion and Philosophy in Germany*: *'Thought precedes action as lightning precedes thunder. German thunder ... will come ... you [will] hear a crashing such as never before has been heard in the world's history ... A play will be performed in Germany which will make the French Revolution look like an innocent idyll.'* I wonder how many people of his day thought his notions exaggerated, if not altogether absurd. Certainly, history attests to the fact that too few, if any at all, took heed of the philosopher's predictions.

ECONOMIC DECLINE

Heine's predictions would find their fulfilment during the economic decline, which resulted from the Great War. Europe's fist came down heavily on Germany for instigating what was a costly war of gross dimensions. The nation resented signing a 'war guilt' clause at the Treaty of Versailles in 1919 and was bitterly opposed to forking out 132 billion Reichsmarks in reparations, which shattered its economy. Additionally, Germany's national pride took a blow when forced to divide some of its land with neighbouring countries. And so, against this backdrop of shame

---

Europeans surveyed blamed Jews for the global financial crisis. This is hauntingly reminiscent of European attitudes of times past.

[294] See 'Heinrich Heine' article, Wikipedia, under subheading: 'Legacy' (8 October, 2015).

and bitterness, poverty and fear, a national hero emerged with the know-how to revive the industrious Fatherland. Here was a man who boldly predicted in 1933, *'History will judge us according to whether we have succeeded in providing work.'* The innovative measures taken by the newly elected German Chancellor, Adolf Hitler, would reduce unemployment rates from six million in 1932 to two million in 1936, until finally in 1939 Germany 'had full employment.'[295] An amazing accomplishment no doubt, Herr Hitler, but at whose expense?

GERMANY'S SCAPEGOATS

Hitler had already planted the notion that the Jews were responsible for Germany's defeat in World War I.[296] All that was needed was to persuade the nation to put this (enviously successful) minority group 'in its proper place'. In summary, what began with stereotyping in German publications (including school textbooks) and boycotts of Jewish businesses, soon turned to: exclusion from roles in the civil service, laws that forbade German-Jewish intermarriage (by penalty of death!), entitlement to vote withdrawn, and the enforcement of dress laws. By the time Jewish people were prohibited from entering public parks, cinemas and theatres, the majority of Germans were desensitised to the discrimination. To see it from the Jewish perspective: Renata was a teenage girl who lived in Berlin. In 1938, she wrote in her diary: *'Papa explained that the Nazis ... are ... using Jews as scapegoats for Germany's problems, taking away all we have.'*[297]

INDICTMENT

Anti-Semitism did not make its first appearance in the twentieth century. Our elder brothers of the faith have seldom been offered

---

[295] Sean Delap & Paul McCormack, *Uncovering History* (Dublin, 2007), p. 289.
[296] This is plainly stated in his autobiography, *Mein Kampf.*
[297] Marilyn Taylor, *17 Martin Street* (Dublin, 2011) p. 11. This real-life account, which was translated from German, is found in the prologue of the novel.

the right to a fair trial. One might anticipate discriminative conduct from an uneducated minority, but not from theologians, of all people! Alas, there is much evidence to indict both shepherds and flock. Historical accounts of the teachings and influence of Church Fathers can be found in the insightful book, *Healing the Past: Catholic Anti-Semitism*, of Dublin-born teacher, Ena Gray, who explains, *'The period of the Fathers of the Church stretches from the time of the Apostles to the death of St Augustine (430).'*[298]

CHURCH FATHERS EXPOSED

Justin Martyr hails from as far back as AD 100. He is the pioneer of the long line of theologians who voiced anti-Semitic sentiments. His accusation that the Jews murdered Christ was the destructive seed that would result in harmful fruits. Building upon this condemning statement, Origen spoke of their permanent rejection as the Chosen People of God. By the time the Archbishop of Constantinople, John Chrysostom, came onto the scene in the fourth century, anti-Semitic ravings were rampant. *Adversus Judaeos* is a collection of homilies delivered by Chrysostom in an attempt, it is believed, to protect his flock from being lured into Judaism. In his own words, he described the Hebraic people as: *'Inveterate murderers ... possessed by the devil ... Why are the Jews degenerate? Because of their odious assassination of Christ ... there is no pardon ... Christians may never cease to seek vengeance on the Jews and they must live in servitude forever ... God always hated the Jews and whoever has dealings with the Jews will be rejected on judgement day.'*[299] Even Augustine of Hippo (AD 354–430) was guilty in this regard. He not only equated the Jewish community with Judas (the one who betrayed Christ), but accentuated the notion that they ought to suffer humiliation by being subservient to the Church.

---

[298] Ena Gray, *Healing the Past. Catholic Anti-Semitism: Roots and Redemption* (2nd edn, Dublin, 2010), p. 25.
[299] Ibid, p.29.

REPLACEMENT THEOLOGY

These flawed early teachings have led to the misunderstanding that the Church has replaced Israel as God's Chosen People. In the words of Messianic Jew Adam Eliyahu Berkowitz, *'Christian replacement theology, also called supersessionism, holds that the Christian Church has succeeded the Israelites as the definitive people of God.'*[300] Replacement Theology, at its embryonic stage, somehow granted its advocates the superior right to judge and chastise the ethno-religious group, as we can see from the following excerpt: *'The next event of historical note was the Christianisation of Europe under Emperor Constantine in the fourth century and the official beginning of state-sponsored anti-Semitism, on the pretext that the Church had supplanted the Jewish people as 'God's chosen' and therefore the Jews 'must be utterly rejected by God', giving the Church the right to 'carry out God's will' in persecuting Jews at every opportunity.'*[301]

How eerie, incidentally, is the adoption of this warped agenda by followers of Islam. In their misguided fervour, many Muslims lay claim to replacing not just Jewish, but Christian rejects of God. As God's final representatives, they see it as their duty to deal with these 'infidels', and have assumed the role of judge and executioner. This is another shocking 'history repeat', if ever there was one.

CALENDAR ADJUSTMENTS

The Fathers of Roman Catholicism moved our religious calendar away from its Jewish roots, in the direction of pagan feast days, incongruous with the Christian faith. They changed names of feasts and holy days, and moved the celebration of the birth of Jesus from the historical date to a day much later in the year, which coincides hideously with the Roman day of Saturnalia (25

---

[300] *Breaking Israel News*, 20 April 2020.
[301] Maltz, *Many Names*, p. 86-87.

December), *'a day of orgy and revelry.'*[302] The traditional day of rest ordained by God (the Sabbath) would no longer fall on Saturday, but Sunday, *'a pagan Roman day of sun worship'.*[303] Author Don Finto explains how the name *Easter* was adopted in place of *Passover*, the Jewish feast that historically coincided with the Lord's crucifixion.

> *'Emperor Constantine ... in AD 325 ... wanted to make sure the Church had once and for all separated herself from these "polluted wretches" who had stained their hands with a "nefarious crime". They needed a resurrection celebration date other than Passover. Passover was too Jewish! ... The Roman calendar had conquered! The annual celebration ... would now have a new name – Easter – strangely similar to Eostre, the Teutonic goddess of spring ... And the Church was further estranged from her roots and her spiritual "parents".'*[304]

JEWISH JESUS

The Church of Jesus Christ, once filled with the descendants of Jacob, was being urged to separate completely from Judaism, and from the traditions in which the Lord Himself had willingly partaken. It's not easy to see how this was overlooked. The Gospels are full of the Jewishness of Jesus. He and His disciples celebrated Passover and the Feast of Tabernacles. He observed the Sabbath on Saturday, went to Synagogue and read publicly from the books of Moses and the prophets. As opposed to rejecting or even suppressing the Jewish culture into which he was born, He completely embraced it – fully aware that these customs were passed down His generational line from Moses, who had received them from Father God Himself.

---

[302] Ibid, p. 82.

[303] Ibid.

[304] Don Finto, *Your People Shall Be My People. How Israel, the Jews and the Christian Church Will Come Together in the Last Days* (California, 2001), p. 88-89.

DIVISION

What on earth had become of the Church that she deliberately deviated so far from the Lord's customs? All that we can deduce from this unchristian behaviour is that a cunning deceiver was at work behind the scenes pulling the strings. And the only reason Satan had a hold over the Church was because of our envy and religious pride. The calculated alterations made by the Church Fathers led to the desired outcome: Christians and Jews, now suspicious of one another, would stay as far away from each other as possible. What a shame!

SERIOUSLY SUSPECT

'Their synagogues should be set on fire ... Their homes should likewise be ... destroyed ... Their rabbis must be forbidden under threat of death to teach anymore ... travelling privileges should be absolutely forbidden ... Let the young and strong Jews and Jewesses be given the flail, the axe, the hoe, the spade, the distaff and spindle, and let them earn their bread by the sweat of their noses.'[305]

A German of incredible influence penned these words, although not the Führer, as you may have thought. It is an extract from 'On the Jews and Their Lies' – a 65,000-word publication from 1543 by the Reformer Martin Luther. Although this professor of theology was not always a Jew-hater, and initially drew his followers' attention to the Jewishness of Jesus, it seems that he eventually became embittered by his failed attempts to convert Jews to Christianity. If you find it difficult to believe that the founder of the Reformation became a source of inspiration to one of the cruellest dictators of history, then you must not have heard that Hitler initiated his great scourging of the Jews on 10 November

---

[305] Ibid, p. 72.

1938 – Martin Luther's birthday. This was the 'Night of Broken Glass' (Kristallnacht) when, in accordance with Luther's wishes, synagogues were set alight, Jewish homes and businesses were vandalised and looted, and thousands of Jewish men were marched off to concentration camps to labour *'by the sweat of their noses.'*

LUTHERAN 2020 BIBLE

While in Israel in 2006, I was surprised to learn from some German friends that the Lutheran church is still awash with anti-Semitic undertones. It's alarming that the world's condemnation of the horrendous Holocaust apparently did not evoke deep soul-searching and repentance in Lutheran hierarchy. The Danish Bible Society, which is run by the Lutherans, has recently produced a revised translation of the Bible. The 2020 Bible, as it is called, has made some major and controversial changes to the original text. Liberties have been taken to replace, for example, 'New Testament' with 'New Agreement'. It is in this very 'New Agreement' that controversy arises, because all 73 references to 'Israel' therein have either been changed or removed altogether. In place of 'Israel' you will now read 'Jews', 'Land of the Jews', or neither.

At first glance, this might seem innocuous, but it is in fact a subtle undermining of the people of Israel; most of whom agree that throughout history antagonists have disparagingly referred to them not as Jewish people but as 'Jews'. It is a derogatory term which might, for example, be compared to referring to black people as 'the Blacks'. Thus, the 2020 Bible is a shameful piece of evidence proving supersessionism is alive today. As one rabbi commented, *'This translation of the New Testament is an important reminder that replacement theology is not a problem of the past ... some segments of Christianity still have a replacement theology problem.'*[306] The excuse for the deliberate alterations, according to the publishers, is that they do not see any correlation between the

---

[306] *Breaking Israel News*, 20 April 2020, citing Rabbi Tuly Weisz, founder of *Israel365*.

Israel of today and the Israel of Bible times. Their exclusion of the word 'Israel' from the text is, in all truth, a damning statement of their rejection of the Jewish nation and State of Israel.

The 2020 Bible seriously lacks 20–20 vision. It is beyond belief that the Global Council Chairperson of the Bible Society, Elaine Duncan, takes pride in the fact that this translation has already been downloaded to almost a hundred countries and sees this accomplishment as a step in the direction of (in her own words) a *'global church.'*[307] If this is the basis for the unification of Christian denominations worldwide it is veering from the foundational apostolic teachings of the church.

2020 SCAPEGOATING

'Since the beginning of the COVID-19 pandemic there has been a significant rise in accusations that Jews, as individuals and as a collective, are behind the spread of the virus or are directly profiting from it ... The language and imagery used clearly identifies a revival of the medieval "blood libels" when Jews were accused of spreading disease, poisoning wells or controlling economies.'[308] What you will not hear from propaganda pushers is that in the early days of the pandemic (and by 10 March 2020) Israel had already donated 250 COVID-19 testing kits to the PA and convened a joint training session for Israeli and Palestinian medical staff. On various online platforms the State of Israel made available an Arabic translation of the Health Ministry's guidelines on self-quarantining.[309] The BDS movement (which in 2019, incidentally, was classified by the German parliament as an anti-Semitic movement, with the backing of Angela Merkel's leading CDU party along with the Green Party, Social Democrats and the Free Democratic Party[310]) has been busy churning out fake news

---

[307] Ibid, Adam Eliyahu Berkowitz: 'Lutherans Publish New Version of the Bible Without the Word "Israel" in it'.

[308] *VFI News*, 24 April 2020, 'Coronavirus brings sharp spike in Anti-Semitism'.

[309] Ibid, 10 March 2020, alluding to an article in the Jerusalem Post.

[310] *New York Times*, 17 May 2019, Katrin Bennhold, 'German Parliament deems BDS movement anti-Semitic'.

regarding Israel's treatment of Palestinians during the pandemic. Meanwhile, Jackie Goodall and the Ireland Israel Alliance (IIA) team have been working around the clock bringing the true facts to the fore and shining the spotlight on official World Health Organisation statistics. In fact, on the IIA Twitter page Goodall commented: '#Israel has been praised by the UN for its #COVID19 cooperation with the Palestinian territories.'[311]

RELEASE THE SUSPECT

With regard to life in the homeland, the last thing the Jewish people want is conflict. Their Scriptures throughout the centuries have assured them of better times to come, with the second half of the following prophecy not yet fulfilled: *'I will assign a place to my people Israel; I will plant them there, so that they can live in their own place without being disturbed anymore. The wicked will no longer oppress them ... instead, I will give you rest from all your enemies.'*[312] The dream of returning to the land of their forefathers was forever tied to the prospects of finally being left alone. The Chosen People presumed they would at last be respected as a people group as soon as they were out of everybody else's backyard. To the contrary, attacks against them have increased since their return.

OPERATION CAST LEAD

Is it not shocking that, as a result of making efforts to protect civilians from daily death threats, Israel is branded the tyrant? Cast Lead was a military operation undertaken by the IDF which commenced in late December 2008 and finished in early 2009 and came about as a result of Hamas terrorists in Gaza raining missiles into Israel on an ongoing basis – something which is so freakishly

<https://www.nytimes.com/2019/05/17/world/europe/germany-bds-anti-semitic.html> (27 October 2020).
[311] Ireland Israel Alliance Twitter page, 14 May 2020.
[312] 2 Samuel 7:10-11; CJB.

normal in the south of Israel that the world seems to have become desensitised. Yet, you can be guaranteed that the residents, including the children of the nearby Israeli cities of Sderot, Ashkelon, Ashdod, and Beersheva have not acclimatised to this endless precipitation. Hela Crown-Tamir implies how reluctant the Israeli government was to go to war. *'Since the Gaza disengagement*[313] *in 2005, approximately 5,700 rockets and 4,000 mortar shells have been fired from Gaza into Israel. Hamas operatives fired over 2,000 rockets and 1,600 mortar shells in 2008 alone.'*[314]

The objective of the operation was to reduce rocket fire into Israel and to hinder arms smuggling into the Gaza Strip. Allegations of genocide attributed to Israel are utterly unjustified, as the following report demonstrates: *'IAF*[315] *pilots always try to avoid civilian casualties, even if this means to abort a strike. In 2007, during air strikes on militants in the Gaza Strip, the civilian casualty ratio was 1:30 (one civilian casualty for every thirty combatant casualties). Commentators have noted that, "No army in history has ever had a better ratio of combatants to civilians killed in a comparable setting."'*[316]

JACOB'S ALIBI

This might explain why a native Israeli priest of non-Jewish descent is so much in support of Israel in its fight against terror that he is actively involved in recruiting Arab-Israelis. Father Gabriel Nadaf is the, *'spiritual head of the Israeli Christians Recruitment Forum, a body that encourages young Arabic-speaking Israelis to join the Israeli army and fully integrate with Israeli Jewish society'.* Not only is he 'proud' to live in Israel, but this Greek Orthodox priest insists that, *'Israel is a shining example*

---

[313] Israel ceded *governance* of the Gaza Strip to the Palestinian Authority.

[314] Hela Crown-Tamir, *Israel. History in a Nutshell* Highlighting the War and Military History (Jerusalem, 2011), p. 204.

[315] IAF: Israeli Air Force.

[316] Crown-Tamir, *In a Nutshell*, p. 22.

of human rights in the Middle East.'[317] Before we turn our attention to a couple of other trustworthy witnesses, may we briefly consider an ongoing oversight on Israel's part which is costing her dearly?

DEFENCE COUNSEL DECLINED

According to Scripture, Israel will not reach her ultimate destiny of peace and tranquillity, until she reconciles with God by receiving her Messiah.[318] When she chooses to come under His covering, she will be fully protected and safe forevermore.[319] In the meantime she sadly remains an exposed target of the enemy of the God of Israel, Satan himself, whose bloody attacks are intensifying. Regardless of her unimpressive size, Israel is considered a formidable nation. Her army is one of the strongest in the world and she is renowned for consistently holding her forefront position in both technological and scientific advances. Nevertheless, Israel is in great danger of leaning into self-reliance, instead of looking to the One who brought her into existence; instead of turning to her Messiah, who said: *'"Come to Me all you who labour and are heavily burdened, and I will give you rest ... rest for your souls".'*[320] She may not realise it, but Israel can't stand alone in trial without a defence representative to act on her behalf.[321]

And, for those of us who honour and love the Chosen People, may we exercise discernment and wisdom, ensuring that our prayers and assistance don't hinder the plans of Almighty God? In the words of a Messianic Jew, *'How we need to be careful ... that we do not in fact work or pray in a way that would further cement Israel's self-confidence instead of driving her closer into the arms*

---

[317] *JNN* editors, 1 January 2014, alluding to *Ryan Jones* and *Israel Today*.
[318] See Zechariah 12:10–11; 14:11; Ephesians 2:14-16; Romans 9:5; 11:15, 22–24.
[319] See Zechariah 14:11; Joel 3:16–17, 20; Psalm 18:2; Zephaniah 3:13–17; Revelation 21:27; 22:3–5.
[320] Matthew 11:28–30.
[321] See Psalm 18:30; 35:1; John 14:16–17.

of the God of Israel.'[322]

SON OF HAMAS

In our quest for truth regarding the Israeli/Palestinian conflict let us call to the stand an ex-member of Hamas as a witness for the defence. Known for his best-selling book, *Son of Hamas*, Mosab Hassan Yousef is informing the world of the organisation's vice. His father was a founding member of Hamas, and the young Yousef was groomed to take a leadership position. That changed, however, when he had a life-changing revelation of the deity of Jesus Christ. Following his radical conversion, Yousef left Hamas and spent a decade working as a *Shin Bet*[323] agent, undertaking covert missions to unveil terrorism. In a live interview on *CNN Tonight* he explained that Hamas' goal goes beyond eliminating Jews from Israel to the common Islamic objective of taking over the world:

> *'Hamas does not care about the lives of Palestinians … They consider dying for the sake of their ideology a way of worship … Hamas is not seeking co-existence and compromise … And, by the way … the destruction of the State of Israel – is not Hamas' final destination. Hamas' final destination is building the Islamic 'Khilafah,'[324] which means an Islamic State on the rubble of every other civilization … In the mosques Hamas taught us that without shedding innocent blood for the sake of the ideology, we won't be able to build an Islamic State. They were preparing us from … as young as five years old … And, honestly, it's impossible almost for anybody to … be able to leave … As you see in my case, I had to lose everything just to say 'no' to Hamas.'[325]*

---

[322] Johannes Facius, *Hastening the Coming of the Messiah* (Kent, 2001), p. 78.
[323] *Shin Bet*: Israel's internal security service.
[324] I.e. Caliphate.
[325] *CNN Tonight* interview with Mosab Hassan Yousef, 24 July 2014; available on YouTube.

When interviewed by a Church leader in the United States, the same Palestinian author made the following daring comments about the legitimacy of Islam: *'The religion of my people is a fake religion ...The god of Islam is a liar and he calls [himself] 'Deceit' in the Koran ... and people worship him every day ... It [Islam] is not more than [a] Satanic religion.'*

TRUSTWORTHY WITNESS

The Bible calls the Son of God: *'Jesus Christ, the trustworthy Witness.'*[326] In the Scriptures, we are assured of His rock-solid dependability: *'"the Everlasting of Israel does not lie or repent; for He is not a man to change His mind."'*[327] Of all people in the world, the believer in Jesus not only has the advantage of understanding the foundations and future developments of the Middle East crisis, but he is obliged, as Christ's ambassador, to share the truth.

Would you be a faithful witness? It's not easy swimming against the tide, and far easier to go with the flow. Thankfully, the author of *Son of Hamas* made the right decision to abandon the dead religion of his people, but it did not come without a price. The eldest of nine children, Yousef lost everything, including contact with his family and friends. The choice is ours, to follow the crowd or follow the Christ; to succumb to the majority or heed the voice of Truth.

IRELAND'S GLORY DAYS

There was a glorious moment in Irish history, when a bishop answered the call of God to return to the island that had once enslaved him. Were it not for God's mercy upon this our little nation; were it not for the obedience of that man from Roman Britain, I dread to think of the present state of our once pagan land. Thanks to St Patrick, Ireland became the land of saints and scholars, sending thousands of monks and missionaries overseas

---

[326] Revelation 1:5.
[327] 1 Samuel 15:29.

to spread the light of the one, true God.

When the Roman Empire was conquering the world and imposing the Roman calendar on its subjects, Ireland was not only one of the countries that remained free of the empire's grip, but it also steered clear of its pagan calendar. It is regrettable that we later succumbed to the majority and adopted both the calendar and the religion of the empire.

In his final address to *muintir na hÉireann* in 1803, the visionary, Robert Emmet predicted Ireland's future glory: *'When my country takes her place among the nations of the earth.'[328]* Emancipation from English rule was that to which the condemned man was referring. Nevertheless, may I suggest that his words were of a prophetic nature? It is only when our ancient homeland for the second and final time turns her back on darkness and false gods that she will be counted among the greatest of the world's nations.

UNTIL PROVEN GUILTY

Fir agus mná na hÉireann, as outlined above, Israel has been accused of many crimes, presumed guilty and arbitrarily convicted from time immemorial. But, as any defence lawyer would ask, how many could be verified in a court of law?[329] Whatever happened to her legal rights of being 'innocent until proven guilty'? Don't you agree, it's time we swallowed our pride and dropped the charges? And it's high time the obsessed and self-righteous global 'police' pursued a new line of enquiry.

---

[328] Edel O'Donovan & Fiona Kirwan, *Take the Plunge* (Dublin, 2005), p. 102.
[329] In 1892 while in court, the legal recorder of Belfast city made a snide remark regarding the Jews and their lack of integrity. When challenged for making the comment, Frederick Faulkiner confessed that in reality he had never known any Jewish person to be 'implicated at the criminal side of the court.' See Rivlin, *Jewish Ireland*, p. 38.

9

In The Line Of Fire

The story of *The Boy in the Striped Pyjamas* reminds us that persecution, like a sinister shadow, has followed the Jews throughout the ages. In the following scene the Commandant's son, Bruno, quizzes a frail Jewish slave: *'"When did you arrive at Out With?" asked Bruno. Pavel put the carrot and the peeler down for a few moments and thought about it. "I think I've always been here," he said finally in a quiet voice.'*[330] We explored in the previous chapter how the deceived early church was responsible for sowing seeds of anti-Semitism. Now it's time to examine the damage. The rotten fruits of their work are such that the people of Israel have been targeted incessantly throughout the Christian era.

'CHRISTIAN' CRUSADES

The Christian Crusades, undertaken by the 'Holy Roman Empire' between the years 1096 and 1291, were guilty of much blood shedding. By order of the Pope, Christian knights set out for the Holy Land, to rescue the Christian community from Muslim persecution. It seemed right to the Crusaders, however, to deal first with the supposed infidels on their doorstep, before engaging with foreign enemies of God. As they made their lengthy journey eastward, they left behind a long trail of Jewish blood. Accompanied by fervent common folk, the Crusaders attacked one Jewish community after another along the river Rhine, with no regard for children and infants. *'Throughout the crusades,*

---

[330] Boyne, *Striped Pyjamas*, p. 84.

which were thought to be a pious undertaking for God, Jews who were unwilling to submit to baptism were put to death. Many Jewish people were burned, beaten, and crucified on a cross as onlookers yelled "Christ Killers!"[331]

In Jerusalem, the defenceless souls tried hiding themselves in a synagogue, which the merciless Crusaders set aflame. This incident is described in a supplementary article written for the *Sunday Times* which records that during the first Crusade (in CE 1099): *'This synagogue in which the city's Jews were sheltering was set on fire to burn them alive, while, "full of happiness and weeping with joy", the crusaders went to worship Christ in the Church of the Holy Sepulchre.'*[332]

Taking part in the Third Crusade of 1187, England also set about massacring her own Jews, reports Ena Gray. Referring to the observations of Flannery[333] she says, *'It is significant, in terms of the motives for the attacks, that all records of debts due them were destroyed by the attackers.'*[334] Thus, religious zeal was not the only motive. These rampages gave begrudging 'Christians' the opportunity to clear their debts, albeit by wiping out their creditors.

LUDICROUS LIBELS

Meanwhile, propaganda was adopted to justify the ill-treatment of the Jew – a line of attack which has had devastating effects on the Jewish community right up to the present day. Historians attest to three common libels. One was host desecration. The absurd allegation claimed that Jews were guilty of deliberately either piercing or stamping on stolen communion hosts. Another libel was ritual murder: Jews were falsely accused of sacrificing Christian children, instead of the Passover lamb. Yet another was

---

[331] Silver, *Train Coming*, p. 180.
[332] Richard Girling *(ed.)*, Eleventh Century, Part 1: 'THE TYRANTS' CHARTER. Pope Urban II's Sermon at Clermont', *The Sunday Times* 'Pages from History' supplement.
[333] Monsignor Edward Flannery, *The Anguish of the Jews: Twenty-three Centuries of Anti-Semitism*, p. 119.
[334] Gray, *Healing the Past*, p. 46.

well poisoning: Jews were blamed for poisoning the wells and water supplies of Europe. This was the fabrication of suspicious minds affected by the devastating 'Black Death'. Ignorant of the cause of the epidemic, the usual suspect was targeted as the scapegoat. In the town of Basel, Switzerland, as many as 600 Jews were burned at the stake on suspicion of well poisoning. Similar myths led to the arrest and torture of countless innocent Jewish people in various parts of Western Europe.[335]

There is current evidence to suggest that Europeans still support malicious slander of Jews. Note the following response to a modern-day libel. In June 2016, PA President Mahmoud Abbas was given a *standing ovation* by European lawmakers following a speech in which he accused a group of rabbis of plotting to poison Palestinians' water supplies. His information had come from a Turkish news report. Subsequent investigations found that neither the accused 'Council of Rabbis' (mentioned in the report), nor the chairman Rabbi Shlomo Mlma exist. Having achieved the desired outcome, the Palestinian Authority leader retracted his allegation.[336]

INQUISITION

The roots of the Inquisition go back as far as 1233, when the pope established the first tribunal of its kind. So clearly unethical was this endeavour to eliminate heresy from Christian Europe that within twenty years, the succeeding Holy See (Pope *Innocent* IV) authorised the use of torture to obtain confessions.[337]

Under threat of exile, torture or death, it's hardly surprising that 'tens of thousands' of Jewish people in Spain converted to Catholicism,[338] especially after 6,000 had been massacred by fanatic mobs in the country at the time. In Portugal, 700 Jewish children were forcibly removed from their families and sent to live

---

[335] Ibid, p. 77.
[336] *JNN*, 26 June 2016, alluding to an article in *Israel Today*.
[337] Ibid, see pp. 55-56.
[338] Ibid, citing Monsignor Peter Hocken, p. 59.

in Christian homes on the island of Sao Tome off the west coast of Africa. The brutal tribunal that commenced forty years later prompted many Portuguese Jews, like their Spanish counterparts, to flee to South America. Sadly, they were not given the dignity to celebrate their religion and culture there either. Nevertheless, the Iberian Jews who sought refuge in Ireland were not only admitted, but free from all racist regulations imposed on the continent. This was a great relief for them.

POGROMS

Aside from the various inquisitions that have taken place in Europe and South America, pogroms (i.e. violent riots) have ignited in various parts of the 'civilised' world at different times throughout history. Often state-sponsored, these vicious attacks have involved pillage, arson, rape, mutilation, murder and massacre of Jewish communities. In Czarist Russia alone, between the years 1881 and 1884 *'one hundred Jewish communities were attacked.'*[339] As recently as 1920, at least three million Russian Jews are known to have fled the country. Some of these desperate souls found refuge in Ireland.[340]

TARGETS ABROAD

After examining the cruel and sanctimonious standards of our Christian ancestors, the current social climate requires attention. Although the national media pay little heed, there has been a rising tide of anti-Semitic incidents in recent years, especially in Europe, Russia, the United Kingdom and America. Along with harassment via various media platforms, verbal and physical attacks have taken place on streets, in Jewish public buildings, and in national universities. To give some idea of the range and regularity of these incidents let's take an overview of one

---

[339] Gray, *Healing the Past*, p. 75.
[340] The Jewish community of Ireland mainly owes its existence to the arrival of Russian Jewish asylum seekers, which began in the 1880s; the majority came from Lithuania.

particular year, 2012.[341]

FRANCE

A *Kosher*[342] foodstore was blown up in Paris in September 2012. France (home to the largest Jewish community in Europe) witnessed a number of violent attacks on Jews that year, not least of which was the murder in Toulouse of three Jewish children and their teacher. Residents of the town of Aix-les-Bains near Lyon received tracts in their letterboxes in October, which referred to Jews as, *'the main people responsible for the decadence of the White People and the invasion of sub-races.'*[343] As one reporter rightly expressed, *'These are modern-day pogroms.'*[344]

HUNGARY

A shocking situation erupted in Hungary in November, 2012. Parliamentarian Marton Gyöngyösi called for a list to be drawn up of all people of Jewish ancestry, as he shamelessly argued they might pose a threat to national security. Jobbik, the successful political party of which he is a leader, has been accused of being neo-Nazi and anti-Semitic. Within just a month, another Hungarian was detained by the police for setting an Israeli flag aflame at a demonstration in Budapest – he too was a member of parliament.[345]

---

[341] To check their validity, please research the following sources: *AFP; Arutz 7; CNN; Debka; Ha'aretz; ICEJ; INN; Israel Today; Jerusalem-On-The-Line; Jerusalem Post; Newsmax; New York Times; Reuters; Washington Post; Ynet;* … Sadly, Irish news sources are absent from the list.

[342] *Kosher* signifies that, according to Jewish religious law, food is fit for consumption.

[343] *JNN*, 29 October 2012, alluding to reports from *INN* and *Ha'aretz*.

[344] Howard Flower, 'Help Jews Fleeing Violence in France', *ICEJ*, June 2013, p. 9.

[345] Here's a troubling fact: In the 2014 local elections, far-right *Jobbik* rose from being the third largest to the second largest political party in Hungary, gaining control of 14 cities and towns. See *JNN*, 20 October 2014, alluding to *Arutz-7*.

DENMARK

It's sad to think that the country and kingdom to which the most credit is due for rescuing and publicly defending Jewish people in the Second World War has begun to change its tune. In Denmark's 'wonderful' Copenhagen, at least thirty-nine anti-Semitic criminal offences were reported in 2012.

BULGARIA

A tour bus was targeted in Bulgaria in August 2012 by Hezbollah. All on board were Jewish except the driver. He, the suicide bomber and five Israelis were killed, while other passengers sustained multiple debilitating injuries.

UNITED STATES

Another disturbing attack that should not go unmentioned took place that year in Michigan in the US. When a 19-year-old student, Zach Tennen, was approached near the university campus and asked if he were Jewish, he was first subjected to anti-Semitic taunts[346] before having his jaw broken and being knocked unconscious. Then his assailants, *'stapled his mouth shut through his gums'.*[347]

THE WILD WEST

It is of no little significance that in 2013 Chancellor Angela Merkel was compelled to caution her people against anti-Semitism, prior to the 75th anniversary of the 1938 *Kristallnacht* pogrom. She expressed in her podcast how necessary it is in Germany *today* to provide police protection for Jewish institutions on such occasions.[348]

---

[346] The attackers were *'making Nazi and Hitler symbols'*.

[347] *JNN*, 1 September 2012, alluding to *Jerusalem Post* article.

[348] In 2014, police protection was required for all Jewish institutions in Germany during 'Yom Kippur'.

All of the above is but the tip of the iceberg. Later, we will analyse how much further the situation has deteriorated in Europe. Let's now turn our focus to issues of home security in Israel.

MODERN ISRAEL

The strategic planting of explosives in densely populated places to impose maximum damage, is a terror tactic that has devastated the people and cities of Israel. Sadly, the world has a tendency to forget the business customers and bus passengers, young and old, who have taken the blow of merciless blasts. Statistics show that aside from all other forms of terror inflicted, 170 suicide attacks shook the nation between the years 1989, when the first of its kind took place, and 2008 inclusive. Meanwhile, bomb attacks claimed the lives of a total of 804 Israeli civilians. The international community has been rattled in recent years by jihadist attacks on Europeans, and has expressed deep sympathy for the victims. It is imperative that we open our eyes to the parallels.

JERUSALEM UNDER FIRE

On the corner of Jaffa and King George Street, the heart of Jerusalem's modern city, now stands a bakery. It was once however, a pizza parlour and the target of a life-shattering suicide bombing, which killed fifteen civilians and injured 130 others, among whom were young families and adolescents.[349]

When I lived in Jerusalem for the best part of a year, Ben Yehuda Street often reminded me of Grafton Street. The vibrant, pedestrianised piazza, surrounded by upmarket boutiques, teems with fun-loving, young Israelis. Tragically, two suicide bombers and a car bomb were the instruments of a major terrorist attack

---

[349] The Sbarro pizzeria suicide bombing, for which Hamas and the Islamic Jihad claimed responsibility, took place during the Al-Aqsa Intifada on 9 August 2001. Seven children and a pregnant woman were among the fifteen civilians who were killed. For a comprehensive list of lives lost to terror attacks from as far back as 1993 to the current day visit the online encyclopaedia www.jewishvirtuallibrary.org.

which occurred there, killing thirteen and injuring 188 others. Imagine if Munster[350] experienced a barrage of as many as forty-seven bomb attacks in one year. How complacent would the bereaved communities of the province be if it had lost 457 lives at the hands of terrorists, as Israel did in the year 2002?

DEFENCE MEASURES

Life could not go on like this. For the sake of the survival of local businesses and the tourism industry, and for the safety and sanity of the people themselves, Israel began to build a protective barrier to run between it and the West Bank. The fence (which in certain vulnerable areas – only five per cent in total – consists of concrete wall) has successfully reduced the number of entry points to Jerusalem. Consequently, hundreds, if not thousands, of Jewish men, women and children have been spared the trauma of additional bomb attacks.

PROTECTIVE BARRIERS

The idea of building protective barriers is nothing new. It has been done since time immemorial. The farmer builds a chicken pen to keep foxes out. Is his motive to aggravate the fox, or is it to protect the chicken from attack? Farmers have nothing against foxes, per se. But they do have issues with them targeting their livestock, and will make every effort to prevent that from happening. Prison walls are built to restrain convicted criminals from having free access to society. Are law-abiding citizens likely to want to tear down those walls, or are they safer and less anxious with that barrier in place?

SECURITY FENCE

Concrete evidence proves how successful the anti-terrorist fence

---

[350] Munster, you will recall, is approximately the same size as Israel.

has been in diminishing the number of explosive attacks.[351] At the height of the onslaught in 2002, 451 Jewish lives were lost to Palestinian terrorists.[352] The completion, in August 2003, of the first section of the fence was instrumental in decreasing the number of fatalities, by more than 50 per cent, to 208 by the end of the year. As further sections were constructed, fewer lives were struck down. By 2005, the number had dropped to fifty-three fatalities.[353] This positive trend continued until there were 'only' sixteen Jewish lives eliminated by terrorists in 2008.[354] Today, Israel continues the work of erecting security fences in vulnerable areas. There is one that now runs along the southern border, due to the volatile activity of ISIS and other Islamic terrorists in the neighbouring Sinai Peninsula. The weekly violent 'March of Return' demonstrations at the Gaza border have necessitated the construction of a 20,000-ton, 20 feet high galvanized steel barrier. Its 'smart fence' feature will additionally be able to detect the construction of underground terror tunnels. This particular defence barrier will come at an approximate cost of $833 million to the Israeli taxpayer.[355] Hezbollah's subterranean network of attack tunnels has led to the construction of yet another security fence along the northern front.

BERLIN WALL

In ignorance, some have compared these walls and fences to the Berlin Wall. The communist structure was unquestionably a divisive barrier that violated the human rights of those it imprisoned. I can testify personally to this, having visited Germany in 1990, the year after the Iron Curtain was torn down. The stark contrast between west and east left a lasting impression. The

---

[351] Not all assaults involve the use of explosive materials; others include guns, knives, hammers, axes, hatchets and other instruments.

[352] This includes a total of 220 massacred in suicide bomb attacks.

[353] Twenty-three of those murdered in 2005 were killed by suicide bombing.

[354] Only one, and still one too many of course, was assassinated by a suicide bomber in that year. All of the above statistics were provided by Israel's Ministry of Foreign Affairs.

[355] *JNN* editors, 6 February 2019, alluding to a *CBN* news report.

modern West was green and lush. Lined with grey apartment blocks, the East seemed to be shrouded in dullness. I have no recollection of seeing trees and parks; cars were sparse and outmoded. It was like entering the set of a musty old film.

In complete contrast, the reason for anti-terrorist fences in modern, high-tech Israel is to preserve life and to progress as a nation, enabling law-abiding citizens to conduct their daily affairs without the constant threat of terror invasions. The unavoidable ramification, however, is the inevitable separation of people and land, which unfortunately impacts on Arabs and Jews.

THE LESSER OF TWO EVILS

From my Theology studies in Maynooth University, I have committed to memory the following lesson: when faced with a moral dilemma choose 'the lesser of the two evils.' In other words, when a difficult choice must be made, select the option that is least harmful to human life. Israel's options were to either continue to allow the lives of her defenceless Jewish civilians to be snuffed out by free-roaming terrorists, or to take costly steps that would increase restrictions on terrorist movements. By choosing the latter and constructing the fence-cum-wall boundary, which inevitably impedes the lives of numerous Arabs (as well as Jews, let's not forget), Israel has done the best she could, given the dire circumstances. To her credit also, the Israeli Supreme Court has made a ruling which facilitates the adjustment of the fence in order to be of less hindrance to the lives and work of local Arabs. *'Palestinians living in the West Bank are able to appeal to the Israeli Supreme Court against the route of the fence where it causes disruption to lives, and have successfully done so in many cases. Attempts are made to minimise disruption caused by the fence, for example by building agricultural gates that allow Palestinian farmers to access their land.'*[356] The heavy burden placed by this defence measure on the economy and taxpayer is a

---

[356] See Britain Israel Communications & Research Centre: *www.bicom.org.uk.*

subject we will shortly broach. First, let's consider the emotional effects of terrorism.

TERRORISED

To give an idea of the intimidation experienced by Israelis *before* the fence was erected, this is what a Jewish civil servant had to say, *'I tell you this as a police officer. I don't come to Jerusalem with my children anymore ... I'd give over my bank account to live in peace.'*[357] During an interview in Jerusalem's King David Hotel, history professor, Benny Morris, explained, *'The Palestinians say they have found a strategic weapon, and suicide bombing is it. This hotel is empty. The streets are empty. They have effectively terrorized Israeli society. My wife won't use a bus anymore, only a taxi.'*[358] Life was bleak. Many Israelis avoided socialising in public places and grew accustomed to staying at home instead. That was one place terrorists weren't targeting.[359] Another objective of the terror attacks was to strike hard at the nation's economy. Not only did the tourism industry take a hit but, it was vital that local businesses use alternative means to keep their customers. McDonalds, for example, was one of many restaurants that launched a home delivery service.

ON THE BREADLINE

And while we are on the subject of food ... Did you know that *'One fifth of Israelis ... suffer from food insecurity?'*[360] For a long time, citizens of Israel have been folding under the weight of high living costs. Housing, retail and food prices are very high. *In fact, 'the*

---

[357] Bruce Hoffman, *The Atlantic Monthly*, June 2003, cited in John Maszka, *Terrorism and the Bush Doctrine*, pp. 102–3.

[358] Google: 'Living with suicide bombing in Israel', *http://factsanddetails.com*.

[359] This is something which we can no longer take for granted. There have been countless vicious attacks made on Jewish people in their homes and on their property in recent years. Perhaps you heard of the Itamar Massacre perpetrated by two Arab teens? In March 2011 a Jewish father, mother and three of their children – aged 11, 4 and 3 months – were stabbed to death in their beds at night.

[360] *VFI News*, 3 January 2020.

cost of living in Israel is among the highest of developed nations.[361] They must also carry the burden of heavy taxes, largely due to a cumbersome defence budget. A report released in December 2019 by the Organisation for Economic Co-operation and Development (OECD) revealed that Israel's poverty rate exceeds that of all its thirty-five member states.[362] Out of a population of 9,136,000, as many as 2.3 million Israelis live below the poverty line. While I have heard numerous people pass ignorant and offensive remarks about "the wealthy Jews" the reality is that almost a quarter of the population of Israel are struggling to make ends meet.

In terms of the most vulnerable: A third of Israel's children suffer from food insecurity – meaning they do not have sufficient food on a consistent basis.[363] 'The latest children's poverty rates place Israel as second to the highest in the OECD countries'[364] with one million living under the line of poverty. 2020 statistics reveal that poverty among the elderly stands at 18.8% and is on the increase.[365] Sadly, the 192,000 Holocaust Survivors in Israel, who mainly live alone, feel the pinch more than the rest of their peers. Various reports over the last few years reveal that over two-thirds of survivors are subsisting off a meagre income which is 'less than the typical monthly rent price for a studio apartment in Jerusalem and Tel Aviv.'[366]

TEMPLE MOUNT

Israel is under tremendous pressure to cede territory to the Palestinians. Each time the Israeli government yields, it backfires on her. While she keeps her side of the agreement, the Abbas administration lets her down. Jerusalem's much disputed

---

[361] Ibid.
[362] Ibid, 18 December 2019.
[363] Ibid.
[364] Ibid, 3 January 2020.
[365] Ibid.
[366] JNN eds, 25 April 2014.

territory, the Temple Mount (on Mount Moriah), is a prime example. This is the location where the temple of Yahweh God stood;[367] it is the precise place where Jesus was dedicated as a baby by Joseph and his mother Mary.[368] And, let's not forget that took place more than five centuries before Muhammad was conceived and before the religion of Islam was envisaged. Muhammad never once visited Jerusalem, and the Dome of the Rock[369] is not the holiest site of Islam, nor indeed the second holiest. Mount Moriah is the place where father Abraham, many centuries before, offered up his son Isaac, in obedience to God.[370] Addressing the Israeli Knesset on 'Jerusalem Day', PM Netanyahu clearly justifies their claim to this site, the epicentre of the Middle Eastern conflict:

"'Since our very beginning as a people, our existence was tied to Jerusalem … Our forefathers visited the Temple Mount 3,800 years ago. The two temples of the Jewish people stood on the Temple Mount for one thousand years. King David made Jerusalem our capital 3,000 years ago, and ever since, the Jewish people have prayed in the direction of the Temple Mount. Does anyone claim that the pyramids in Giza have no connection to the Egyptians? That the Acropolis in Athens has no connection to the Greeks? That the Colosseum in Rome has no connection to the Italians? We, the people of Israel, have a primal claim on Jerusalem. Our roots here are deeper than any other people, and the same is true about the Temple Mount.'"[371]

---

[367] See 2 Chronicles 3:1.
[368] See Luke 2:21–24.
[369] Dome of the Rock: the sacred rock on Mount Moriah, around which the Muslim shrine was built.
[370] See Genesis 22:2.
[371] JNN, 4 June 2016, citing a press release from the Prime Minister's Office.

1967 RELINQUISHMENT

For some years prior to the war of 1967, east Jerusalem and the Temple Mount were under Jordanian control. (The Hashemite Kingdom of Jordan had in fact illegally annexed the area in question in the year 1950, while the United Nations along with the rest of the world turned a blind eye.) Then the powerful nation of Egypt, along with Syria and backed by Jordan and Iraq, called for Jihad on Israel. In the words of Egyptian President Gamal Abdel Nassar: *'The objective will be to destroy Israel.'*[372]

Much to the dismay of Nassar and his allies, the Six-Day War of 1967 would miraculously turn in Israel's favour, despite her comparatively low resources of arms and manpower. *'They outnumbered Israel five to one in troops, three to one in tanks and nearly three to one in combat aircraft.'*[373] Israel not only thwarted their evil plans, but *regained* control of areas that had not been hers for almost two millennia, including the Temple Mount. *'By the end of the week, Israel had captured Sinai and the Gaza Strip from Egypt, the West Bank and the rest of Jerusalem from Jordan, and the Golan Heights from Syria.'*[374]

Regrettably, in the hopes of appeasing her Arab neighbours, Israel later waived her rights to the Temple Mount. Fooled into believing she could persuade her enemies to make peace with her, she yielded. This decision has cost Israel dearly. Not only is the Jordan-controlled Temple Mount not accessible to Jewish visitors, but *'No Jewish or Christian prayer is allowed on the mountain and such prayer is subject to arrest.'*[375] With intention to kill, rocks and stones have been hurled by Arab men from this elevated position at Jewish men, women and children praying at the Western Wall below. Such malicious conduct was a feature of the Al-Aqsa *Intifada*[376], which began in the year 2000. The uprising was sparked by the visit of the then Prime Minister, Ariel Sharon,

---

[372] Crown-Tamir, *In a Nutshell*, p. 104.
[373] Maltz, *Many Names*, p. 125.
[374] Ibid, p. 125.
[375] *JNN*, 8 March 2019, alluding to a *Jerusalem Post* article.
[376] The Arabic word 'intifada' means 'shaking off'; it refers to a Palestinian uprising.

to the holy site.

GUSH KATIF

Gaza has been home to Jewish people since long before the Six-Day War. *'During much of the Biblical, Second Temple and Roman/Talmudic periods, the Middle Ages and the era of modern Zionism, there had been a Jewish presence in the Gaza region.'*[377] The twenty-two Israeli settlements of Gush Katif in the strip had for almost forty years been a hub of agricultural productivity. *'The total value of exports from the greenhouses of Gush Katif reached 200 million US dollars per year and amounted to 15 per cent of Israel's total agricultural exports.'*[378] In relation to conflict, there was relative peace in the coastal enclave until a tragic road accident led to rumours among Gazan Arabs which, along with further provocations by the PLO and religious leaders, sparked the first Palestinian Intifada of 1987. *'False charges of Israeli atrocities and instigation from the mosques played an important role in starting the intifada.'*[379] The uprising, which spread to the West Bank and Jerusalem, would last for six long years. (A concise and factual account of the First Intifada can be found at www.jewishvirtuallibrary.org.) Shortly thereafter Gush Katif would fall victim to even more gruesome terror tactics in the Second Intifada. To take but a couple of examples: Jewish women and children were targeted by Palestinian snipers as they journeyed home from work and school; a yellow school bus was bombed, killing the driver and one of the teachers, and leaving several Jewish children bereft of limbs and body parts.[380]

---

[377] Lewin, E. (2015). The Disengagement from Gaza: Understanding the Ideological Background. *Jewish Political Studies Review, 27*(1/2), 15–32. Retrieved May 21, 2020, from www.jstor.org/stable/43868412.

[378] Ibid.

[379] www.jewishvirtuallibrary.org. Israel's Wars and Operations: First Intifada (1987–93). Retrieved 20 May 2020.

[380] Lewin, E. (2015). The Disengagement.

GAZA DISENGAGEMENT

It was during the Second Intifada that Israel made further concessions. Under the administration of Prime Minister Ariel Sharon the drastic decision was made to evict all Jewish residents from the Gaza Strip[381] and implement the complete withdrawal of IDF forces, leaving the governance and welfare of the enclave completely in the hands of the Palestinian Authority. Understandably, the evacuation in August 2005 was met with resistance by many members of the Gush Katif community, some of whom were literally dragged from their homes by IDF soldiers. It must have been devastating for them to have to walk away from their vast and thriving glasshouses and dairy farms and even more so to witness the demolition of their 2,500 homes, along with their schools, kindergartens and religious institutions.

In the pull out, Israel vowed to continue providing the Palestinian population of the strip with electricity, communications, water and sewage systems. Regarding customs, *'imports from Israel to Gaza are not taxed, exports from Gaza to Israel are taxed.'*[382] The Jewish state has kept her side of the bargain while, at the same time and for obvious security reasons, retaining control of Gaza airspace and coastline.

COST OF YIELDING

The uprooting from their land and demolition of their homes had a demoralizing effect on the *9,000* Jewish citizens of Gaza, who felt they had been betrayed by their government. Even as late as 2016 the effects of their diminished morale were manifest: *'Many residents of Jewish communities expelled during the 2005 Gaza Disengagement are still unemployed and living with their families in cramped caravans or small overcrowded apartments.'*[383]

With the IDF now out of the equation, Hamas speedily expanded

---

[381] Along with four settlements of northern Samaria.
[382] Crown-Tamir, *In a Nutshell*, p. 197.
[383] *JNN* editors, 2 March 2016, alluding to *Washington Post* and *Ynet* articles.

its control over the region and, by means of a putsch in June 2007, *'neutralized the military and political power of the Palestinian Authority and set up a radical Muslim entity in the Gaza Strip, often referred to as Hamastan.'*[384]

In its oppressive government of the Strip, Hamas has continually failed to use foreign aid funds to improve infrastructure and medical centres, and provide social benefits for their citizens. On the contrary, the bulk of the abundant acquisition is spent annually on arms purchases, and on the construction of illegal tunnels into Egypt and Israel. The withdrawal of the Israeli Defence Forces served to exacerbate this problem. To see it in perspective: During 2012, terror rockets were fired into Israel from the coastal enclave at a rate of two per day.[385] It is therefore little wonder that wars broke out between Israel and Gaza terrorists in 2012, and also in 2008 and 2014 for the same reason.

Furthermore, Israel relinquished the vast Sinai Peninsula, in exchange for peace with Egypt. The 'Sinai Disengagement' of 1982 made vulnerable the southern border of Israel. This territory is now illegally occupied by militant Muslim groups (including ISIS) who regularly attempt to penetrate the Jewish state. Thus, it is proven time and again, in an honest desire to procure peace, Israel has made concessions and sacrifices, only to be met with broken promises and malicious attacks by a substantial contingent of her Muslim neighbours. This is the cost of yielding to the unreasonable demands of terrorists. When will the international community recognise this, and cease putting unfair demands on Israel?

FROM ANOTHER ANGLE

One must wonder why so little attention is paid to Egypt's handling of terrorist activity in the region. While Israel is expected to sit back and let her enemies tear her to pieces, Egypt appears

---

[384] Lewin, E. (2015). The Disengagement.
[385] *JNN* eds, 19 October 2012.

to be allowed to defend itself against these same terrorist entities. Following two separate terrorist attacks which killed 33 Egyptian soldiers in Autumn 2014, the Egyptian military closed Gaza crossings into Egypt. The world was relatively quiet and was not concerned that a humanitarian crisis might ensue for these Palestinians. Not long after, thousands of Gazans were forcibly evacuated from their homes, which were subsequently exploded by the Egyptian army, yet there was no international outcry and not a mention of Egypt perpetrating 'human rights violations'.

Egypt has made no apologies but has rather defended its right to create a security zone, ten kilometres long and a *half kilometre wide* between the Gaza Strip and the Sinai Peninsula. Egyptian Army spokesperson, Tamer al-Rafai, explains that it was because of the terror tunnels that this drastic measure was taken: *'In 2015, the Egyptian government made a decision to establish a buffer zone along the border with the Gaza Strip … These tunnels were used to threaten Egypt's national security, including the infiltration of terrorists, smuggling of weapons, ammunition, goods, narcotic drugs and vehicles.'* The same spokesman revealed that since 2015 the Egyptian army has destroyed more than 3,000 illegal tunnels along the border with Gaza, many of which were three kilometres in length and 30 metres deep. During numerous military operations over that same period it has targeted and struck down hundreds of terrorists in the Sinai Peninsula, and arrested 266 suspects. Al-Rafai concluded: *'The Egyptian armed forces are working round the clock to combat terrorism and secure our borders … We have scored many achievements … including the destruction of the terror infrastructure.'*[386] Why is it when Israel attempts to quell the activity of terrorists and strike their supplies the whole world is in uproar?

---

[386] *Jerusalem Post,* 4 May 2020, Khaled Abu Toameh: 'Egypt says it Destroyed more than 3,000 Gaza Tunnels', citing Egyptian military spokesman Tamer al-Refai from an interview on the Egyptian news channel *Extra News* on 3 May 2020.

FLASHBACKS

Jerusalem has in recent years introduced a tram network similar to the *Luas* design. The majority of passengers in that capital city, however, are not as carefree as they scud along. Some have flashbacks of an explosion they narrowly escaped; for others, memories revive of loved ones lost or maimed; while most share the unspoken fear of the tram being the target of another terror attack.

And if that weren't enough to be worried about, the following extract throws light on the fact that other means of terror are being utilised to debilitate business and social life in the capital. *'The company that runs Jerusalem's light rail system, City Pass, reported that its fleet of 23 railway cars had been effectively reduced to 14 as a result of repeated rock throwing in Arab neighbourhoods. On Sunday, four rail cars were damaged in five rock throwing incidents.'*[387] Does it not seem that Israel is forever in the line of fire?

---

[387] *JNN* eds, 20 October 2014, referring to an article in *Israel Hayom*.

10

Line Up! Attention!

In 1982, Irish poet Michael O'Siadhail gained world-wide acclaim for *The Gossamer Wall*, his prize-winning book of poetry that focused on the Holocaust. The poem 'Faces', quietly pleads with us never to forget.

'Neat millions of pairs of abandoned shoes …
Faces both stare and vanish. Which ghetto?
Warsaw, Vilna, Lodz, Riga, Kovno.
Eight hundred dark-eyed girls from Salonica …
Tread the barefoot floor to a shower-room.
Each someone's fondled face. A named few ….
I'll change their shame to praise and renown in all
The earth … Always each face and shoeless footfall
A breathing memory behind the gossamer wall.'

In a book review, Fred Johnston of Books Ireland commented, *'Ó Siadhail personalises both captives and victims … to … give them back to us as real human beings and not numbers … This is … a book of windows into terror we in our soft Irishness cannot begin to imagine.'*

ANARCHY IN THE MIDDLE EAST

In a visit to Auschwitz concentration camp, Israeli Prime Minister Benjamin Netanyahu asserted, *'One of the key lessons the Jews took from the Holocaust was not to be complacent in the face of threats of annihilation. We must not bury our heads in the sand or allow others to do the work for us.'* Israel is in the line of fire and cannot afford to be a sitting duck. In the words of the Premier: *'If the Arabs lay down their arms there will be peace, but if the Jews lay down their arms, there will be no more Israel!'* The Jewish state is surrounded by danger on every side, with increased terror activity for the last decade on the Golan border since the Syrian civil war broke out, Iran's undeterred, unabashed nuclear threats, and, not to forget, the now underground brutal ISIS entity.

SIGNS OF THE TIMES

It is a well-known fact that Adolf Hitler unveiled his wicked schemes long before WWII. 1925 saw the publication of his aforementioned racist book: *Mein Kampf,* which indoctrinated the crumbling Weimar Republic with skewed political ideologies. 1933 – the year Hitler was elected Chancellor of Germany – witnessed the construction of concentration camps for the detainment of political prisoners. Eager to embrace employment opportunities made available by the construction of vast roads and concentration camps, the majority of Germans did not oppose the growing dictatorship. It is little wonder that the Nazis made rapid, monstrous progress! Today, the Iranian theocratic regime poses an even greater threat. As someone rightly pointed out, *'with just one bomb, Iran can do to the Jews in 12 minutes what Hitler did in 12 years.'*[388]

ON THE FIRING RANGE

As we witness history repeat itself, our world is suffering selective memory loss. Both Mahmoud Ahmadinejad (former president of Iran) and the country's Supreme Leader, the *Ayatollah* Ali Khameini, have unashamedly spewed countless threats of obliteration at Israel. Yet, of all the places which should know

---

[388] *JNN,* 2 March 2015, alluding to *Wall St Journal* article.

better, Europe is inexcusably betraying the Jewish nation, whose life is in grave danger (this time at the hands of fanatical, fundamentalist Muslims) while at the same time bending over backwards to appease Ali Khameini and his cohort. The fact that Arabs have monopoly over the oil market has been an undeniable influencing factor. Greed and self-preservation prove yet again to be the shameful components driving the apathetic engines of the world's 'developed' nations.

ISLAMIC REPUBLIC

Before addressing the current political climate of Iran, it will help to review her historic agenda. Over forty years ago, the goal of the Islamic Republic was set forth by her founding ruler, the Ayatollah Ruhollah Khameini: *'We will export our revolution to the entire world, until the cry, "There is no god but Allah" will echo throughout the world.'*[389] Reiterating these sentiments, commander of the regime's ruthless Revolutionary Guards, Major General Mohammad Ali Ja'afari, declared, *'Our duty is to prepare the way for an Islamic world government.'*[390] In other words, the goal of the Islamic Republic of Iran is to build a world-dominating Islamic empire (aka caliphate). Do we in the West think that this will be brought about peaceably? Former Muslim terrorist Kamal Saleem is not so naïve: *'Every Muslim must commit Jihad. It's the sixth pillar of Islam. It's the invisible pillar that nobody talks about, except the Iranians.'*[391]

---

[389] Excerpts from Speeches and Messages of Imam Khomeini on the Unity of Muslims', p. 108. <http://en.wikipedia.org/wiki/Political_thought_and_legacy_of_Ruhollah_Khomeini> (9 June 2016)

[390] Cited by Prime Minister Benjamin Netanyahu in his UN General Assembly speech, 29 September 2014.

[391] *Jewish Voice*, Daystar Television (Viewed 20 October 2015).

TRACK RECORD

It is no secret that the Islamic Republic of Iran is arming terrorist organisations, such as Hezbollah of Lebanon and Hamas in Gaza. In fact, the US State Department acknowledges that Iran has been the leading exporter of terrorism for the last four decades.[392] Her support of Syria's dictator, President Bashar al-Assad, is widely known. The regime's attempts to control Yemen have made world news.

Iran's leadership continues to voice existential threats at public rallies and on social networking sites regarding Israel and 'the Great Satan' (America). With that in mind, the following candid description of the Iranian regime would be difficult for any European leader to rebut: *'Any nuclear agreement that allows Iran to maintain a native uranium-enrichment capability is a dicey proposition; in fact, any agreement at all with an empire-building, Assad-sponsoring, Yemen-conquering, Israel-loathing, theocratic terror regime is a dicey proposition.'*[393] Ever since the Iranian revolution of 1979 and the birth of the Islamic Republic of Iran, it is not unusual for Friday prayers at the mosque to conclude with crowds chanting 'Death to America' – which even continued, incredibly, while in the process of negotiating a nuclear deal with the USA!

IRAN'S NUCLEAR HISTORY

The Islamic Republic has had a nuclear research and development programme since the 1950s. She signed the Nuclear Non-Proliferation Treaty[394] thereafter and became subject to the International Atomic Energy Agency (IAEA). What sparked a United Nations investigation in 2002 was the disclosure of the covert construction of two nuclear sites. The following year, the IAEA was alarmed to discover that Iran had been carrying out

---

[392] I.e. since the *Ayatollah*/Supreme Leader along with the new Islamic Republic of Iran took the nation by force, ousting the Shah's historical monarchy.
[393] *The Atlantic*, 1 March 2015.
[394] Proliferation is the distribution of nuclear weapons.

research and experiments at the various stages of nuclear weapons development. Thus, international negotiations with the Iranian administration were convened in 2003 to deter her quest for nuclear capability.[395] Due to increasing concerns in 2006[396], the United Nations Security Council demanded that she suspend her uranium enrichment programme. Iran's non-compliance resulted in the enforcement of UN sanctions.

EXTREMIST SECURITY COUNCIL

The regime's current President Hassan Rouhani once declared that *'Israel is "a wound on the body of the Islamic world", echoing the words of ... Ayatollah Ali Khameini that the Jewish state is a "cancer" that must be removed'.*[397] Desperate nonetheless, to have international sanctions lifted which were choking the economy, President Rouhani has taken a different approach to his antagonistic precursor and set out to beguile world media with supposed passivity. Were we not to have seen his *Curriculum Vitae*, we might be fooled by his renowned 'charm offensive'. *'Far from being an enemy of terrorism, Rouhani's record shows ... He headed Iran's Supreme National Security Council from 1989–2003. During that time Iran committed a series of terrorist attacks, including ... murdering 85 people at the Jewish community centre in Buenos Aires, and blowing up the Kohbar Towers in Saudi Arabia, which left 19 American soldiers dead among other victims.'*[398]

---

[395] Nuclear capability is defined as a 'country's possession of, and ability to use, nuclear weapons'.
[396] From 2006 to mid-2015 the P5+1 nuclear negotiation was in operation. It was led by the Obama administration and comprised five Security Council nations: the United States of America, France, the United Kingdom, Russia and China; plus Germany.
[397] David Parsons, 'Iran Seeking Second Route to Nukes', *ICEJ* publication, September/October 2013, p. 25.
[398] Barry & Batya Segal, Joseph Storehouse publication, October 2013.

NUCLEAR ARMS RACE

States which had a *Sunni* majority in the Middle East at the time of the nuclear negotiations voiced their concerns over the Iranian nuclear deal, greatly fearing the possibility of nuclear weapons in the hands of their *Shi'ite* neighbours. A number of Arab nations have been, in this regard, unashamed to say they are of one mind with Israeli Prime Minister Benjamin 'Bibi' Netanyahu. Columnist Dr Ahmad Al-Faraj made the following remark about the head of the negotiations, former American president Barack Obama, in the Saudi daily *Al-Jazirah* in March 2015: *'Obama … is the ally of political Islam, which is the caring mother of all terrorist organizations, and he is working to sign an agreement with Iran that will come at the expense of America's long-time allies in the Gulf … I am very glad of Netanyahu's firm stance.'*[399] Here's another unexpected article by Faisal Abbas for *Al-Arabiya* news, *'Bibi got it right when it came to … Iran. What is absurd … the only stakeholder that seems not to realize the danger of the situation is President Obama, who is now infamous for being the latest pen-pal of the supreme leader of the world's biggest terrorist regime.'*[400]

Iran's success in achieving nuclear capability would inevitably lead to a race to produce nuclear arms in the surrounding unstable Arab nations. It is little wonder that Saudi Arabia, fearing for her life has begun to explore the same avenue. Could anybody possibly deny that a nuclear arms race in the Middle East would mean perilous times ahead both for the region and the world?

NUCLEAR DEAL FINALISED

In July 2015, following twelve years of negotiations, a deal was reached. Considering it had not mended its ways, one would have expected the dismantling of at least some of Iran's nuclear sites. Yet, all of the nation's nuclear facilities would continue to operate. The agreement failed to stipulate that Iran end its

---

[399] *JNN*, 5 March 2015, alluding to *Jerusalem Post*.
[400] Ibid.

aggressiveness and support of global terrorism. Almost all economic sanctions imposed over the previous decade would be lifted; Iran would gradually receive almost $150 billion dollars in sanctions relief.[401] Additional bonuses for the Theocratic regime included the elimination of ballistic missile sanctions after eight years and the lifting of the UN weapons embargo after five.[402] And, to put the icing on the cake, Iran would be granted 24 days' notice prior to IAEA inspections of nuclear sites. In short, the Iranian regime emerged triumphant; the negotiations were a farce. Instead of hindering her nuclear progress, western powers in all probability bolstered Iran's prospects of nuclear capability.

Could nothing have been learned from failed acts of appeasement in the past, such as the 1938 Munich Agreement which according to British Prime Minister Neville Chamberlain, guaranteed *'peace for our time'*? Had the Obama administration so quickly forgotten President Clinton's regrettable nuclear deal with North Korea's dictator in the 1990s?

INITIAL FALLOUT

What came as no surprise was the continued belligerence of the Iranian leadership. Immediately after the deal was reached, Rouhani's administration increased its defence budget by 32.5%;[403] Iran resumed funding terror organisations, such as Hamas and Islamic Jihad.[404] Also, *'Iran has gone on a shopping spree for military hardware, purchasing Russian missiles, submarines, tanks and fighter aircraft.'*[405] It is unfathomable that the Obama administration could have been at ease with the Ayatollah Khamenei's 'America Suicide' tweet, which featured a

---

[401] Upon implementation of the deal in January 2016, Iran immediately received access to 'tens of billions of dollars in unfrozen assets', *JNN*, 17 January 2016, citing a *Jerusalem Post* article.
[402] *JNN*, 24 August 2015, alluding to *Algemeiner*.
[403] *JNN*, 17 July 2015, alluding to *Times of Israel*.
[404] *Ibid*.
[405] *JNN*, 27 April 2016, alluding to *INN*.

silhouette of the US president pointing a gun to his own head.[406] In January 2016, President Rouhani ordered the increase of missile production.[407] A month later, US intelligence confessed: *'We judge that Tehran would choose ballistic missiles as its preferred method of delivering nuclear weapons.'*[408]

On 10 October and 21 November 2015, and again on 9 March 2016, the Islamic Republic carried out ballistic missile tests. This is a deliberate violation of UN Security Council Resolution 2231 which was passed a day after the nuclear accord was signed.[409] Yet, contrary to Obama's threats to re-impose sanctions if Iran breached the deal, no action was taken. On the other hand, we can be sure to take the Supreme Leader of Iran seriously when he, just short of a year after the deal was reached, declared: *'The future is missiles, not negotiations.'*[410]

COME UP TRUMPS

Thankfully, the succeeding president of the United States was alarmed by the deal's failure to curb Iran's nuclear aspirations and took a major step in 2018 by pulling America out of the deal. After several warnings to the Islamic Republic, which continued undeterred in its nuclear pursuit, he also re-imposed necessary sanctions. In his address to the UN General Assembly that year former President Donald Trump justified the action taken:

> *'"The Iran deal was a windfall for Iran's leaders. In the years since the deal was reached, Iran's military budget grew nearly 40 per cent. The dictatorship used the funds to build nuclear capable missiles, increase internal repression, finance terrorism and fund havoc and slaughter in Syria and Yemen. The United States has launched a campaign of*

---

[406] *JNN*, 29 July 2015, alluding to *Arutz-7*.
[407] *JNN*, 2 January 2016, alluding to *Times of Israel*
[408] *JNN*, 12 February 2016, citing *Arutz-7/US Institute of Peace*.
[409] *JNN*, 19 March 2016, alluding to *INN*.
[410] *JNN*, 1 April 2016, alluding to *INN*.

economic pressure to deny the regime the funds it needs to advance its bloody agenda.'"[411]

These sanctions, which have hit the banking and oil industries, have had a crippling effect on Iran's economy and are apparently bringing to the surface the true colours of the purportedly composed Iranian President. From a podium at an annual Islamic Unity Conference in Tehran, Rouhani struck the League of Nations (aka United Nations) and Israel with one rhetorical blow: *'one of the ominous results of World War II was the formation of a cancerous tumour in the region.'*[412]

PEOPLE AFTER PROFIT

It is terribly unfortunate that the regime is weighing heavily on the Iranian people. Months before the first round of sanctions were restored Iranians took to the streets in protest against their leaders. The petition to their government was that it *'Leave Syria'* (i.e. pull out its troops and quit interfering in the civil war) and focus instead on their own people's needs. Iranian Saeed Ghasseminejad explains: *'The regime is selling oil to fund terrorist groups and its military adventures in the region while Iranians become poorer and poorer every day.'*[413]

What has also sparked flares of social unrest in the Islamic Republic has been the government's failure to disburse months of hard-earned salaries. Teachers, truck drivers, farmers and factory workers have been particularly vocal in expressing dissatisfaction with the state of affairs. While some overlooked and underappreciated protestors have shown their disenchantment

---

[411] Former USA President Donald Trump's full address to the 2018 UN General Assembly may be viewed on YouTube <https://www.youtube.com/watch?v=hO-fSfKq8vI> (27 May 2020).

[412] <https://www.aljazeera.com/news/2018/11/iran-rouhani-calls-israel-cancerous-tumor-rare-outburst-181124093929399.html> (26 November 2018).

[413] *JNN*, 28 June 2018, citing a Wall St Journal article. Ghasseminejad is Senior Iran and Financial Economics Advisor at the Foundation for Defence of Democracies.

by shouting: *'They say our enemy is America, when the real enemy is right here'*[414], crowds of others have taken to the streets chanting: *'Death to the dictator! Death to Khamenei! Death to Rouhani!'*[415] The appearance and spread of sinkholes in the capital city and beyond has also been a cause of great concern to the Iranian people. With cracks appearing on walls and water pipes bursting, many are afraid that poorly built apartment blocks and houses will collapse. An international airport, an oil refinery and a major highway are also at serious risk. Aerial photographic evidence leaves no more room for denial: *'Iranian authorities now openly acknowledge: The area around Tehran is literally sinking.'*[416] Although drought is undoubtedly a contributing factor, man's interference with the earth's resources is probably also to blame. *'Excessive water pumping creates a series of underground air pockets which then implode, creating cracks or massive holes in the ground.'*[417] Vast quantities of water are required for nuclear power production. Yet the Iranian administration has bulldozed ahead in its determination to reach nuclear capability, despite the fact that the people of Iran have been enduring a 30-year drought!

ISLAMIC STATE

After focusing on one major security threat in the Arabian Peninsula, it would be remiss not to mention ISIS. This militant Islamist group displays complete callousness at the slaughter of innocents, and has proved it will stop at nothing to achieve its desired outcome: an Islamic caliphate.[418] In July 2014 the self-declared caliph of ISIS, Abu Bakr Al-Baghdadi announced: *'A day will soon come when the Muslim will walk everywhere as a*

---

[414] *JNN*, 4 January 2019, citing a *New York Post* article.

[415] *JNN*, 11 August 2018, citing a *Fox News* report.

[416] *Associated Press*, 24 January 2019, by Mehdi Fattahi. <https://www.csmonitor.com/World/Middle-East/2019/0124/Sinkholes-spread-across-Iran-triggered-by-drought-and-excessive-pumping> (28 May 2020).

[417] *JNN*, 4 February 2019, alluding to an article in the *Jerusalem Post*.

[418] The idea of a theocratic one-world government is beginning to sound all-too-familiar, with the Islamic Republic of Iran and the Islamic State of Iraq and Syria competing for the position of world domination.

master. The Muslims will cause the world to hear and understand the meaning of terrorism ... and destroy the idol of democracy.'[419] The ISIS leader may now be dead and hundreds of his operatives in Syria and Iraq may have been overpowered militarily, but the vision has not died. Thousands have gone underground. A UN report reveals that in early 2018, ISIS rallied 20,000–30,000 members in the two countries.[420] Some from the same sadistic group emerge from hideouts in the Sinai Peninsula and wreak havoc wherever possible. Others have successfully infiltrated and occasionally rattle the cities and towns of Europe.

COMMON OBJECTIVE

Ask yourself if Irish citizens should feel threatened by the following statement made by a leader of another radical fundamentalist organisation, Khaled Meshaal: *'We say this to the West ... By Allah you will be defeated. Tomorrow our nation will sit on the throne of the world.'*[421] Are these the sentiments of a freedom fighter? This Islamic leader is responsible for the merciless slaughter of civilians in Israel. Prime Minister Netanyahu outlined Hamas' target ambition which he equated with that of ISIS' here below:

> *'As Hamas's charter makes clear, Hamas's immediate goal is to destroy Israel. But Hamas has a broader objective. They also want a caliphate ... That's why its supporters wildly cheered in the streets of Gaza as thousands of Americans were murdered on 9/11. And that's why its leaders condemned the United States for killing Osama Bin Laden, whom they praised as a holy warrior. So, when it comes to*

---

[419] Quoted by PM Netanyahu, UNGA speech, September 2014.

[420] *Fox News*, 15 August 2018, Adam Shaw, 'Al Qaeda Returns? UN Panel Warns of new bin Laden Threat' <https://www.foxnews.com/politics/al-qaeda-returns-un-panel-warns-of-new-bin-laden-threat> (4 June 2019).

[421] Ibid.

their ultimate goals, Hamas is ISIS and ISIS is Hamas. And what they share in common, all militant Islamists share in common.[422]

According to the then government head of the only functioning democracy in the Middle East, there is a common thread that unites Jihadist organisations: Islam. If this were not so, why would an Islamic religious leader from the Galilee region in Israel call these vicious Islamic State terrorists 'brothers'? In a sermon delivered in October 2014, Imam Ahmad Badran goaded: *'For us, there is no difference between Australia, Sweden, Japan, Russia, or the US. They are all one army united against Islam. It will take ancient Islam not more than ten years to rule the world.'*[423]

FORMER MUSLIM: BROTHER RACHID

To think that certain world leaders distinguish ISIS (aka ISIL) from Islam seems farcical. The following is an extract from a speech by Brother Rachid, addressed to the then American President Barack Obama. Rachid is a former Muslim, who spent more than twenty years studying Islam, and whose father is an Imam.[424]

'Mr President ... You said, "ISIL speaks for no religion." I'm a former Muslim ... ISIL speaks for Islam ... Its name stands for "Islamic State." ... Their leader, Abu Bakr Al-Baghdadi holds a PhD in Islamic Studies ... He was a religious leader in one of the local mosques in Baghdad ... ISIL's 10,000 members are all Muslims. None of them is from any other religion ... They implement Sharia [law] in every piece of land they conquer ... They are willing to die for their religion. They are following the steps of Islam's Prophet Muhammad to the letter.'[425]

---

[422] Ibid.
[423] *JNN*, 8 October 2014, referencing an article in *Arutz-7*.
[424] An imam is a religious leader of Islam.
[425] Brother Rachid, 'A Message to President Obama from a Former Muslim', 2

Brother Rachid, who for his own safety cannot disclose his full name, draws a parallel between the activities of ISIL's operatives and those of the 'prophet' Muhammad. Not only is the beheading of non-believers in the Islamic faith commanded in the Quran (Surah 47, verse 4), but Muhammad had at least 600 Jewish men from the Banu Kurayza tribe decapitated in one day. Following in the footsteps of the founding father of Islam (who was guilty of abducting females) ISIS, on their destructive rampage through Iraq and Syria, kidnapped women and used them as sex slaves.

ISLAM UNCOVERED

The Islamic State is not a new phenomenon; rather it is another offshoot of the imbalanced system of indoctrination that is tragically ingrained in the Islamic community. Listen to Brother Rachid's personal testimony:

> '*I grew up in Morocco, supposedly a moderate country, yet I still learned at a young age to hate … Jews and Christians … We have been brainwashed to hate all of you in our sacred texts, in our prayers, in our Friday sermons, in our educational systems. We were ready to join any group that one day would fight you and destroy you and make Islam the religion of the whole world, as the Quran says. This is what I and millions like me have been taught.*'[426]

It follows then that in order to achieve consistency in the international response to terrorism, it is essential to recognise Islamic jihadist parallels. If we don't expect that sitting down to peace talks will work with the Islamic State, why would we expect it to work with Hezbollah, Hamas or Fatah?

September, 2014. <https://www.google.com/search?sourceid=navclient&ie=UTF-8&rlz=1T4TEUA_en_IE504&q=A+Mes sage+to+President+Obama+from+a+Former+Muslim> (19 September 2014).
[426] Ibid; for Arabic speakers see www.islamexplained.com.

ATTENTION, WORLD LEADERS!

By way of concluding this section, we will recall the warning delivered by the Israeli Premier to the American congress in March 2015: *'To defeat ISIS but let Iran get nuclear weapons would be to win the battle but lose the war.'* As intimidating and ferocious as the Islamic State (IS) may be, let's not forget that it is *not* the biggest sponsor of terrorism in the world – the Islamic Republic (IR) is. May we also bear in mind that IS is not in pursuit of nuclear capability. IR is. To quote Middle East special envoy and former UK prime minister Tony Blair: *'If you had a benign regime in Iran, all of the problems in the Middle East would be resolvable.'*[427] Despite the ongoing devastation inflicted by the Islamic State, the biggest threat to world peace is still the Islamic Republic of Iran. Watch this space.

KRISTALLNACHT II

As referred to in Chapter 8, the infamous *Kristallnacht* of 1938 was that fateful night when the terror tempest tore across Germany and Austria. Nazi stormtroopers emerged looting thousands of Jewish businesses and burning hundreds of synagogues, plundering and destroying hundreds of Jewish homes, breaking bones and morale, snuffing out more than a thousand Jewish lives and marching 30,000 Jewish men to concentration camps. Thus was the unleashing of that sinister season in history. Did Europe ever imagine she would witness the likes of it again?

An ominous storm has been brewing in recent years. Flashes of evil outbursts have been experienced in much of the world at an incredible rate of increase, but most especially in Europe. In one year alone,[428] hate crimes against Jews on the Continent

---

[427] *Algemeiner*, 26 March 2017, Barney Breen Portnoy
<https://www.algemeiner.com/2017/03/26/ex-british-pm-tony-blair-at-aipac-conference-if-iranian-regime-were-benign-all-problems-in-middle-east-would-be-resolvable/> (29 March 2017).
[428] From October 2013 to October 2014.

increased by 436 per cent.[429]

2014: PARIS

January 2014 witnessed a demonstration on the streets of Paris of no less than 15,000 anti-Israel activists; some were wielding Israeli flags with the Star of David replaced by the Nazi swastika.[430] A few months later, on 13 July, what appeared to start out like other anti-Israel protests in the capital escalated rapidly. The following news article is alarming:

> 'This was the first time since World War II that an anti-Semitic pogrom took place in France ... the call for "Death to Jews" was picked up by the crowd. Demonstrators also shouted slogans in favour of a man who had murdered Jewish children: "We are all Mohamed Merah." Merah shot and killed a rabbi and three Jewish children at close range in a schoolyard in Toulouse in 2012 ... This was the first time in France that a large crowd proudly identified with a murderer of Jewish children ... 'Dozens of windows of Jewish shops and restaurants ... were broken and covered with yellow labels saying, "Boycott Israel."
>
> '... several hundred protestors armed with iron bars, machetes, axes and firebombs ... marched to the nearby ... Synagogue ... They shouted, "Let's slay the Jews," "Hitler was right," and "Allahu Akbar." Only six police officers were on hand, who were quickly overwhelmed ... [There were] 200 Jews present inside the synagogue. Even after the police reinforcements arrived, the synagogue was besieged for nearly two hours.'

---

[429] *JNN*, 14 October 2014, alluding to *Arutz-7*.
[430] There was *no* war taking place in Israel at the time – apart from the one-sided usual rocket fire into Israeli territory by Gaza terrorists.

Any group trapped in a building by a threatening throng would suffer trauma. Imagine how terrorising it would be when some of your ancestors had perished in buildings set alight by such mobs. Even if you are still convinced that Israel is guilty of perpetrating war crimes, the fact that these Jewish people don't live in Israel means this is none other than anti-Semitic violence. It is fuelled by hatred of the Jew. Columnist, Guy Millière, continues:

> 'Although the government banned the next demonstration ... it took place anyway, and soon turned into a riot. When thousands of protestors gathered again ... throwing stones, Molotov cocktails ... using iron bars. Garbage cans were burned. Bus stations, dozens of them, and billboards were destroyed ... This was the first time that riots in France looked like an Islamic uprising ... the vast majority of demonstrators and rioters were Muslim.'[431]

And, if that weren't enough, the following day the largest Jewish community of the suburbs was ransacked. 'All the Jewish stores' and numerous cars were either wrecked or set alight. This all happened as recently as 2014. How apt is the caption *Paris's Kristallnacht* for the above article?

2014: GERMANY

A recent report has revealed an exponential rise in anti-Semitic and anti-Israel crimes in Germany, from a total of forty-one in 2013 to 575 the following year.[432] Monika Friesel, of Berlin's Technical University, studied thousands of anti-Semitic emails sent in 2014 to various Jewish institutions, only to make a disconcerting discovery. *'We saw that more than 60% of the writers, who clearly evoke anti-Semitic stereotypes, come from the*

---

[431] Guy Millière, 'Paris's Kristallnacht', *Gatestone Institute*, 26 July 2014.
[432] *JNN*, 10 June 2015, alluding to the *Jerusalem Post*.

middle of society and many of them are highly educated.[433] (This description bears an eerie resemblance to the Nazi engineers, scientists and doctors guilty of perpetrating ethnic cleansing, as well as performing brutal experiments of the vilest kind). The worrisome climate of increased animosity was witnessed at an anti-Israel protest that occurred in July 2014 on the streets of Berlin. With heated vehemence the mob chanted: *'Jews to be gassed, to be slaughtered, to be burned!'*[434]

ALONG THOSE LINES

Outside of the Middle East, Europe is proving to be the most anti-Semitic place in the world. It's sad to say that Ireland, not unfamiliar with anti-Israel remarks and all-too familiar with pro-Palestine assertions, is considered one of the most hostile environments in Europe, from the Jewish perspective. Yet, this comes as no surprise to a teacher on our island who has experienced demoralisation both in classroom and staffroom: *'In the 1980s a Jewish secondary teacher who met anti-Semitism in every Dublin school she taught in, had a door slammed in her face by a colleague. 'I'm not talking to the likes of you!' he declared. Erasing her pupils' anti-Semitic graffiti from the blackboard became routine until her retirement in 1999.*[435] Somehow, I imagine she carried the hurt of the maltreatment without making a formal complaint, as this has been the typical response of the people group in question.

FORMER ISLAMIST: DR TAWFIK HAMID

Jewish people are tired of conflict and generally want to get on with life. By contrast, a lot of time and energy is spent by the Palestinian people lamenting their plight. Similar to their counterpart they have valid reason for complaint, but are directing

---

[433] *JNN*, 6 October 2014, alluding to *CBS*.
[434] Ibid.
[435] Rivlin, *Jewish Ireland*, p. 50.

the blame not to the source of their troubles but to Israel.[436] A prominent former Islamist agrees. In the words of Dr Tawfik Hamid:

> *'You have one million Arabs living in Israel with the Jews, and they are not suffering like the Arabs who are actually controlled by Arabs [elsewhere in the Middle East]. To be honest, the suffering of the Palestinians is because of their leadership and the wrong decisions of leaders like Hamas, not Israel ... The moment the Palestinian leadership stops its arrogance and its barbaric attitude towards the Jews then you will see that things will change and you will see that no Palestinian will be suffering there.'[437]*

Some Palestinians and many of their supporters are (either literally or figuratively) hurling rocks in the wrong direction and damaging the reputation of Israel as a result.

THE WHEEL THAT SQUEAKS

Nineteenth-century American humourist Josh Billings once remarked: *'The wheel that squeaks the loudest is the one that gets the grease'*. In other words, whoever talks the loudest will not go unheard. Similarly, Shakespeare's clever saying: *'The empty vessel makes the loudest sound'*, is true more often than not in the average classroom. However, it does not mean that the most vocal are the most sincere. But, they certainly get our attention and we remember them. If we were to imagine Israel as a great classroom (of Palestinians and Jews), I wonder whose voice would shout the loudest? Former US Ambassador to the United Nations, John C. Danforth once observed: *'The loudest voices we hear are those who advocate conflict, divisiveness.'*

---

[436] It could prove to be dangerous for them to make accusations against their own authorities.

[437] *JNN*, 29 March 2014, citing *Israel National News*.

11

Front Line Miracles And Wonders

EXODUS

Novelist Leon Uris takes his readers on the turbulent voyage through European Jewish history that necessitates the great escape on the weary sea vessel, the *Exodus*. The year is 1946. Both fictional characters in the following excerpt represent two types of Israeli: the sceptic and the believer. Ari and David are on a covert rescue mission on the island of Cyprus, which contains detention compounds that stretch for miles. These are packed full of thousands of illegal immigrants who failed to run the British blockade of Palestine. Frail and destitute, the Jewish adults and children have barely survived the horrific Holocaust. Many were among the millions displaced on the continent after the war, with no homes and no place to turn. As a result of trying to find refuge in the homeland of their forefathers, they are imprisoned in camps enclosed by ten-foot walls of barbed wire, with watchtowers, controlled by British soldiers wielding machine guns. Let me repeat: the war is over, and the atrocities of the Holocaust are widely known. Yet the Jews are now caged by the British. Ari and David are on a mission to free them.

'Ari Ben Canaan stood a head taller than David Ben Ami. He smiled down at the younger man as a father might smile at an over-enthusiastic son. "... Oh yes, the Bible and our history are filled with wonderful tales and convenient miracles. But this is real today. We have no Joshua to make the sun stand still or the walls to come tumbling down. The British tanks will

not get stuck in the mud like Canaanite chariots, and the sea has not closed in on the British Navy as it did on Pharaoh's army. The age of miracles is gone, David."

"It is not gone! Our very existence is a miracle. We outlived the Romans and the Greeks and even Hitler. We have outlived every oppressor and we will outlive the British Empire. That is a miracle, Ari."[438]

Despite all the odds stacked against her, the Jewish race has indeed outlived the British Empire.

CONSCRIPTION

Israel time and again has been forced to face enemies she'd rather not oppose. As the target today of Islamist militant groups, the Israelis are left without a choice. Submission would be suicide. Yet, you can be sure mums and dads would be relieved *not* to see their sons and daughters conscripted into the Israeli army – not knowing if they will return alive or in one piece; fearful that while on patrol duty they might be kidnapped by terrorists and tortured to death. Imagine what it would be like if Irish school leavers were obliged to serve two or three years[439] in an army that is confronted daily by jihadist Muslims. The traumatising scenarios in which these young people would find themselves don't bear thinking about.

OFF DUTY

As we in Ireland are accustomed to spending holidays with family and friends, Israel too celebrates her customary days of rest, worship and festivity at home in the local community.[440] On one

---

[438] Leon Uris, *Exodus* (London, 1992 edn), p. 25.
[439] Israeli girls are conscripted into the IDF for two years; boys are conscripted for three.
[440] As a matter of interest, most of Israel's national holidays are God-ordained, as the Scriptures attest.

such holy day – the most solemn of the Jewish calendar – vulnerable Israel came under attack. This was the Day of Atonement (*Yom Kippur*) 1973, when Syria and Egypt breached her borders. With much of the Israeli army on holiday leave, Israel was at an immediate disadvantage and suffered many blows at the start of the war. Similar to previous campaigns that sought her ruin, the odds were against her. Including reserves, the entire Israeli army was outnumbered by a ratio of two-to-one.

YOM KIPPUR WAR

The situation for Israel looked grave indeed. Thankfully, she had more than her natural ability to sustain her. If you have not yet heard that the Israelis experienced miracles that ultimately shaped the outcome of the war, then I challenge you to open your heart to the following historical description:

> '*Two episodes stand out. The first Egyptian tank division that crossed over the Suez Canal faced nothing to prevent it and the ones that followed behind from advancing into central Israel. Yet, inexplicably, it stopped. To the north of Israel the Syrians poured out of the Golan Heights, yet when they got within sight of the Israeli HQ and the Sea of Galilee they also mysteriously halted. What makes this story amazing is that the HQ was manned by just ten men and two tanks! Another story concerns an Israeli captain, a man without any religious beliefs. As he was fighting in the Golan, he looked up into the sky and saw a great grey hand pressing downwards as if it were holding something back.*'[441]

This is the same powerful and caring God, after all, who historically performed miracle after miracle for His people, and not just in New Testament times either.

---

[441] Maltz, *Many Names*, p. 126–127.

DISPATCH

In the book of Kings we read of how the mighty hand of God intervened when His people were in danger. The king of Syria was frustrated because his schemes to conquer Israel were being thwarted. Israel's success was attributed to her God, who was forewarning her of the attacks through His prophet Elisha. When the foreign king was made aware that Elisha was the informant, he immediately dispatched troops to descend upon the town where the prophet was lodging. Naturally, Elisha's servant was alarmed when he saw the encompassing enemy. His master was not fazed, as he was seeing the situation from another perspective. Elisha was seeing with the eyes of the spirit and he asked God to enable his servant to do so, too. *'Then Elisha prayed, "O LORD, open his eyes and let him see!" The LORD opened the young man's eyes, and when he looked up, he saw that the hillside around Elisha was filled with horses and chariots of fire.'* (2 Kings 6:17; NLT) Thus, Elisha's servant witnessed the host of angels who had been called upon to protect them. He then understood that irrespective of how threatening the Syrian army appeared, they were in safe hands.

MILITARY ADVANCE

As we revert to the Yom Kippur War, let us consider its conclusion. Instead of being crippled by the enemy, the small nation of Israel defied the odds and rose to victory. In the northeast, after reclaiming the Golan Heights territory from Syria, she continued taking ground. Meanwhile, in the south she had the Egyptian army surrounded. Israel had regained territory west of the Suez Canal and was pressing forward in the direction of Cairo, when the UN finally intervened, calling for a ceasefire. The war had lasted a mere twenty days.

IN DEFENCE

Can we please remember who started the Yom Kippur War? Israel was not the aggressor. At the Arab Summit of October 1973, Yasser Arafat declared: *'The goal of our struggle is the end of Israel, and there can be no compromises or mediations. We don't want peace, we want victory. Peace for us means Israel's destruction, and nothing else.'*[442] Golda Meir, the fourth Prime Minister of the State of Israel, was in office at the time and had this to say about the aspirations of her people: *'We do not rejoice in victories. We rejoice when a new kind of cotton is grown and when strawberries bloom in Israel.'*[443] Before we reflect on other wars of the State of Israel's formative years, we ought to consider the geographical and political setting of nineteenth/twentieth century 'Palestine'.

WELCOME HOME!

At the turn of the twentieth century, Arab leaders took a different approach to the return of the Jews. For example, a prominent figure had this to say in a letter written in 1919: *'We Arabs … look with deepest sympathy on the Zionist Movement … We will wish the Jews a most hearty welcome home.'*[444] While in London with his adviser and interpreter[445] this same spokesman, Emir Faisal, who later became King of Iraq, acknowledged: *'Of course we want Zionists to come to Palestine. They will bring large sums of American … money … They will bring in their great scientists in the world; they are all Jewish. The desert will be transformed; it will blossom like a rose. We shall borrow their experts.'*[446]

---

[442] Crown-Tamir, *In a Nutshell*, p. 136.
[443] Ibid, p. 137.
[444] Ibid, p. 65.
[445] Faisal's advisor was Lawrence of Arabia.
[446] Crown-Tamir, *In a Nutshell*, p. 66.

ENVIRONMENTAL BACKGROUND

In order to value the impact of the above statement it's necessary to know the condition of Palestine prior to the Jewish homecoming. The land had been barren and virtually uninhabitable for many centuries. By 1900, all the trees had been cut down. Mark Twain was so deeply impacted by his visit to Palestine in 1866 that it inspired him to write his first book, *Innocence Abroad*. A *'desolate country'* and a *'mosquito-infested swampland'* is how he described it. *'Given over wholly to weeds ... a silent mournful expanse ... we never saw a human being on the whole route ... hardly a tree or shrub anywhere. Even the olive tree and the cactus, those fast friends of a worthless soil, had almost deserted the country.'*[447] Inhabited by a small number of Arab peasants and Bedouins, the land was in need of much work to transform it into the fertile and thriving nation that it is today. But it was not they who had the initiative to develop it. The gruelling groundwork was laid by Jewish immigrants.

KIBBUTZ WORK

Inspired by the Zionist political movement that was birthed in the late 1800s, small colonies of Jewish people began to arrive from Europe. I doubt they realised what lay ahead of them. Some lost their lives to malaria and other diseases; others to violent attack by local Arabs; while the rest toiled to resurrect the land and produce arable soil. These colonies formed special agricultural communities[448]. Much of the laborious elementary work was accomplished by the time agricultural and irrigation specialists arrived from America in the twenties and thirties. One such expert, Professor Walter Clay Lowdermilk, made the following observation in a 1942 publication: *'A great movement has been under way for the redemption of the Promised Land by Jewish settlers, who have wrought wonders in draining swamps, ridding them of malaria and planting them to thriving orchards and fields*

---

[447] Ibid, p. 42, citing *Innocence Abroad*.
[448] I.e. the Israeli *kibbutz*.

... *reforesting the desolate and rocky slopes, and in the improvement of livestock and poultry. The work of the Jewish colonies is the most remarkable reclamation of old lands that I have seen in three continents.*[449] In summation, necessary environmental foundations and structures were in place, to be built upon and developed in the years that would follow.

POLITICAL BACKDROP

Politically speaking, particular steps were taken by leading nations that helped pave a way for 'Israel' to be on the map once again. The signing of the *Balfour Declaration* by the British parliament in 1917 – which had the approval of the American President – was one of these key initiatives. Issued to the Zionist Federation, the core of the letter reads: *'His Majesty's Government view with favour the establishment in Palestine of a national home for the Jewish people, and will use their best endeavours to facilitate the achievement of this object.'*[450]

DIVIDING THE SPOIL

Then came the San Remo Conference in 1920, where the Allied Powers convened after the First World War to divide the spoil. With the Ottoman Empire[451] gone, they agreed to allow France to govern Syria[452], while Britain would oversee both Palestine (an area which includes Israel and Jordan of today) and Iraq. The *Balfour Declaration* was an integral part of the *San Remo Resolution*, which was signed by over fifty countries and assumed by the League of Nations. The resolution specifically states that

---

[449] 'Conquest of the Land Through Seven Thousand Years', cited in Fachler, *Errand Boys*, p. 74.
[450] Fachler, *Errand Boys*, p. 52. You will recall from the first chapter that 'Palestine' was the derogatory name bestowed by the Romans on 'Israel' – the land of the Jewish nation.
[451] The Turkish Empire controlled parts of the Middle East, Africa and Europe for at least four centuries.
[452] This would incorporate Lebanon on today's map.

exclusive political and legal rights in Palestine were to be granted to the Jews, while the Arabs would retain those same rights in the rest of the Middle East. To the shame of both Great Britain and the United Nations, this resolution was never properly implemented.[453]

QUESTIONABLE ALLEGIANCE

In subsequent years, with Palestine under the British Mandate, increasingly difficult restrictions were placed on Jewish settlers. Furthermore, despite far-reaching news concerning the dire mistreatment of Jews and the renowned Jewish refugee crisis in Europe, the *1939 White Paper* of Britain severely limited the quota of Jewish immigrants to Palestine. Suffice to say, this contradicted their commitment to the 1920 resolution and seriously questioned their loyalty to the *Balfour Declaration*. A mere quotation from Uris' novel exposes both the motive of such ventures of betrayal and the object of British allegiance:

> '[English General Sir Clarence:] *"It is not for you and me to argue the right or the wrong of this question. The only kingdom that runs on righteousness is the kingdom of heaven. The kingdoms of the earth run on oil. The Arabs have oil."* [English Brigadier Sutherland replies:] *"... Sir Clarence. It seems that all of life itself is wrapped up in those lines. All of us ... people ... nations ... live by need and not by truth."'*[454]

THE BRITISH BLOCKADE

One would think that by the time the war had ended and the full extent of the horrific Holocaust was made known that the empire in question would have eased her tight restrictions on Jewish

---

[453] The United Nations descends from the League of Nations.
[454] Uris, *Exodus*, p. 31.

entry. Desperate, many survivors attempted illegal entry. The majority were caught and confined there in British-controlled camps. Thousands of other emaciated victims hoping to seek refuge by arriving (without arms and ammunition) on overcrowded prohibited ships, were not only denied access, but were mistreated and on some occasions attacked by the British Navy. Contemptibly, it soon became the official policy that all on board would be immediately transferred to Royal Navy prison ships and returned to their port of origin. Two shiploads were made to return to Dachau – then a camp for displaced persons, but previously a Nazi concentration camp.[455] Another ship, the *Patria*, which was refused entry by the British and exiled to the Mauritius actually sank off the coast of Palestine, drowning hundreds of Holocaust survivors on board.[456] The British Mandate for Palestine, overwhelmed by this issue of illegal Jewish immigrants running the blockade, also resorted to confining these survivors in British army detainment camps in nearby Cyprus, where they suffered appalling conditions. This whole scandalous, surreptitious affair led to the *Exodus* mission which would ultimately free these innocent inmates by drawing the attention of the international press. The Christian clergyman Rev John Stanley Grauel in 1947 was instrumental in heralding the injustice to the world. *'These British are imprisoning our people in the same types of camps in Cyprus as they suffered in Hitler's Europe.'*[457]

BRITISH MANDATE

The general approach of the British for Mandate Palestine seems to have been the ignoring of pogroms and violent attacks made on the Jewish community by Arabs. It is said that the darkest part of the night is just before the dawn. In the following extract, the Reverend Willem J.J. Glashouwer of 'Christians for Israel' directs our attention to a time when attacks on the Jewish settlers

---

[455] Ibid, p. 154.
[456] Ibid, p. 296.
[457] Fachler, *Errand Boys*, p. 119.

intensified. This coincided with the mounting expectation of state recognition and reunification. *'Between 1947 and May of 1948 hundreds of Jews were murdered on the roads and in the fields of Palestine each month, but the British would not permit the Jews to be placed in convoys for safety. They turned a blind eye to the Arab murderers.'*[458]

INTERNATIONAL INVESTIGATION

The first glimmer of hope came when an international committee was set up by the United Nations in 1947 to investigate the troubled situation. This was followed by Britain's pronouncement to withdraw their mandate from Palestine, which would take effect on 14 May 1948. The committee was instructed to suggest a solution for both people groups represented in the land. Not unlike today, the UN was unsympathetic to the predicament of the Jew. In spite of their making deliberate efforts to prevent it, nonetheless, the delegation was exposed to the truth on a number of occasions.[459]

Contrary to UN wishes also, the delegates went to Palestine to assess the situation and to visit camps for displaced persons in Austria and Germany. These field trips influenced their final recommendation, to partition the land and establish a Jewish state alongside a Palestinian one (while retaining economic union). The proposal was well received by the Jewish community, considering that what they were being offered was far less than the area prescribed by the *San Remo Resolution*. It would not include Judea and Samaria or their historical capital, Jerusalem (the latter was to come under international jurisdiction). I believe they accepted the decision because they were exhausted from incessant incoming attacks and relieved to have security in sight.

---

[458] Willem J.J. Glashouwer, *Why Israel?!* (Virginia, 2001), p. 70.
[459] See Fachler, *Errand Boys,* pp. 108-9, 118-30.

1947 UN VOTE

It was put to a vote in the UN General Assembly on 29 November 1947. Unexpectedly, the majority of representative nations voted in favour of the two-state recommendation. The Jewish people were jubilant to finally have a safe place to call 'home'. They had less than six months to wait before they would see their dream fulfilled. The Arab nations went berserk and refused to accept the decision. They were being handed the opportunity to have their own Palestinian state alongside that of Israel, but refused it.

A MIRACULOUS DAY

The historic liberation of the ancient land of Israel from foreign (Gentile) control had finally come. Through the mouths of numerous prophets, God had promised the return of the Jewish people to their land following many agonising centuries of exile. He said he would rebirth the nation in a single day. It would be a truly unexpected and miraculous event. *'Who ever heard of such a thing? ... Shall a land be brought forth in a single day? Shall a nation be born in a moment? Yet Zion had hardly travailed, when she gave birth to her children.'*[460] Merely a skeletal remnant of the nation would reclaim the holy soil that day. Little did the ancient Hebrews realise that masses of their gaunt descendants would pass through the valley of the shadow of death in Nazi Europe before being resurrected, as it were, and reunited as a people group in the land of their ancient forefathers. *'Thus says the Lord God: Take note! I will open your graves, raise you ... and ... I will settle you in your own land ... Observe! I am taking the children of Israel from among the nations ... and will gather them from every quarter and bring them into their own land; and I will make them one nation in the land, upon the mountains of Israel.'*[461] It almost seemed too good to be true. The enemy of the God of Israel would certainly concoct a plan to strike the vulnerable and defenceless embryonic nation with a fatal blow.

---

[460] Isaiah 66:8.
[461] Ezekiel 37:12, 14, 21-22.

A PACK ATTACK

It didn't come as a surprise to the Israelis that their celebration would be short lived. The Arabs had been amassing their armies and tanks alongside her borders for some weeks in anticipation of the day when the British would withdraw their final troops. The armies involved represented seven nations on today's atlas: Lebanon, Syria, Jordan, Iraq, Saudi Arabia, Yemen and Egypt. They planned to destroy the Jews and take possession of the land. On her birthday, 14 May 1948, the vulnerable new-born state was forced to the front line of battle. How on earth was she to survive such an extensive, ferocious attack as inexperienced and ill-equipped as she was?

ON A WING AND A PRAYER

The military equipment which the State of Israel had at her disposal left a lot to be desired. As they did not possess enough guns or rifles, soldiers often shared them. Incredibly, Israel in total wielded two tanks (stolen from the British) and four planes (two of which were shot down on the first day). According to historian Steve Maltz, they resorted to using Molotov cocktails and improvised armoured vehicles. Rather than provide assistance to the Jews, the British handed over their military posts (often along with weaponry) to the Arabs.[462] To say that all the odds were against the infantile state would indisputably be an understatement.

> *'The odds were 200 to 1: seven Arab nations with a population of over 140 million against one fledgling Jewish nation with 650,000 people. The Arabs driven by hatred and pride, the Jews driven by the need for survival and the desire to put the Holocaust behind them. The Jews had no backing from any other country. The Arabs had, amongst other advantages, a British-sponsored army called the Arab Legion. Israel was fighting on four fronts: Transjordan to the*

---

[462] Glashouwer, *Why Israel*, p. 70.

east, Lebanon to the north, Iraq and Syria in the north-east and Egypt in the south.[463]

1948: WAR OF INDEPENDENCE

The War of Independence raged for months. After Israel gained the upper hand on all fronts, armistice agreements were settled with her next-door neighbours: Egypt, Jordan, Syria and Lebanon. Somehow, in dire circumstances, she managed to regain extensive territory. Maltz describes the triumph:

> *'The Israeli victory was such that only a quick intervention by British delegates in the UN saved the Arabs from a more disastrous defeat. The war that was provoked by the Arabs to annihilate the new State of Israel not only brought a pride-thrashing defeat for them but rewarded the Israelis with over 40 per cent extra land over and above that promised to them through the UN Partition Plan, including West Jerusalem!'[464]*

For Israel to have come out of the War of Independence with her head above water was truly a marvel, not to mention the fact that she emerged triumphant.

WARTIME MIRACLES

The first Israeli Prime Minister David Ben Gurion, in an interview in 1956, openly declared: *'In Israel, in order to be a realist you must believe in miracles.'* The following account defies human reason:

> *'Every Israeli war has seen its miracles. There was a time in the 1967 Sinai campaign when two Israeli tanks topped a*

---

[463] Maltz, *Many Names*, p. 122.
[464] Ibid, pp. 122–123.

sand dune and found themselves facing a complete Egyptian tank unit. With no explanation, the Egyptians stopped, opened their turrets, jumped out and began to flee through the desert. After the Egyptians were captured, they explained their actions, telling stories of "hundreds of Israeli tanks" they had encountered.[465]

It's a wonder also that the Israeli army has consistently suffered fewer fatalities than the forces assailing her in each annihilation attempt. There is no logical explanation for this, other than the fact that God is still working on Israel's behalf. Even her enemies attribute her protection to the God of Israel! The following report was written during Israel's war against Gaza terrorists in 2014: *'Hamas has become frustrated with Israel's miracles. As one of the terrorists from Gaza was reported to say, when asked why they couldn't aim their rockets more effectively: "We do aim them, but their God changes their path in mid-air."'*[466] Might this not suggest that those Hamas projectiles that have occasionally been known to backfire are the result of God's intervention?

TO THE FORE

It's insightful to look at the extent to which Israel is flourishing. The progress they have made is phenomenal. True to the predictions of Emir Faisal, Jewish scientists have indeed wrought wonders in Israel, while at the same time sharing their extensive breakthroughs in medical science. Under the caption: *In you all the Families of the Earth will be Blessed.*[467] JNN editors highlight the following:

'When Israel was founded 64 years ago, it was a barren country with no natural resources, little water, and more

---

[465] Finto, *My People*, p. 117.
[466] JNN, 22 July 2014, alluding to *Inquisitor News*.
[467] Genesis 12:3.

than half of its land mass desert ... the Israelis have turned their country into an oasis of technology and innovation ... attracting international giants to its shores. Additionally, the amount and quality of medical research coming out of Israel is astounding. Advances have been made in treating cancer, asthma, diabetes, sepsis and neurological diseases ... From health breakthroughs to technology, agriculture, the environment, the country's innovations are transforming and enriching lives everywhere.[468]

When God was pronouncing blessing over the descendants of Abraham, through Isaac and Jacob (Israel), He didn't forget the nations. As the Scriptures confirm, His vision extended to the Gentiles.

ACTIVE TROOPS

The front line of battle is where the greatest level of resistance is met. Israel needs to know who's behind her; a rear-guard is required. When others, in their ignorance, are quick to slate her, Christians should be the ones to share the true facts of the matter. On a practical level, they can show solidarity and defy the BDS movement by buying Israeli products. Spiritually speaking, those who have a personal relationship with Jesus Christ have a direct line of communication to the Creator of the universe. Apparently, if a sea vessel or airplane is in a life-threatening situation and is unable to signal for help, another vessel can send the emergency signal on its behalf. Christians can send out a 'Mayday!' signal on behalf of Israel and can 'stand in the gap' for her as spiritual sons of Abraham.[469] Knowing how alone she feels, tossed about in the tempest which the nations have invoked, would you consider throwing her a line?

---

[468] *JNN*, 30 September 2012, alluding to an article in *JTA*.
[469] Those of us who have put our faith in the Jewish Messiah have become Father Abraham's spiritual progeny. *'But if you are Christ's, then you are the offspring of Abraham; you are heirs in agreement with the promise.'* Galatians 3:29.

ACTION STATIONS

Israel could be likened to a lone naval ship in murky enemy waters. A dense fog descends; an eerie calm pervades the taut atmosphere. One could almost hear a pin drop – or even a torpedo. Suddenly, out of the fog appears an enormous menacing fleet of enemy warships. Israel is surrounded. Surrender would be suicide. 'Mayday! Mayday! Mayday!' Alarms sound aboard the ship. Hearts skip a beat. Captain Jacobs alerts crew members to report to station and prepare for action. 'Battle Stations!' The frantic struggle for her survival ensues ...

12

Plumb Line Perspective

An encouraging true story was circulating on the internet in recent years. Polish social worker Irena Sendlerowa was in her late twenties in 1939 when the Nazis invaded Poland. Unlike many of her contemporaries, this empathetic mother of two set out to save lives.

WARSAW GHETTO

Irena Sendler (as she is known) made it her business to obtain a special pass which enabled her to make multiple entries into the rat-infested Warsaw ghetto. Cruelly overcrowded, the ghetto incarcerated nearly half a million Jews in an area less than half the size of Phoenix Park. Almost a quarter died from starvation and disease. Irena headed an 'underground' team who successfully rescued Jewish children from within, as other youngsters who were in hiding with their families outside the ghetto walls. The number of children and babies brought to safety totalled almost 2,500. Irena kept a coded record of their names and of the foster families into whose care they had been placed, in the hope that one day she would be able to reunite them with their parents.

'RIGHTEOUS AMONG THE NATIONS'

Irena was eventually arrested by the infamous Gestapo. To her credit, she endured three months of torture without disclosing the whereabouts of the children. Due to be executed by firing squad, Mrs Sendler managed to escape, with the help of a bribed

Nazi guard. After the war, Irena faded into obscurity – that is until 1965 when she was recognised by Israel as 'Righteous Among the Nations.'[470] Later, she was nominated for the 2007 Nobel Peace Prize.[471] On 13 May 2008, a *New York Times'* headline read: *'Irena Sendler, Lifeline to Young Jews, is Dead at 98.'* Meanwhile, a journalist for the UK *Daily Mail* commented: *'Irena Sendler saved twice as many Jews from death as the celebrated Oskar Schindler, who inspired Steven Spielberg's film.'*

SEWER ROUTE

Irena deserves to be remembered not only for having put her life on the line, but for employing resourceful means of rescue. To name but a few: children were hidden in sacks and cases and wheeled out in trolleys; those who could recite Catholic prayers, were smuggled out via the church beside the ghetto. Even sewage pipes were used as a means of escape.[472] We gain insight into Irena's altruistic worldview from an interview carried out by the *New York Sun* in which she explained: *'If someone is drowning, you have to give them your hand. When the war started ... those who were drowning the most were the Jews. And among the Jews, the worst off were the children. So I had to give them my hand.'*[473] I think it would be fair to say that Irena took the 'plumb line perspective.'

WHAT'S A PLUMB LINE?

Our judgements can't always be trusted. In a sermon titled 'The Plumb Line' delivered in 1876, the late Charles Spurgeon remarked: *'Do not let us judge either ourselves or one another*

---

[470] 'Righteous Among the Nations' is the official title awarded to Gentiles who put their own lives at risk in order to rescue Jews during the Holocaust.

[471] The award was given to former American Vice President, Al Gore together with the 'Intergovernmental Panel on Climate Change'. Incredible that the environment should take precedence over the value of human life.

[472] For further details, google 'Irena Sendler project: Life in a Jar'.

[473] *New York Sun*, 29 January 2007.

simply by the eyes. I have frequently thought that a building was out of the perpendicular when it was not ... The human eye is readily deceived, but the plumb line is not – it drops straight down and at once shows whether the wall is upright or not.[474] In Scripture, the plumb line is usually associated with judgement. Perhaps we should visualise it. A plumb line is an ancient device, consisting of string with a lead weight (called a plummet or plumb bob) attached to one end. One of its functions is to determine whether or not a line is vertical.

GOD'S PERSPECTIVE

The plumb line perspective is the viewpoint of the most trustworthy being that exists; it cannot be *manipulated* to suit man's circumstances. *'Thus says the Lord God, "Behold I lay in Zion ... a precious cornerstone ... I will make justice the measuring line and righteousness the plummet."'*[475] God's standards were met in the person of Jesus Christ, who is Justice and Righteousness personified. Jesus is the plumb line by which we measure the standards of God. If we wish to ascertain God's thoughts on a particular subject, we look to the written Word of God. On the other hand, Jesus is the standard by which God measures man. Dear friends, not a single person has ever existed who has measured up to Christ's standard. We all fall short.[476] Suffice to say, we all need to come under Jesus' covering and authority, so that we won't come under God's judgement.

UNPOPULAR

Not many are willing to take the 'plumb line perspective', because God's way is contrary to man's.[477] The true disciple is willing to lay down his own will and allow God's will to reign in his life. There is

---

[474] Metropolitan Tabernacle Pulpit, vol. 50, sermon 2904, [consulted at www.spurgeongems.org].
[475] Isaiah 28:16–17.
[476] See Romans 3.
[477] See Isaiah 55:8-9; Matthew 7:13–14.

a cost involved when we choose to adopt the divine point-of-view. No wonder it's unpopular. Yet the eternal rewards obtained far outweigh the sacrifice entailed – as Jesus knows well. *'Jesus … who, in view of the joy that lay ahead for Him, submitted to the cross, thought nothing of the shame, and is seated at the right hand of the throne of God.'* [478]

As we evaluate the subject of Israel, the plumb line – that which defines truth – ought to be our guide. Israel is not a hidden concept in the Word of God; it's there from beginning to end – from Genesis to the Book of Revelation. Yet, how askew is the average person's estimation of Israel? Let's take a look at how tilted the scales have been in times past and present.

NOTRE DAME

I am grateful for the fact that I had the opportunity to visit the famous thirteenth-century *Notre Dame* of Paris before much of the colossal iconic structure was engulfed in flames by the 2019 inferno. While it is a shame to witness the near destruction of this monumental building, a lesser known, dark aspect is depicted in its portals. The bigotry portrayed in the imposing Gothic architecture of what was once the largest cathedral in France is shameful.

A statue of a woman is set in each pillar on either side of the impressive entrance. The lady to the right exudes an air of triumph. She wears a crown and a halo; she holds up a cross-topped staff in her left hand, and in her right a chalice. This statue is called 'Ecclesia' (Latin for 'church') and it symbolises the glory of the Roman Catholic Church. To the left of the entrance is the statue of a disgraced woman. On her stooped head is what appears to be a dunce cap encompassed by a snake; in her left hand she holds a broken staff, while her crown lies at her feet. The title given to this statue is 'Synagoga', which is Latin for 'synagogue'. Should anyone question what Synagoga signifies, the five stone tablets in her lowered right hand dispel all doubt. These

---

[478] Hebrews 12:2.

symbolise the Torah (the five books of Moses), which is the bedrock of Judaism.[479] This glorious representation of the Roman Catholic Church and shameful personification of the Jewish community undoubtedly influenced the masses.

ILLEGAL FLOTILLA

Let us fast forward the tape of history to recent anti-Zionist events and focus our lens on the east coast of the Mediterranean Sea. You may recall the 2010 flotilla incident. A view was projected in the media that the IDF was heavy-handed in its reaction. Was Israel not within her legal rights to intercept six Gaza-bound ships attempting to break the Israeli naval blockade? Certainly, the UN deems the blockade a *'legitimate security measure'* which *'complies with the requirements of international law.'*[480] Remember, Israel would have no need to patrol Gaza's coastline, were it not for the security threat posed by terrorists and their misguided sympathisers.

ALL ABOARD

It is necessary to examine the Israel Defence Force handling of the matter. Expecting to encounter human rights activists on board the *Mavi Marmara* ship, a number of lightly armed Israeli soldiers were lowered from a helicopter onto the deck. Upon landing, each was set upon by hidden IHH operatives[481] who emerged in bulletproof vests and were armed with weapons which included iron rods, iron chains and knives. After severely wounding the IDF soldiers, two were thrown to the deck below – breaking the arm

---

[479] Torah (the Greek for which is Pentateuch) comprises the first five books of the Old Testament.
[480] Sir Geoffrey Palmer, Report of the Secretary-General's Panel of Inquiry on the 31 May 2010 Flotilla Incident, p. 3, September 2011. <http://www.un.org/News/dh/infocus/middle_east/Gaza_Flotilla_Panel_Report.pdf> (25 June 2016).
[481] IHH (*Insani Yardim Vakfi*): a Turkish-founded 'humanitarian relief organisation' with ties to Hamas, al Qaeda and the Muslim Brotherhood. Its militant leader, Bülent Yildirim, organises jihadist activities.

of one soldier. During the brutal attack, a soldier was shot in the knee, while another received a bullet in the abdomen. An Israeli commando was stabbed in the stomach, while another was stabbed in the ear. Some were beaten unconscious. Three of the wounded Israelis were taken hostage and moved below deck, where they were subjected to stabbings and choking. Were it not for the intervention of non-violent passengers on board, there would surely have been a number of Israeli fatalities.

Eventually the soldiers received permission from their commander to use their pistols in self-defence. During the intense struggle that ensued, the lives of nine Turkish extremists were lost. There is documented evidence, cited by a number of sources, that proves seven of the fatalities and many of the wounded terrorists had expressed the desire to become a *shaheed* (i.e. Islamic martyr).[482] When the IDF gained control of the situation, passengers witnessed how humane they were in the treatment of all aboard the ship, including the extremists who were slating them. Subsequently, a number of passengers, one of whom was a doctor, gave statements describing how the Israel Defence Force treated their assailants professionally and with care.

TURKISH WITNESS

The above outline of events has been corroborated by a Turkish journalist, Şefik Dinç, who was a passenger on the vessel and witnessed the assault made on the Israeli soldiers. In the book he consequently wrote, *Bloodstained Mavi Marmara*, are a number of photographs captured that day. The following caption is linked to one of those: *'The [Israeli] soldiers who slid down ropes met with resistance ... The first three soldiers were captured and beaten with iron bars...'*[483] Dublin writer and historian Ruth

---

[482] Gilead Ini, 'Backgrounder: The Human Rights Council Flotilla Report', CAMERA, 30 September 2010.
<http://www.camera.org/index.asp?x_context=2&x_outlet=118&x_article=1930> (27 June 2016).
[483] <http://www.crethiplethi.com/testimonies-from-idf-naval-commandos-who-participated-in-the-raid-on-the-mavi-marmara/israel/2011/> (14 October 2014).

Dudley Edwards wrote an insightful article in the *Irish Independent* in June 2011 which shed light on the flotilla mission, and in which she synopsised the Turkish journalist's testimony: '*the ship carried no humanitarian aid, but had on board a large number of Islamist activists spoiling for martyrdom. Dinc's first hand testimony and photographs show definitively that violent, heavily armed men set upon and viciously beat Israeli soldiers who had come on board to check for weapons: the shots were fired to save their lives.*'

PUBLICITY STUNT

In the above article (*Gaza-Bound Vessel Really a Ship of Fools*), Ruth attempted to forewarn the *MV Saoirse's* crew of the absurdity of their upcoming mission: '*Whether they know it or not, anti-Semitism is driving these activists on a "mercy mission."*' Yet, the Irish vessel ploughed ahead and (with a crew of fourteen Irish citizens) set sail in November. They would join another ship from Turkey. It is good to know they subsequently received criticism for the 'publicity stunt'.

What we watch and listen to affect our worldview. If we want to have balanced judgements, we will need to carefully monitor what we visually and audibly absorb.

OUT-OF-FOCUS

It's also true that our world view filters and interprets what we see and hear. An obscure, out-of-focus world view will result in erroneous judgements.

In the last chapter we mulled over the angry reaction of the Arab nations in 1947 to the UN decision to form a two-state solution, one for the Arabs of Palestine and another (of smaller dimensions) for the Israelis. While Arab nations were amassing their troops and tanks along the borders of Mandate Palestine in preparation for the annihilation of Israel, two other sinister strategies were under way, the consequences of which are still sorely felt.

PALESTINIAN REFUGEES

The first is that, the Arabs of Palestine were advised by *their leaders* to flee temporarily into other Arab nations. The approximate 700,000 who took heed of this advice were promised they could return, after the 'Jews' had been wiped out. In the words of a *white South-African* anti-apartheid activist, *'The Palestinian refugee problem was thus caused by Arab hatred against Israel. The Arabs, even to this present day, acknowledge this!'*[484] After Israel's miraculous victory in 1948, the Arab refugees were cast aside by their own leaders and their plight ignored. *'Despite the vast Arab territory, Arab refugees were intentionally neither absorbed nor integrated into the Arab countries to which they fled ... theirs is the only refugee group in the world that has never been absorbed or integrated into their own people's lands.'*[485] This explains why, generations later, Palestinians continue to inherit their refugee status from their ancestors. Instead of liberating them, their Arab leaders decided to use them as pawns for their own agenda. While the people have been enduring a confined, substandard life, their leaders have been busy gaining the sympathy of the world (along with millions of dollars per annum from international aid funds aforementioned). Had the donations in their entirety reached the needy people in question, they would long ago have been released from the refugee camps and enabled to sustain themselves. Why can't the world see this? Are we refusing to look at the facts?

WITNESS: SYRIAN PRIME MINISTER

In his memoirs, former Prime Minister of Syria, Khaled El-Azim, wrote:

> *'Since 1948 it is we [Arab leaders] who demanded the return of the [Palestinian] refugees to their country, while it is we who made them leave it ... Is this wise and established*

---

[484] Hedding, *Understanding Israel*, p. 160.
[485] Crown-Tamir, *In a Nutshell*, p. 21.

policy? ...

We brought disaster upon ... Arab refugees, by inviting them and bringing pressure to bear upon them, to leave their land, their homes, their work ... We have rendered them dispossessed, unemployed ... We exploited them in executing crimes of murder, arson and throwing bombs upon houses and vehicles carrying men, women and children – all this in the service of political purposes in Lebanon and Jordan.'[486]

I cannot but admire the courage of this Arab statesman for exposing the truth that Arab leaders have exploited their own people in goading them to attack and murder Jewish civilians.

UNITED NATIONS RELIEF AND WORKS AGENCY (UNRWA)

It is not just Arab leaders who have been responsible for the deterioration of the Palestinian refugee situation, the United Nations is every bit as much to blame, if not more so. This brings us to a very important question: What is the reason for having two separate UN refugee agencies – one, to handle refugee cases worldwide, the United Nations High Commissioner for Refugees (UNHCR), and the other to deal solely with refugees from just one particular people group? The latter, the United Nations Relief and Works Agency (UNRWA) was established in 1949 for the Arabs of Palestine. So, what has the UNRWA been doing for the last seventy-two years? Surely by now they should have enabled the original refugees to move on with their lives. Why were the refugee camps not dismantled decades ago? Here is Yemini's answer to those questions: *'The purpose of the UNHCR is to help refugees start a new life and end their refugee status; the goal of UNRWA is the opposite – to perpetuate it.'[487]* Rather than assist the original 700,000 refugees to assimilate, the UNRWA has made it so that it is almost impossible for the descendants of these

---

[486] Memoirs of Khaled El-Azim, cited in Hedding, *Understanding Israel*, pp. 160–61.
[487] Yemini, *Industry of Lies*, p. 87.

refugees to lose their status. This is explained in a damning article titled, *UNRWA Closely Embedded with Hamas – perpetuates Refuge Status*:

> *'While The UNHCR is tasked with treating and resettling all refugees in the world, UNRWA exists separately and solely to deal with "Palestinian refugees", and has been exposed to be closely embedded with the Hamas terrorist organization as seen in last summer's [2014] war with Israel, when rockets where found at UNRWA clinics. Uniquely, "Palestinian refugee" status is "inherited" by the descendants of the original refugees, meaning that today the number of "Palestinian refugees" numbers five million in total. Instead of resettling them and helping them to rebuild their lives, UNRWA operates an extensive network of "refugee camps" in which residents are encouraged not to integrate into their host countries. Even in Gaza, those living in "refugee camps" are forbidden from purchasing land outside the "camps."'[488]*

To add fuel to the fire, a report, which was compiled during the Obama presidency, reveals that merely 20,000 of the original "Palestinian" refugees from 1947–48 are still alive and displaced from their homes.[489] Twenty thousand is a far cry from the 5.1 million supposed recipients of international aid. Here is an added deception which ought to alarm Irish taxpayers: *'40% of the "refugee" recipients are not refugees at all, having been given citizenship in Jordan, Syria and Lebanon. Yet their numbers still*

---

[488] *JNN*, 11 June 2015, alluding to *Arutz-7*.

[489] *The Washington Free Beacon*, 12 July 2018, Adam Kredo: 'Congress Demands State Department Release Secret Report Busting Myth of Palestinian Refugees.' <https://freebeacon.com/national-security/congress-demands-state-department-release-secret-report-busting-myth-palestinian-refugees/> (19 August 2018). Although the US Congress has demanded that the classified report be released, to my knowledge this has not yet occurred.

appear in the UNRWA and Palestinian Authority ledgers.'[490] If it is truth we are after, we will acknowledge that it is absurd to blame Israel for the Palestinian refugee problem.

UN BIAS

There are many known militant Islamic factions. If there is one thing that unites them, it's their hatred of Israel; if there is one thing they can agree on, it is to eliminate the Jewish nation. Could it be true that the United Nations set up this special agency to appease those who are in possession of (in all probability) two-thirds of the world's oil resources? Could this have been the influencing factor that brought about the establishment of the UNRWA? Some world leaders have been expressing serious concerns. Former Canadian Minister for Justice, Irwin Cotler, in January 2014 called for the disbanding of the UNRWA: *'Jurisdiction over the Palestinian refugees should be transferred from UNRWA, which frankly, continues to engage patterns of incitement against Israel and in misrepresentation of the truth.'[491]* This special UN agency is not funded by Muslim countries, incidentally. It is funded almost entirely by Western taxpayers. In August 2018 the USA announced its plans to discontinue funding the UNRWA. This would mean a loss of $300 million plus per annum. It has been the largest contributor, supplying almost 30 per cent of the agency's budget.[492] In addition to that, the following year the same administration called for the dismantling of the organisation. In the words of USA advisor Jason Greenblatt, *'The UNRWA model has failed the Palestinian people.'[493]* More recently, the British government in 2020 has: *'pledged to urgently review the tens of millions of dollars in aid the UK provides to the UN agency for Palestinian refugees, after an investigative report*

---

[490] *JNN*, 18 January 2019, alluding to *INN*.

[491] *JNN*, 20 January 2014, alluding to *Jerusalem Post* article.

[492] *New York Post,* 31 August 2018, Bob Fredericks: 'Trump Cuts Funding for UN Palestinian Refugee Agency'. < https://nypost.com/2018/08/31/trump-cuts-funding-for-un-palestinian-refugee-agency/>(4 September 2018).

[493] *JNN*, 27 May 2019, alluding to *Arutz-7*.

found that a majority of the funds have been going to schools in the West Bank and Gaza Strip which use textbooks that incite violence against Israelis.[494] Meanwhile, along with donating €360 million annually to the Palestinian Authority, Europe also contributes a hefty €158 million to the UNRWA. Are we Irish happy to be a part of that?

JEWISH REFUGEES

The second issue of injustice that came into play in the months leading up to the 1948 War of Independence was the mistreatment of Jewish communities in Arab nations. Not only were thousands physically attacked and hundreds killed in *'government-condoned rioting,'*[495] but the majority were forced out of these countries, after having their wealth and property confiscated. At least 820,000 Jews[496] were banished from the Arab world at this time. So, why don't we know more about it? And why haven't we heard about generations of Jewish refugees? This is because Jewish refugee camps don't exist. 590,000 were absorbed into the new State of Israel, and the rest found refuge in America and elsewhere. None of the descendants of these people have ever called themselves refugees and neither have their leaders treated them as pawns. You'll notice that there were originally somewhere in the region of 100,000 more Jewish refugees than there were "Palestinian". Yet, *'No UN organization was established to aid the 850,000 Jewish refugees who fled or were expelled from Arab countries following 1948.*[497] Are we beginning to see a clearer picture emerge?

---

[494] *The Times of Israel*, 22 February 2020, TOI Staff: 'Count the Martyrs: UK to Review Funds for Palestinian Schools whose Books Incite'. < https://www.timesofisrael.com/uk-to-review-funds-for-palestinian-schools-using-textbooks-encouraging-violence/> (3 June 2020).

[495] See Maltz, *Many Names*, p. 133.

[496] This is a conservative estimate. A number of sources say as many as 850,000.

[497] *JNN*, 11 June 2015, alluding to *Arutz-7*.

LITERAL OR ALLEGORICAL?

Our overall comprehension of Scripture will be deficient if we are not using the correct lenses of interpretation. Were we to interpret certain passages of the Old Testament allegorically, then our image of the power and sovereignty of God would be skewed. Although there are numerous poetic writings and some symbolic accounts in the Old Testament, even these are based on historical facts and serve to show how individual Israelites grappled with divine instruction. *'In the 1920s, liberal theologians were promoting the idea that the Old Testament was not the inspired Word of God, but just a history book of the Jewish people, and a collection of beautiful poetry and exciting myths.'*[498] It stands to reason that, if Old Testament miracles and promises cannot be trusted, neither can those of the New. And, who gets to decide which parts are figurative and which literal? With chunks of the first and second section of the Bible effectively discarded we are left with a fragmented body of Scripture, like a jigsaw puzzle missing many of its pieces. Is it really any wonder there is so much confusion in the church today, when so many interpret Scripture allegorically? Johannes Facius makes the point that this, *'widely accepted view ... became the background for stripping the Jewish people of their divine election and calling.'*[499]

CAN GOD BE TRUSTED?

If the Almighty's oft-repeated promise to be the God of Israel for all time is not to be interpreted literally; and if He actually has wiped His hands clean of them forever, then could He not also do the same with New Covenant believers? If He's as elusive and undependable as the allegorical interpreters make Him out to be, then we may all put away our Bibles forever.

However, if Creator God can be trusted to fulfil all of the promises He made to Israel, then He can be trusted to bring about all of His

---

[498] Facius, *Days of Noah*, p. 48.
[499] Ibid.

promises to the Church. I am grateful that He is trustworthy. It is also a relief to know that we don't have to labour hard over the meaning of Scripture when the Holy Spirit is available to assist. *'No prophetic Scripture can be explained by one's unaided mental powers ... no prophecy ever came by the will of man; instead, men spoke from God as they were carried along by the Holy Spirit.'*[500] Without seeing the Word of God through the eyes of the Spirit, we are sure to be led astray.

DRAINING DYNAMICS

'The old adage retains its validity: the first casualty of war is truth.'[501] Satan, the 'Father of Lies', who is the eternal instigator of wars, has historically taken every opportunity to target truth. When you consider the intelligence and education of modern man, it is staggering that this well-known line of attack is successfully utilised in conflict zones today. Quite disconcerting is the fact that Hitler's blatantly fascist *Mein Kampf* is currently listed an international e-book bestseller!

NAZI PROPAGANDA

Propaganda is a caustic weapon that rapidly corrodes the public image and dignity of the victim. The German Minister for Propaganda, Josef Goebbels, craftily used every medium at his disposal to bring disrepute upon people considered intolerable to the Nazi administration. Goebbels was responsible for the widespread dissemination of an inexpensive radio set, the People's Receiver. This served to indoctrinate the general public with Hitler's venomous speeches and Nazi propaganda. With only a short wavelength, the cheap radio could not be tuned into other broadcasting stations. Unfortunately, many Germans were

---

[500] 2 Peter 1:20–21.

[501] Enda McDonagh, 'From *Shoa* to *Shalom*: The Case for Abolishing War in the Twenty-first Century,' in Dermot Keogh & Diarmuid Whelan (eds), *Gerald Goldberg: A Tribute* (Cork, 2008), p. 167.

brainwashed into believing the lies, thus solidifying the Nazi mentality.

HITLER YOUTH

School textbooks were altered by the propaganda pushers to elevate the Nazi regime and to undermine the contemptible minorities. Hitler Youth was a sinister strategy adopted to brainwash German children. This exclusive youth camp served to boost pride in the Aryan race and inspire the young to join the army or the civil service as soon as they were of age. A special movement was established for the girls also – boosting pride in the nation and trust in the Nazi leadership.

PALESTINIAN CLASSROOMS

Has it occurred to you that the same strategies are in use today? Did you know that the schools of Gaza, the West Bank and those in Palestinian refugee camps in Syria, Jordan and Lebanon are managed by the UNRWA? According to the official agency website: *'Through its education system, UNRWA aims to ensure* [emphasis added] *that Palestine refugee students develop their full potential and become "confident, innovative, questioning, thoughtful, and open-minded, to uphold human values and tolerance, proud of their Palestinian identity and contributing positively to the development of society and the global community".*[502] It would be liberating to the youth if the agency even partially fulfilled this aim and made certain that *'human values and tolerance'* were upheld and that children in their school system were *'open-minded'* and encouraged to *'contribute positively to the development of society'.* Yet the glorification of terrorists is part of the ethos of these establishments of which the UN agency is well aware. A school in Tulkarem in the West Bank is named after Salah Khalaf, the mastermind of the 1972 Munich

---

[502] UNRWA website <https://www.unrwa.org/what-we-do/education> (4 June 2020).

Massacre that killed eleven Israeli athletes.[503] In 2017 media watchdog *PMW* revealed that seventy-five Palestinian Authority schools are either named after terrorists or Nazi collaborators, or they honour 'martyrs/martyrdom.'[504] This is a travesty of justice. School outings have included visiting the homes of terrorists who perpetrated often multiple wicked acts of violence against Israeli men, women and children.[505] To present terrorists as role models and heroes to young children is criminal.

It is the responsibility of the same UN agency to employ the Palestinian teaching staff. (If you are not already aware, school textbooks are usually written by teachers.) In these primary- and secondary-level classrooms textbooks do not place Israel on the world map. Palestinian children are led to believe that Jewish people are illegal immigrants and human 'leeches' in the land. Here are just a couple of '*the dozens and dozens of examples of incitement that litter Palestinian schoolbooks,*' according to former British MP Joan Ryan:

'The incitement is pernicious and pervades subjects across the curriculum and across every age group. Children of 13 are taught Newton's second law through the image of a boy with a slingshot targeting soldiers. For the avoidance of any doubt, I have here the textbook and can show ... the relevant photograph. The evidence is not difficult to come across. Children of 10 are asked to calculate the number of martyrs in Palestinian uprisings in a maths textbook, and I have that here too.'[506]

---

[503] *The Times of Israel*, 26 October 2016, Dov Lieber: 'PA Governor Defends Naming School after Black September Chief'. < https://www.timesofisrael.com/pa-governor-defends-naming-school-after-black-september-chief/> (20 March 2020).
[504] *Palestinian Media Watch*, 27 September 2017, Itamar Marcus. <https://palwatch.org/page/13015> (20 March 2020).
[505] *JNN*, 10 August 2015, alluding to *PMW*.
[506] House of Commons Hansard, Volume 644, 04 July 2018. <https://hansard.parliament.uk/Commons/2018-07-04/debates/427DEF14-43F1-4090-98D6-742499164690/PalestinianEducationSystem> (4 June 2020).

The above was part of a debate held in the House of Commons in July 2018 on the subject of the Palestinian education system.[507]

RADICALISATION IMPACT

Indoctrinated by the curriculum and deceived as they are by respected authority figures, one could hardly blame the students for carrying hatred in their hearts. Sadly, radicalisation is having the desired effect, Palestinian children are inflicting terror. On 12 May 2020 an Israeli soldier, Amit Ben-Ygal, was deliberately killed in a rock-throwing incident. It occurred *'in the predawn hours'* as his unit was leaving a village in the West Bank following an arrest raid. Although the assailant may have been an adult, moments prior to the incident, youths were involved. *'As the troops were making their way out of the village on foot following the arrests, a small group of roughly 10 Palestinian youths began throwing rocks at them.'*[508] Apart from anything else, one must ask why these children were outside of their homes before dawn. The twenty-one-year-old Ben-Ygal was an only child.

In 2016, knives were confiscated from two eight-year-old Palestinian boys on their approach to an Israeli settlement in Judea and Samaria. When questioned by security, they said a man had given them the knives and told them to perpetrate a stabbing attack.[509]

---

[507] In March 2020 a parliamentary debate was scheduled to discuss a report on the 'Radicalisation in the Palestinian School Curriculum'. See House of Commons Library, 6 March 2020, Anna Dickson & Nigel Walker: Radicalisation in the Palestinian School Curriculum'. <https://researchbriefings.files.parliament.uk/documents/CDP-2020-0046/CDP-2020-0046.pdf> (4 June 2020).

[508] *The Times of Israel*, 12 May 2020, Judah Ari Gross: 'IDF Soldier Killed by Rock Thrown at his Head during West Bank Arrest Raid'. <https://www.timesofisrael.com/idf-soldier-killed-by-rock-thrown-at-his-head-during-west-bank-arrest-raid/> (14 May 2020).

[509] *Haaretz*, 27 October 2016, Gili Cohen: 'Two Eight-year-old Palestinian Boys Arrested with Knives in Israeli Settlement'. <https://www.haaretz.com/israel-news/two-eight-year-old-palestinian-boys-arrested-with-knives-1.5453757> (30 October 2016).

INTERNATIONAL RESPONSE

The education system in question has undergone international scrutiny in recent years and has led to policy adjustments. Belgium has been a key European donor, sending millions of Euros annually to the PA for school equipment and construction. In 2017, Brussels was alerted to the fact that an all-girls primary school in Hebron, which had been constructed in 2012–13 with the use of Belgian aid funds, was later renamed 'Dalal Mughrabi elementary school'. Mughrabi was a female terrorist who was involved in the infamous 1978 Coastal Road Massacre, in which thirty-eight civilians were killed, thirteen of whom were children. The Belgian government promptly demanded the name of the school be changed. Although the Palestinian Authority eventually yielded (a year later, following much diplomatic pressure), it spitefully renamed another elementary school 'The Martyr Dalal Mughrabi elementary school', while at the same time naming the foundations of yet another school after the same murderer.[510] As a result, in autumn 2018 Belgium became the first European country to withdraw funds from the PA education system. The following is a statement by Belgian Foreign Ministry spokesperson Didier Vanderhasselt: *'Belgium has long since been an important partner of the Palestinian Authority's strategic plan for education. Belgium endeavours to promote a culture of respect for human rights, human dignity and tolerance. This should be reflected in curricula taught at schools funded abroad by Belgian taxpayer's contributions as well as in the names and logos of such schools.'[511]*

The EU is a major financial aid donor to the Palestinian Authority. Having studied an extensive range of school textbooks for children of all ages, a bill was passed by the legislative body of the EU to

---

[510] *JNS*, 25 September 2018, Itamar Marcus & Nan Jacques Zilberdik: 'Belgium Suspends Aid to PA Education Ministry for Naming Schools after Terrorists'. <https://www.jns.org/belgium-suspends-all-support-for-pa-education-for-naming-schools-after-terrorists/> (27 October 2018).
[511] *EJC*, 10 October 2017, 'Belgium Halts PA Education Funding because School Named after Terrorist'. <https://eurojewcong.org/news/communities-news/belgium/belgium-halts-pa-education-funding-school-named-terrorist/> (27 October 2018).

freeze €15 million to the PA until it is willing to reform the schoolbooks and curricula. *'"The textbooks published by the PA in 2017, which are financed by the EU ... contain, across all subjects, numerous examples of violent depictions, hate speech – in particular against Israel – and glorifications of jihad and martyrdom," the bill states.'*[512] Despite promises made by the PA to comply, in recent years there have been numerous reports in various European newspapers proving that the material, which shapes the minds of 1.2 million Palestinian children, is in fact becoming more radical. This leads us to the question: what is Ireland's contribution?

THE GIFT OF THE IRISH

'Improving the opportunities for young Palestinians to access quality education has been a priority for Ireland in our work in Palestine for many years.' [emphasis added] These are the words of former Tánaiste and Minister for Foreign Affairs and Trade, Simon Coveney TD. Indeed, in the same February 2019 press release from the Tánaiste's office (which heralded the *'Launch of Ireland-Palestine Scholarship Programme'*) the following editorial note was added: *'Ireland's funding to the Palestinian people has traditionally had a strong focus on the education sector.'*[513]

JOINT FINANCING ARRANGEMENT

In 2010 a Joint Financing Arrangement (JFA) was established by five EU states to support the development of the Palestinian education system, both financially and practically. Belgium is one

---

[512] *Jerusalem Post*, 27 September 2018, Lahav Harkov: European Parliament Committee Votes to Freeze €15 million to PA over Inciting Textbooks. <https://www.jpost.com/arab-israeli-conflict/european-parliament-committee-votes-to-freeze-15m-to-pa-over-inciting-textbooks-568172 > (8 June 2020).
[513] 'Tánaiste announces launch of Ireland-Palestine Scholarship Programme', Govt. press release, 11 February 2019. <https://www.dfa.ie/ie/nuacht-agus-na-meain/preasraitis/press-release-archive/2019/feb/tanaiste-announces-launch-of-ireland-palestine-scholarship-programme-1.php> (9 June 2020).

of the joint financing partners (JFPs), although it suspended its contributions at the end of 2018, for reasons highlighted above. Ireland is another of the five. Between 2010 and 2018 the Irish taxpayer contributed €15.8 million to the JFA pool fund which is sent to the PA and the UNRWA. But that's not all, a *further* four million Irish Euros per annum is donated to the UNRWA Programme Budget for social, health and education services, approximately 54 per cent of which goes to education.[514]

Regarding Palestinian school development planning: As the *'lead nation on textbook development'* [515] among the JFPs, Ireland has no doubt had a critical role to play. What a wonderful opportunity for the Irish – whose highly acclaimed education system prides itself on tolerance and equality – to hugely influence curriculum and textbook reform. Yet, the staggering fact of the matter is that the necessary modifications have not taken place; rather, the latest curriculum that has emerged between the years 2016 and 2018 is even more radical and intolerant than ever.

ACCOUNTABILITY

IMPACT is a watchdog organisation that has been closely monitoring the curriculum in question and alerting the nations of its findings. Alarmed by the intensification of the PA's radicalisation agenda many statesmen have prompted parliamentary debates. *'There has been a great deal of international outrage, and Marcus Sheff, chief executive officer of IMPACT-SE, has been astounded by the silence of Ireland.'* Writing for the Belfast Telegraph Ruth Dudley Edwards asks, *'Has ambition for a high-profile global role corrupted the Department of Foreign Affairs?'*[516] She argues that Ireland's silence or

---

[514] Ibid.

[515] *Belfast Telegraph*, 23 September 2019, Ruth Dudley Edwards, 'Textbook error by Republic of Ireland will just encourage more hatred of Israelis among Palestinian kids', <https://www.belfasttelegraph.co.uk/opinion/columnists/ruth-dudley-edwards/ruth-dudley-edwards-textbook-error-by-republic-of-ireland-will-just-encourage-more-hatred-of-israelis-among-palestinian-kids-38522398.html>(8 June 2020).

[516] Ibid.

inadequate input as the case may be, could actually be a political strategy of the Irish government in its bid to join the 2021-2022 UN Security Council. After all, the twenty-one Arab states (which clearly have a strong Palestinian bias) have significant clout in the UN; they constitute almost 11 per cent of the 193 member states. Compare that to Israel, with its one vote and its uphill battle to gain support from others. In the same article Dudley Edwards quotes the Washington correspondent for *The Irish Times*, Suzanne Lynch, who presents the same argument: *'Ireland's reputation as a strong defender of the Palestinian perspective may secure the support of Arab nations in the Middle East and Africa, while its status as a former British colony is likely to find favour with smaller countries and other former colonies.'*[517] Whether this is the true motive behind our failure to rise to the challenge presented I cannot say. All I can say is that the petition was successful; Ireland was elected and is a member of the current Security Council. In addition, I would seriously question the accuracy of our assertions in the campaign for election to the Security Council, which boast: *'We are by nature bridge-builders. We listen to all sides … Ireland's commitment to hearing and heeding the voices of all … We pledge to work with all Member States* [bearing in mind that Israel is a member state, not 'Palestine'] … *Our path is our own. We bring no partisan agenda to the table.'*[518] If it is true that action speaks louder than words, then we have failed both the Palestinian people and the Israelis on all counts.

For anyone who may be curious to know how the Israeli education system fares, Joan Ryan[519], in her extensive research on the subject, concluded: *'Israeli textbooks see peace as the ultimate goal and depict it as highly desirable and achievable, while war is a*

---

[517] Ibid.

[518] 'Ireland United Nations Security Council', Department of Foreign Affairs campaign brochure. <https://www.dfa.ie/media/dfa/ourrolepolicies/unitednations/Campaign-Brochure-July-2018.pdf> (8 June 2020).

[519] The former MP has a background in teaching sociology and politics. Ryan, who is in favour of a two-state solution, quit the UK Labour party in February 2019 because of the party leader's anti-Semitic bias and joined the new Change UK party.

negative, although sometimes necessary, occurrence.'[520]

YOUTH BOOT CAMPS

It seems that the Palestinian leadership has taken a leaf out of Hitler's book. Their boot camps for youths are frightfully similar to 'Hitler Youth', yet far more militant and are often named after so-called martyrs. The main objective is not just to indoctrinate, but to train the children for violent guerrilla warfare (sometimes using real weapons). The following extract indicates two things in particular. One: these military training camps for youths are far-reaching; and two: support for these camps which indoctrinate and instigate violence comes from the government of Gaza.

> *'13,000 TEENS COMPLETE HAMAS TRAINING CAMPS TO EMULATE SUICIDE MARTYRS: The camps ... are run by Hamas's ministries of education and interior. Some 13,000 students in grades 10-12 participated[521] in the one-week training camps this year, compared to 5,000 last year ... the curriculum includes weapons training, self-defence, and "security awareness" classes on identifying Israeli spies. Hamas PM Ismail Haniyeh, Interior Minister Fathi Hammad and Education Minister Usama Mzeini attended the graduation ceremony last week, each delivering fiery speeches ... "This is a generation which knows no fear. It is the generation of the missile, the tunnel and the suicide operations" [said Palestinian PM Haniyeh].'[522]*

Could you possibly imagine the Taoiseach making the above statement about the young people of Ireland, with the Minister for Education standing alongside him in agreement? At the very

---

[520] House of Commons Hansard, Volume 644, 04 July 2018. See footnote no. 37 above.
[521] Grades 10-12 (approximately aged 15-18 years) are equivalent to High School level in the USA.
[522] JNN, 22 January 2014, alluding to *Times of Israel*.

least, it would be judged to be politically *in*correct.

CASE STUDY: KAMAL SALEEM

As incredible as it may sound, Kamal Saleem's career as an Islamic militant began at the tender age of seven, when he attended his first PLO terrorist camp. In that same year, he carried out his first mission *'sneaking explosives into Israel'*. Saleem lived the next twenty years of his life as a jihadist, during which time he moved to the United States. He later confessed that his motive was *'to infiltrate'* the culture; the term for which, by the way, is 'stealth jihad'. Thankfully, the culture managed to infiltrate him. As a result of converting to Christianity, he acknowledges, *'My family has a fatwa on my head, to kill me … The PLO has a fatwa on my head.'* He also claims that he is one of the top most wanted men on the Muslim American Society hitlist. It is not easy for us, in the West, to comprehend that Kamal Saleem's journey of hatred and violence began in a children's summer camp.[523]

CHILDREN'S TV

Another means used by the Palestinian Authority to corrupt the minds of the young with racial hatred is television programmes. I have personally seen for myself a friendly-looking Arab TV presenter on an interactive children's show undermining Jewish people and encouraging their own Muslim youth to always contend with them and kill as many as possible. The young children present on the set understandably knew no better than to agree with the convincing adult – especially as her co-host was wearing an adorable cartoon-animal costume. In the same parliamentary debate aforementioned Ryan commented on PA TV: *'I fail, for instance, to see how children's television programmes in which poems are recited that refer to Jews as "barbaric monkeys", "wretched pigs" and the "most evil among creations" do anything to advance the cause of peace,*

---

[523] *Jewish Voice*, Daystar Television, 20 October 2015.

reconciliation and co-existence.'[524]

'PALLYWOOD'

You may not have heard of *Pallywood*, but you probably will have seen it. Pallywood is Palestinian drama, Hollywood style. Although rehearsed, these shows are portrayed as real events. You will sometimes have seen it on the news as video footage. Like footballers who feign injuries in order to have the opponent penalised, these actors pull a similar stunt. Using ammunition and real ambulances they succeed in faking injuries received during a staged attack from Israel. And, they are quite convincing. Fortunately, a number of these acts have been confirmed bogus by various media reporters. A 2012 headline reads: *Gaza Man Caught Faking Injuries to Create Anti-Israel Media Bias*. Here is an extract from the article:

> *'Footage from the BBC captured by watchdog group Honest Reporting shows a heavy man lying on the ground and being carried away by residents, apparently after being injured by an Israeli attack. Moments later that same man again fills the frame, except he is walking about and obviously unhurt. The widespread staging of such victim situations is a favoured tactic of Arabs fighting Israel and has come to be known as "Pallywood". Because Israel is stronger militarily, the Arabs cling to the underdog image of poor refugees under occupation and siege by evil Israelis, thus eliciting sympathy.'*[525]

Having seen the unedited video footage, I can personally verify its authenticity.

---

[524] House of Commons Hansard, Volume 644, 04 July 2018. See footnote no. 37.
[525] *JNN*, 17 November 2012, alluding to *The Blaze*.

BIRD'S-EYE VIEW

The plumb line perspective, paradoxically, is the bird's-eye perspective. It is the willingness to understand life's situations from the divine point-of-view, which takes into account historical, current and future dimensions.[526] A courageous ambassador of this outlook was German pastor, Dietrich Bonhoeffer, who once said: *'Silence in the face of evil is itself evil ... Not to speak is to speak. Not to act is to act.'*[527] Bonhoeffer was assassinated by the Nazis in 1945 for his heroic underground activities.

HUMAN PIPELINES

Earlier, we glimpsed the story of the Jewish exodus out of post-Nazi Europe. It's hard to believe that after WWII had ended British consulates were putting pressure on governments to close their doors to Jewish refugees. Neither would they allow them to make their way to Mandate Palestine. The terrorised and malnourished inmates of Auschwitz were now free to leave, but with nowhere to turn, many ended up staying in that haunting, putrid prison.[528]

Uris illustrates how a plot was forged by Jewish secret agents from Palestine to transport the inmates out of war-torn Europe into their Promised Land. This would begin with a seventy-mile gruelling trek through snowy mountains. After bribing the Polish border patrol, the secret agents sought favour in Czechoslovakia for the Auschwitz survivors. A chartered train, which would carry them through Europe, awaited them there. Needless to say, the British were not impressed. When urged by the British Ambassador to Prague to send the Holocaust survivors back to

---

[526] In the final chapter, we will take a look at what is 'in the pipeline' for the Chosen People.

[527] See Bonhoeffer's book, *The Cost of Discipleship*.

[528] Many Jews who returned to their homes in Poland were subjected to anti-Semitic violence by locals, who blamed them for the war. This was how they rationalised looting and bullying the Jews off their own property. 2016 commemorated the 70th anniversary of the Kielce pogrom, in which forty-two Jewish people were murdered. This was one of many post-war pogroms in Poland which killed between 1,500 and 2,000 Jewish people. (*JNN*, 3 May 2016, alluding to *JTA* article).

Poland, the Czech Foreign Minister resisted and, instead, maintained the plumb line perspective. In his own words, Uris portrays the minister's insightful and challenging response: *"'I do not know much about oil pipelines, Mr Ambassador," he said, "but I do know about human pipelines.'"*[529]

---

[529] Uris, *Exodus*, p. 146.

Part Three

Appointed Times And Seasons

13

It's All Lining Up ...

'Former events I declared in ancient times ... then suddenly I did them and they came to pass.'[530]

APPOINTED TIMES

About five hundred years before the angel Gabriel visited the young virgin, Mary, he was sent with a message to Daniel. Seeing into the distant future, he proclaimed: *'I am here to acquaint you with the final events ... for the end comes at the appointed time.'*[531] In the Acts of the Apostles we read: *'He [God] made all the nations ... and He marked out their appointed times in history.'*[532] What these verses have in common is the theme of providence. The world is not abandoned to chance. Pastor JD Farag believes mankind is travelling down a biblical timeline, where: *'Everything is perfectly on time prophetically.'*[533]

LONGSUFFERING

That is not to say that God is uncaring. Natural disasters, plagues and war were not part of God's plan. Man brought these curses

---

[530] God speaking to Israel's prophet: Isaiah 48:3.
[531] Daniel 8:19.
[532] Acts 17:26; NIV.
[533] Mid-East Prophecy Update, 3 August 2014.

upon himself.[534] Neither is the Creator negligent of His sons and daughters (who, by faith, have chosen to come under His protective covering). The Bible tells us that the God of Israel doesn't sleep. Yet, He is not nervously pacing the heavens. He has a plan: *'Salvation – and every spiritual blessing that accompanies it – has come to the Gentiles through one and the same channel: the Jewish people.'*[535] Father God's heart is occupied with saving His precious created ones from the torment of sin and death. The Alpha and Omega[536] is indeed patient and longsuffering.

INTO THE FUTURE

According to the late Derek Prince, *'the Bible has predicted the course of Israel's history accurately for the past 3,500 years.'*[537] During his first official visit to the State of Israel in June 2018 Prince William of the British royal family warned, *'We must never forget what was perpetrated against the Jewish people in the Holocaust'*, before proceeding to praise the modern state of Israel:

'Israel's remarkable story is partly one of remembering this terrible past but, also, looking forward to a much more hopeful future. There is – and I've seen it already – an essential vibrancy to this country. From the early stories of the kibbutzim, to the revival of Hebrew as a living, modern language, to the hi-tech economies that we see around us here in Tel Aviv – the modern story of Israel is one of inventing, creating, innovating and striding confidently into its future.'[538]

---

[534] See Romans 8:18–21.
[535] Derek Prince, *The Destiny of Israel and the Church* (Wiltshire, 1999 edn), p. 119.
[536] The title 'Alpha and Omega' signifies the One who has no beginning or end, i.e. the Eternal One.
[537] Prince, *End Times*, p. 14.
[538] *Jewish News*, 27 June 2018, 'Read the Duke of Cambridge's speech at UK embassy reception'. <https://jewishnews.timesofisrael.com/read-the-duke-of-cambridges-speech-at-uk-embassy-reception/> (28 June 2018).

The revival of the Hebrew language, a little over a century ago, is truly a miraculous fulfilment of prophecy. Consider the magnitude of this accomplishment. No matter how hard we try, there is not a hope that Ireland will return to using Gaeilge as her first language.

THE TRUMPET BLAST

Politics witnessed some major shifts in 2017 with the entrance into the world arena of Donald Trump as the 45th president of the United States of America. Despite the extensive criticism he received, it was refreshing to see a person of his position prove in many ways to be a man of his word. Trump adhered to pre-election vows, borne out by the official recognition of Jerusalem as Israel's historic capital, and the relocation of the American Embassy in 2018.[539] The Trump administration withdrew from the United Nations' educational, scientific and cultural body (UNESCO) in October 2017, due to its longstanding anti-Israel bias; he cut all US funding to the UNRWA, as well as having called for the dismantling of the agency (May 2019). A year previous, Donald Trump followed through on his warnings to withdraw the United States from the UN Human Rights Council (UNHRC), after it failed to abolish 'Item 7' from its agenda. 'Item 7' is unique in that it is devoted entirely to targeting one country: Israel. It would not be unfair to say that the UNHRC is obsessively preoccupied with 'Item 7', to the disgraceful neglect of all other people groups suffering human rights abuses. This is why former Governor of South Carolina and US Ambassador to the United Nations, Nikki Haley, described the UNHRC as *'a protector of human rights abusers, and a cesspool of political bias.'*[540] In late 2019 the Trump administration made a bold and integrous political statement by

---

[539] According to Dr Emmanuel Navon, senior fellow at the Jerusalem Institute for Strategic Studies: *'Dozens of embassies were in Jerusalem before the 1967 war, and even some afterward [such as those of Chile and the Netherlands]. Most left in 1981, after the Knesset declared Jerusalem as the [unified] capital of Israel.' Jerusalem Post*, 17 June 2019, Tara Kavaler. <https://www.jpost.com/israel-news/why-havent-more-embassies-moved-to-jerusalem-analysis-592758> (3 October 2019).
[540] *JNN*, 25 June 2018, citing an article in *INN*.

disqualifying the use of the term 'illegal' in reference to 'Israeli settlements'.

CONSERVATIVE ESTIMATES

I am an Irish woman who loves her country, her native language, her culture and her people. Perhaps I am a little idealistic, but I am not alone in my desire to see the whole island united under the Irish flag, speaking our own language. The idea of inflicting terror to achieve that aim, however, is abhorrent to me. Yes, we should never have been colonised by the British; yet in this day and age I refuse to allow unforgiveness and bitterness to taint how I regard and how I relate to our English neighbours across the sea; and I will give credit where credit is due.

Former prime minister Theresa May has been deemed a *'true friend'* of British Jewry. On her watch, £25 million of Palestinian Authority aid money was suspended in September 2016, because of its use for terrorist salaries. A thorough investigation made by the Department for International Development led to the decision in December of that same year to make some *'critical changes'* to the UK aid programme for the PA. There can be no doubt from the following remark, that the premier supported these decisions: *'Let me be clear: no British taxpayers' money will be used to make payments to terrorists or their families.'*[541] Alerted in 2017 to the serious implications of 'Israel Apartheid Week' in third-level institutions, she charged UK universities to *'investigate and swiftly address'* anti-Semitism on campus.[542]

Her predecessor David Cameron referred to Israel as *'the nation state of the Jewish people'* – a statement which is not, in fact,

---

[541] *Jewish Virtual Library*, The Palestinian Authority: History and Overview. <https://www.jewishvirtuallibrary.org/palestinian-authority-history-and-overview> (10 January 2020).

[542] *The Algemeiner*, 1 March 2017, Lea Speyer: 'British Prime Minister Calls on UK Universities to "Swiftly Address" Campus Antisemitism'. <https://www.algemeiner.com/2017/03/01/british-prime-minister-calls-on-uk-universities-to-swiftly-address-campus-antisemitism/> (12 January 2020).

untrue. You will recall that 1947 witnessed the earliest proposal for a 'two-state solution', which won the majority vote in the UN General Assembly, and would result in a nation state for the Jewish people (which they gladly accepted) alongside a nation state for the Palestinian people (which they strongly rejected). Cameron's government not only increased funding for the protection of the Jewish community in Britain, but it has been said that *'Under him, Britain began drafting laws outlawing the boycott effort against Israel.'*[543]

Theresa May's successor also speaks common sense on the issue. The former London Mayor Boris Johnson in 2015 criticised boycotters of Israel: *'I cannot think of anything more foolish than to say that you want to have any kind of divestments or sanctions or boycott against a country that, when all is said and done, is the only democracy in the region, is the only place that has, in my view, pluralist, open society – why boycott Israel?'*[544] During his tenure as Secretary of State for Foreign and Commonwealth Affairs Johnson declared: *'We support Israel's right to defend itself against any incursions into its territory.'*[545] On behalf of the United Kingdom some months later, he strongly condemned the UN Human Rights Council's obsession with Israel. *'The dedicated Agenda Item 7 focused solely on Israel,'* he declared, *'is disproportionate and damaging to the cause of peace, and unless things change we shall vote next year against all resolutions introduced under Item 7.'*[546] One of the first announcements the British government made under the newly elected Prime Minister,

---

[543] *Times of Israel*, 24 June 2016, Cnaan Liphshiz: 'The Brexit: Six things you need to know'. <https://www.timesofisrael.com/the-brexit-six-things-you-need-to-know/> (12 January 2020).

[544] *The Telegraph*, 11 November 2015, Michael Wilkinson: 'Boris Johnson banned from Palestinian charity visit after branding Israel boycotters "lefty academics".' <https://www.telegraph.co.uk/news/politics/boris-johnson/11988353/Boris-Johnson-banned-from-Palestinian-charity-visit-after-branding-Israel-boycotters-lefty-academics.html> (12 January 2020).

[545] *JNN*, 16 February 2018, citing an article in *Arutz-7*.

[546] *Gov.uk*, 18 June 2018, 'Speech by the Foreign Secretary to the Human Rights Council'. <https://www.gov.uk/government/speeches/speech-by-the-foreign-secretary-to-the-un-human-rights-council> (13 January 2020).

Boris Johnson, in December 2019 was the pledge to prohibit public organisations from supporting the BDS movement, as this was considered a misuse of taxpayers' money.[547]... It is a concern that, regarding this subject, Dáil Éireann is yet to echo the discernment and astuteness shared by these heads of state.

JERUSALEM PREOCCUPIED

'Next year in Jerusalem!' This is the traditional appeal of the Diaspora at the conclusion of the annual Jewish Passover. It signifies the longing in the Jewish heart throughout the ages to be home, in their holy capital. But they are not the only ones to call it home. God Himself calls Jerusalem His 'holy habitation', His 'dwelling place' on earth. Zion, the 'city of God', is where He decided to put His name.[548] 'But now I have chosen Jerusalem for My name to be there.'[549]

Now that we are no longer living in the time of the exile, of what significance is the city to both Jew and Gentile today? To answer this, a brief study of recent history is necessary. In 1950, the Hashemite Kingdom of Jordan annexed East Jerusalem which includes the Temple Mount.[550] With the exception of Pakistan, the rest of the world did not recognise the occupation; yet there was no international intervention or public outcry. It would remain illegally under Jordanian control for almost two decades.

THE SIX DAY WAR

In 1967, Israel was forced into war. Threatened by the armies of Jordan, Egypt, Syria and Iraq, she was once again heavily outnumbered. Her army was only one-fifth of the size of her allied enemies; Israel possessed a little over a third of the military

---

[547] VFI News, 18 December 2019, 'UK to ban BDS'.
[548] See 1 Kings 9:3; 1 Chronicles 23:25; 2 Chronicles 7:15–16; Psalm 132:13–14; Isaiah 18:7d; Joel 3:21; Zechariah 8:3–5; etc.
[549] 2 Chronicles 6:6; NIV.
[550] Jordan also annexed the West Bank at the time.

aircraft used in the war.

The sinister scheme was unveiled in May 1967 when the Egyptian army crossed the Suez Canal into the Sinai Peninsula. *'Within a couple of weeks, this military build-up amounted to some 90,000 men, 900 tanks, 350 planes and great concentrations of artillery.'*[551] They were within striking distance of Israel. President Nassar of Egypt proudly pronounced that the time had come for the eradication of the Jewish nation.[552] On 30 May, Jordan's King Hussein signed a military pact with Nassar. *'An Egyptian general was sent to take command of Jordan's forces ... a wave of excitement was sweeping through the Arab world ... the mosques were preaching 'Jihad'.'*[553]

On the morning of 5 June, the Israeli Air Force made a pre-emptive strike. In three hours, they destroyed over 400 enemy warplanes (mainly in Egypt). Most of these hadn't yet taken off. With much of Egypt's air force (the largest in the Middle East) demolished, the war was effectively over. Israeli tanks struck the stunned Egyptian army and chased them back over the Suez Canal. Meanwhile, Jordan launched a heavy attack on Jerusalem and coastal cities. Although many Israelis were killed, within days they managed to gain control of the situation. Syria struck Israel from the Golan Heights, which was then under Syrian control. By 10 June, the northern enemy was defeated and pushed back as far as Damascus. The war was over, with a sensational victory for Israel. Her spoils would include the ancient capital of King David: Jerusalem.

THE END OF THE AGE

Since 1967 the world has entered into a new era. This is the time in Bible prophecy when Jerusalem is no longer under Gentile control, but back in the hands of the Israelites. It is the season of the return of the Jewish Messiah. *'Then the Lord will go forth and*

---

[551] Crown-Tamir, *In a Nutshell*, p. 104.
[552] Ibid. Egyptian President Nassar: *'the objective will be to destroy Israel'*.
[553] Crown-Tamir, *In a Nutshell*, p. 104.

wage war against those nations ... His feet shall stand in that day upon the Mount of Olives, which is on the east side of Jerusalem.'[554] From there He will rule the world for a thousand years as majestic King (see Zechariah 14:9 and Revelation 20:6) before the world comes to an abrupt end. Paul and Nuala O'Higgins explain it this way: *'Eventually Jerusalem would be returned to Jewish rule (Luke 21:24). This was the sign by which we would know we are at the end of the age. The end of the age should not be confused with the end of the world. It is the end of the present age which began with Jesus' Ascension and will end with His return as King of Jerusalem and King of the world.'[555]* The earth has crossed a threshold into a new phase of her spiritual journey. Concurrent with the rapid deterioration of the world system, is a sovereign move of God, bringing life and liberty into the hearts of many. The exciting effects of this spiritual awakening can be seen in different ways ...

CHURCH REVIVAL

Revival has begun to take place in the Church. Some say the Jesus Movement of the late 1960s came as a result of the victorious reclamation of the Jewish capital. Is it a coincidence that the Catholic Charismatic Renewal began in 1967? Many Bible scholars associate the return of the Jews to their ancient homeland with the prophet Ezekiel's vision (see Ezekiel 37:1-13, 21). *'Just as the Jewish people are being gathered to Israel from their "valley of dry bones" so too is the church rising from its valley of spiritual decline (for the last 1900 years. It has not been totally dead or bereft of the spirit but far from the position of purity and spiritual power which it had in the first generation of its existence).'[556]*

---

[554] Zechariah 14:3-4.
[555] Paul & Nuala O'Higgins, *Christianity Without Religion: The Message that's Changing the World* (Florida, 2003), p. 184.
[556] O'Higgins, *In Israel Today*, p. 198.

RECOGNISING OUR ROOTS

Secondly, the Church is receiving a revelation of God's heart for Israel. *'A love for Jewish people is being sovereignly poured out into the hearts of the Gentile Church … congregations are [being] restored to an appreciation of their Jewish heritage.'*[557] As God is yet to remove the veil of blindness from the nation of Israel regarding her Messiah[558], He is currently removing a veil from His Gentile followers. The New Testament tells us that our love for the Jewish Messiah will stir up jealousy in Israel. *'Salvation has come to the gentiles to make the Jews jealous.'*[559] Extending our love and support to the Jewish nation is vital.

MESSIANIC JUDAISM

Although comparatively few in number, there have always been Jewish believers in Jesus scattered throughout the world. Some scholars directly associate the dramatic increase in number from 1967 onward with the divine fulfilment of the reoccupation of Jerusalem. Meanwhile, the opposition is becoming increasingly agitated. *Yad L'Achim* is an anti-missionary organisation in Israel that is frantically trying to put an end to these conversions. One Orthodox Jew from the organisation pleads: *'how urgent it is to demand legislation against missionary activity in Israel … in the past 19 years, more Jews have converted to Christianity than in the 1,900 years before that.'*[560] These converts are now discovering the joy of marrying their Jewish roots with their Christian beliefs. They like to be called Messianic Jews; they observe the Sabbath and keep Jewish holidays, *'which they understand to have their fulfilment in Jesus.'*[561] Messianic Jewish congregations have been springing up in various parts of the world. *'In 1967, there were no messianic Jewish congregations in*

---

[557] Finto, *My People*, pp. 157, 159.
[558] See 2 Corinthians 3:16.
[559] Romans 11:11; ISV.
[560] *JNN*, 27 March 2015, alluding to *Israel Today*.
[561] Spector, Stephen, 5 November 2008, 'Evangelicals and Israel', Oxford University Press, p. 116.

the world. Today, according to an article in "Christianity Today", there are over 350.'[562] This observation was made over twenty years ago; it would be interesting to know how many Messianic Jewish congregations are in existence now!

PERPETUAL OBSERVANCES

From the earliest church councils (i.e. from AD 100), Jewish believers in Jesus were ordered to forsake the customs and feasts appointed for them by God. Some prescribed customs were eternal and to be practised forever, such as the Sabbath rest. Tabernacles (or 'Booths') is a feast which God commanded the Jewish people to perpetually observe as a reminder to them of His faithful provision and care during their forty years of wandering through the wilderness. During the millennial reign *all people* will be expected to come to Jerusalem to celebrate the feast *every year*. *'So it shall be that all who are left from all the nations, which came up against Jerusalem, shall go up as often as once a year to worship the King, the Lord of hosts, and to celebrate the feast of booths.'*[563] This is yet to happen.

'WARS, WARS AND RUMOURS OF WARS'

In the meantime, wars are inevitable. Former leader of the United Nations, Kofi Annan, would agree. *'The General Secretary of the UN had to admit in a speech little more than a year ago that the world is not entering into peace ... there are more people involved globally in situations of war and conflict today than during the time of the Second World War.'*[564] Israel is increasingly the focus of world news. The most recent full-scale offensive strike at Gaza militants once again drew harsh criticism and evoked strong reactions from a frightfully large number of people – especially in Europe and the US.

---

[562] Finto, My People, p. 143.
[563] Zechariah 14:16.
[564] Facius, The Coming Messiah, p. 91.

2014 GAZA CONFLICT

'Operation Protective Edge' lasted fifty days. It commenced in July 2014, following the kidnapping and brutal murder of three Israeli adolescents, for which Hamas is noted to have taken *credit*.[565] The schoolboys were without military training. Meanwhile, the Gaza situation was overbearing, with Islamic militants provocatively hurling daily projectiles into Israeli towns and territory. Between the Israeli disengagement in 2005[566] and 2014, *'more than 14,800 rockets had been fired into Israel by the group [i.e. Hamas] and its proxies.'*[567] Thus, to Israel, the kidnapping was the last straw.

HOLLYWOOD'S TAKE

We will begin our investigation into the war by turning to the opinion of individuals in the film industry.

> *'A bevy of Hollywood's leading figures ... signed a statement blaming Hamas for the current violence in and around the Gaza Strip. Championed by the likes of Arnold Schwarzenegger, Sylvester Stallone, Minnie Driver, Kelsey Grammer, Seth Rogen, and Sarah Silverman, the letter read: "Hamas cannot be allowed to rain rockets on Israeli cities, nor can it be allowed to hold its own people hostage. Hospitals are for healing, not for hiding weapons. Schools are for learning, not for launching missiles. Children are our hope, not our human shields." ... The statement was signed by no fewer than 187 actors, directors, writers, agents, executives and other Hollywood personalities.'*[568]

---

[565] JNN, 21 August 2014, alluding to a *Jerusalem Post* article.
[566] That is, when the Israeli government made the difficult decision to remove all, i.e. almost 10,000, Israeli residents from the Gaza Strip, as mentioned in chapter 8.
[567] JNN, 26 August 2014, alluding to *New York Times*.
[568] Ibid, 25 August 2014, citing *Israel Today*.

Needless to say, performing artists whose livelihood depends on popularity, must have solid evidence to take such an unpopular position.

EU REPORT

The following statement was made by the European Union in July 2014: *'The EU strongly condemns the indiscriminate firing of rockets into Israel by Hamas and terrorist groups[569] in the Gaza Strip, directly harming civilians. These are criminal and unjustifiable acts … The EU strongly condemns calls on the civilian population of Gaza to provide themselves as human shields.'[570]* During the conflict, the European Union's ambassador to Israel publicly expressed solidarity with the besieged Israeli civilians. Other world leaders who expressed support for Israel included former British Prime Minister David Cameron and German Chancellor Angela Merkel.

HUMAN SHIELDS

Mosab Hassan Youssef claims *'Hamas was born to destroy. It cannot build.'* This Palestinian, who identifies with Israel, continues: *'Let's not forget that our enemy is a barbaric one which uses women and children as human shields, and in these situations we are very limited, because we [in Israel] care about the lives of innocent citizens.'[571]* In the eyes of Hamas, use of their own civilians as human shields is a worthy means to an end. Here is how one spokesman, Sami Abu Zuhri, defends the policy: *'This attests to the character of our noble, Jihad-fighting people. We in Hamas call upon our people to adopt this policy, in order to protect the Palestinian homes.'[572]* The truth of the matter is that Hamas is more concerned about protecting their arsenal inside

---

[569] Another terrorist group which was involved in Operation Protective Edge was Islamic Jihad.

[570] *JNN*, 23 July 2014, alluding to *Jerusalem Post*.

[571] Ibid, 24 November 2012, alluding to *INN*.

[572] Ibid, 11 July 2014, alluding to *Israel Today* and *Ryan Jones* articles.

and beneath these buildings. Photographic evidence from Operation Protective Edge reveals Hamas leaders making their way around the city in ambulances full of children, thereby preventing the IDF from striking them.

GOVERNMENT EXECUTIONS

If Northern Ireland was governed by the IRA or UVF, we might have an inkling of the severity of the situation. For fifteen years, Gaza has been officially governed by Hamas. This is a government system in which loyalists are promoted and dissidents eliminated. During 'Operation Protective Edge', at least thirty-eight male and female suspected Israel collaborators in the Gaza Strip were publicly executed by the government in question. These took place out in the open for all to witness – young and old alike. The United Nations' *Universal Declaration of Human Rights*[573] states that all persons charged with a penal offence are entitled to a fair trial. In that case, the Palestinian government is guilty of war crimes.

UN SECRETARY GENERAL

In a public statement, former UN Secretary General, Ban Ki-moon, criticised the violent activity of Gaza terrorists. *'We condemn strongly the rocket attacks, and these must stop immediately ... We condemn the use of civilian sites, schools, hospitals and other civilian facilities for military purposes.'*[574] On the same day I read this report, I witnessed the UN leader making the first part of this statement on *RTÉ News*. The TV report was edited in such a way, however, that you were led to assume he was condemning Israel. It also failed to include the following commendation of Israel by the Secretary General: *'Even in the darkest hour the people of this country have such a tremendous capacity for generosity and good.'*

---

[573] See Article 11.1.
[574] *JNN*, 23 July 2014, alluding to *Jerusalem Post*.

UNRWA HYPOCRISY

During 'Operation Protective Edge', terrorist rocket caches were discovered in at least three schools run by the *United Nations Relief and Works Agency* (UNRWA). Following one of the discoveries, the agency made a statement: *'UNRWA strongly and unequivocally condemns the group or groups responsible for this flagrant violation of the inviolability of its premises under international law.'*[575] However, they then returned the projectiles to Hamas, rather than hand them over to the UN. This behaviour seriously questions their allegiance to the UN charter for Human Rights, when it is commonly known that such missiles are used to target Israeli civilians – especially children. In fact, the mortar attack that killed a four-year-old Israeli boy in August 2014 was, *'fired by terrorists from within an UNRWA school in northern Gaza.'*[576] The following questions beg to be asked: On whose side are these Gaza-based UN agents? And, just how serious are they really about the business of uniting nations?

TERROR TUNNELS

The illegal construction of tunnels linking Gaza to Israeli territory is thought to have begun in 2010. By 2014, the 'terror tunnels' had reportedly consumed 40 per cent of Hamas' budget.[577] In an interview with *Sky Arabic*, the Israeli Prime Minister pinpointed Hamas' agenda: *'They [Hamas] have taken billions of dollars [from international charity funding]. Instead of building kindergartens with it, they're building tunnels, concrete tunnels to blow up our kindergartens. They are the enemies of the Palestinians.'*[578] Even Hamas' Minister for Foreign Affairs, Osama Hamdan, did not conceal his government's violent strategies, *'"In the next campaign ... we will plan the liberation of the land inside Israel ...*

---

[575] Ibid, 23 July 2014, alluding to *Jerusalem Post*.
[576] Ibid, 23 August 2014, alluding to *Ynet*.
[577] Ibid, 12 August 2014 referring to *Times of Israel* report.
[578] Ibid, 22 July 2014, alluding to articles in the *Jerusalem Post* and *Arutz-7*.

and we will attack them by land.'[579] The IDF succeeded in eliminating thirty-two of these tunnels during Operation Protective Edge. It is no surprise, however, that tunnel construction resumed shortly after the war ended, as did rocket production and arms smuggling.

Had Gaza any concern for its vulnerable citizens, it would have sheltered them underground. Instead, those who were found to be in hiding in the terror tunnels during the ground incursion were Hamas operatives. On the other side of the fence, Israel was protecting her civilians in bomb shelters. Is it any wonder that Israelis sustained fewer fatalities?

WAR CRIMES?

That the United Nations set up an inquiry to assess whether *Israel* is guilty of war crimes is a complete travesty of justice. Thousands of flyers were air-dropped by Israel into Gazan neighbourhoods prior to IDF strikes, along with: *'broadcast warnings in Arabic on Palestinian television ... to enable Palestinian civilians to evacuate targeted areas.'*[580] Buildings were marked because they contained arsenals of projectiles.[581] Over 100,000 calls and texts were sent warning Gazans to evacuate the area in which the ground invasion was to take place. This is a humanitarian step that is costing the Israeli tax payer. Is it any wonder the UN Secretary General praised Israel's generosity?

Photographic evidence proves that enemy leaders encouraged civilians to stand on their roofs in order to deter the Israeli Air Force (IAF). In such cases, the IAF was left with little choice but to abort the strike. This explains why they had to resort to a ground offensive.[582] In the eyes of any rational soldier, the Israel Defence

---

[579] Ibid, 17 July 2014, alluding to *Israel National News*.
[580] PM Netanyahu, UN General Assembly, 29 September 2014.
[581] Later, homes of Hamas commanders were struck in an effort to eliminate these organisers of terror.
[582] Another reason, no doubt, was the elimination of terror tunnels.

Force has set an exemplary standard.[583] Former commander of the British forces in Afghanistan, Colonel Richard Kemp made the following statement: *'No other army in the world has ever done more than Israel is doing now to save the lives of innocent civilians in a combat zone ... British soldiers have fought exactly this kind of enemy in Afghanistan and in Iraq. British soldiers understand what Israel is doing.'*[584]

CENSORSHIP

Such are the underhanded ways of the government of Gaza that, although they welcomed international journalists to witness their so-called onslaught by Israel, they made sure these same journalists were not exposed to the true facts of the matter. Any who were found filming or taking photographs of Hamas' missile launch sites were deported from the Gaza Strip. (This fact has been verified by a Norwegian journalist, Pål Jørgensen, and by a Hamas spokesperson on Lebanon's *al-Mayadeen* TV). Could this be because of the strategic positioning of missile launchers beside hospitals, mosques and schools? As the war progressed, more and more reports materialised of Hamas firing from built-up civilian areas. Eventually, the *Foreign Press Association* protested that reporters were being harassed and threatened by Hamas. They made no such complaint about Israel.

HUMAN RIGHTS OFFENCES?

Meanwhile, the IDF set up a field hospital at a Gaza crossing to treat Palestinians. After the IDF medical team treated a wounded Gazan terrorist, Dr Daniel Albo said: *'My team and I saved the life of a terrorist who tried to kill us because we are IDF soldiers and citizens of Israel. We saved him because we are human.'*[585]

---

[583] See Appendix 5 for an article quoting top world generals who have assessed the 2014 war in Gaza.

[584] JNN, 25 July 2014, alluding to *Israel Today* and Ryan Jones.

[585] Ibid, 20 July 2014, alluding to *INN* and *Jerusalem Post*.

Wounded Palestinians, including children, were treated in various hospitals in Israel. During the war, the IDF did not impede the supply of aid and fuel: *'trucks of ... food and basic products passed into Gaza ... including some 200,000 litres of fuel daily, in an attempt to prevent a humanitarian crisis in Gaza.*[586] That Israel would be guilty of human rights offences clearly does not correlate with the above evidence.

Were we to compare this situation with the recent civil war in Syria, we would soon see that when dealing with Israel one is treated humanely. Those dying of starvation in besieged Syrian towns received no such charitable outreach. President Assad's regime is responsible for the routine killing and systematic starvation of Palestinians at the Yarmouk refugee camp in Syria. Is it not alarming that the UN chose to turn a blind eye to this? Meanwhile, Israel (the 'Big Bad Wolf') intervened on behalf of besieged Syrians near the Israeli border, supplying them with food and water. The IDF also evacuated a few thousand wounded Syrians to Israeli hospitals during the course of the long, drawn-out civil war.

CIVILIAN CASUALTIES

Mike Fegelman of *Honestreporting Canada* online, had a letter published in the *Chronicle Herald* in August, 2014 questioning the legitimacy of reported civilian casualty statistics. *'University professor Judy Haiven grossly distorts Palestinian casualty figures by claiming all were "civilians" ... Israel contends it killed some 900 Palestinian terrorists from Hamas, Islamic Jihad, and other terror groups since July 8.'* What the Gaza health authority, along with international media, generally failed to report is that the majority of males killed in the Gaza Strip by the IDF were terrorists.

> *'Even the BBC and the New York Times have acknowledged that Israel's casualty statistics are most likely accurate and that stats from Gaza health officials, AKA Hamas, lack*

---

[586] Ibid, 11 July 2014, alluding to *Ynet.*

credibility due to their strategic interest in inflating the numbers ... Importantly, the United Nations estimates that for conflicts worldwide, such as Afghanistan, there is an average of a three-to-one ratio of civilians to combatant deaths. Fighting in Iraq and Kosovo was higher at four-to-one, and in Gaza, thanks to Israel's surgical pinpoint operations, the ratio was one-to-one.'[587]

ARAB SURGEON'S PERSPECTIVE

In an interview, an Arab doctor, who works in Israel, expressed his solidarity with the Jewish state in their war against terror:

'Dr Rabia Darawasha is an Israeli-Arab surgeon at Barzilai Hospital in Ashkelon, where Hamas rockets land in the vicinity and "Code Red" alerts send staff and Israeli and Palestinian patients scrambling for cover. Asked in a media interview if treating Israeli soldiers was difficult for him, he replied, "Hamas does not represent me. The soldiers represent me." He added, "This is my country; my family is here." Dr Darawasha comes from Iksal in northern Israel. As an Arab, he has never felt discriminated against or treated as a second-class citizen by Israel.'[588]

'PROTECTIVE EDGE' CONCLUSION

Please don't assume that Israel emerged out of the war unscathed. For every terrorist missile struck in mid-air by Israel's ultra-expensive Iron Dome missile defence system, shrapnel fell, wounding Israelis and causing extensive damage to homes, public buildings and infrastructure. Here are some statistics from Operation Protective Edge that will not likely have been reported in Ireland: *'armed groups in Gaza fired 4,564 projectiles at Israel ...*

---

[587] Ibid, 6 December 2013, alluding to *Jerusalem Post*.
[588] Ibid, 23 August 2014, alluding to *National Post Canada*.

Throughout the fighting, 71 people were killed on the Israeli side, including 66 soldiers. 469 IDF soldiers were wounded ... emergency services paramedics treated 842 civilians.'[589]

It seems to me that there is an underlying cynical agenda at work here – to single out the Jew in the global schoolyard and give him a hard time whenever possible. Although she would rather live in peace, Israel had once again, to put up a resistance to the ongoing onslaught from terrorists on her border in Operation Protective Edge.

WE'RE ON COURSE

'As Jesus was sitting on the Mount of Olives, the disciples came to him privately. "Tell us," they said, "what will be the sign of your coming and of the end of the age?"'[590] Jesus' description of the signs of the times is known as the 'Olivet Discourse', during which He says: *'Now learn this lesson from the fig-tree: As soon as its twigs get tender and its leaves come out, you know that summer is near. Even so, when you see these things happening, you know that He [the Messiah: Jesus] is near, right at the door.'*[591] This verse would make no sense were we not to know that in Hebrew thought, the fig tree symbolises Israel.[592] When Israel – the people and the land – begin to blossom again (which they have since their return in 1948, as was eloquently conveyed by Prince William), then we enter a new era. That final lap of the race of history – before the return of Messiah – has begun. In addition to this, Jesus specifies another requirement of the season. It will happen when the ancient capital of Jerusalem is restored to the Jewish people: *'Jerusalem will be trampled on by the Gentiles until the times of the Gentiles are fulfilled.'*[593] This would suggest that since Jerusalem came back into the hands of its rightful owners in

---

[589] Ibid, 30 August 2014, citing *Israel Hayom* and *Jerusalem Post*.
[590] Matthew 24:3, NIV.
[591] Mark 13:28-9, NIV.
[592] See Jeremiah 24 and Luke 21:24, NIV.
[593] Luke 21:24, NIV.

1967, the time for Gentile occupation is over. Soon after, Jesus concluded: *'When these things begin to take place, stand up and lift up your heads, because your redemption is drawing near.'*[594]

SILVER LINING

Winner of three Academy awards, the screenplay *Fiddler on the Roof* captures the exasperation of the taunted Jews. Tevye has just heard that a pogrom is on its way to his Russian village, when he turns his perplexed gaze heavenward, and says: *'I know, I know we are Your chosen people. But, once in a while, can't you choose someone else?'*[595] Just because Israel happens to be the chosen people of God, doesn't mean they've had a life of comfort and repose. Taking on the leadership role was never going to be easy. But, anything that God has allowed Israel to endure has been for her refinement, with salvation in mind. The same could be said of Gentiles. God allows and sometimes orchestrates difficult events in our lives for our ultimate good and for His glory. Someone once made the following observation: Every shadow is produced by light.

---

[594] Ibid, v 28.
[595] The Broadway musical production of the popular tragicomedy celebrated its Golden Anniversary in 2014.

14

Cross The Finish Line

Kick off ... hope ... excitement ... thrills ... foul play ... penalty ... disappointment ... half-time ...

ALL NATIONS

In the upcoming all-nations final, one thing is for sure: Israel will be there. Which final? The final play-out of world history, and the end of life as we know it. End Times prophecy tells us that the Jewish state and her Arab neighbours (especially Iran), along with Turkey and Russia, are nations that will feature prominently in the days ahead. Before we bring closure to our study of the indispensability of Israel, we need to address some questions: What is required for any nation to cross the finish line of history? And, if the Cross of the Jewish Messiah signifies the finishing point, what are the implications of this for Jew and Gentile? First, let's tackle the latter.

'IT IS FINISHED'

At Calvary, Jesus had effectively nailed the sins of mankind to the Cross and become the curse that had separated us from God the Father. By rising from the dead, He opened the way for us to have new life in the Kingdom of God ... A bridge was built between the God of heaven and the believer.

By saying, *'It is finished,'*[596] the King of the Jews was heralding that

---

[596] See John 19:30.

this was the season of 'out with the old and in with the new'. The previous era was completed by the work of the Cross. *'The Law is fulfilled in the Messiah in the same way as the boy is fulfilled in the man, the caterpillar in the butterfly, the bud in the blossom.'*[597] A new chapter of history had begun. A type of *wind* pollination was introduced on Resurrection Sunday. The wind of the Holy Spirit would carry the seed of divine love into the hearts of all who would receive the Son of God. Through the Jewish apostles, the Holy Spirit crossed the divide, drawing Jew and Gentile together in a unique form of 'cross-pollination'.

RECONCILIATION

At the foot of the Cross we find grace to reach out the hand of mercy to those who have wronged us. Figuratively speaking, the Cross is the place where Jew and Gentile meet and embrace. *'Breaking down the barrier that separated Jews and Gentiles He [Jesus Christ] united the two … so that in Himself He might … reconcile them both in one body to God, bringing the hostility to an end by the cross.'*[598] Scripture is clear regarding the destiny of both Jewish and Gentile believers in the Messiah; there will not be a separate neighbourhood for each of these groups in the City of God; rather, this 'one new man' shall spend eternity together in perfect harmony. Has it escaped your attention that not a single verse of Scripture teaches Christians to reject the Jewish people? On the contrary, we are encouraged to honour, comfort and bless them.

ELEVENTH HOUR

In a Root Source broadcast, CEO Gidon Ariel reported that over 800 documented Palestinian attacks (from rock throwing to stabbing and shooting) were perpetrated against Israeli Jews in

---

[597] Paul & Nuala O'Higgins, *New Testament Believers & the Law* (Florida, 2003), p. 53.
[598] Ephesians 2:14–16.

the two weeks from 28 September to 12 October 2015.[599] That is a daily average of *fifty-seven* attacks against random Jewish civilians and security personnel. *'There will be a short period of darkness all over the world, and then that time will arrive. The stage is being set in the Middle East with a re-established Jerusalem in a re-established Israel and a re-established Jewish people.'*[600] With Europe awaiting its next attack by random radical Islamists, a surge in anti-Semitism worldwide, both Iran and North Korea flexing their nuclear muscles, the ongoing global refugee crisis, and dare I forget the Covid-19 pandemic which has brought every continent to a standstill and the global economy to its knees, who could honestly argue other than that the world is in a rapid downward spiral?

HIGHER POWER

In the Bible we learn that Jesus was asleep on a boat during a raging storm. His disciples were terrified. *'A heavy squall of wind came up and the waves dashed into the boat so that the boat was filling, while He was in the stern asleep.'*[601] When they finally approached their Rabbi, the situation took a miraculous turn. *'"Teacher, do You not care that we are sinking?" He rose up, rebuked the wind and said to the sea, "Silence! Be still!" Then the wind fell and there was great calm.'*[602] It may be humbling to admit that we cannot manage on our own but the alternative could be lethal.

THE TEAM IS PICKED

Regarding the people of Israel, the apostle Paul wrote: *'Theirs [are] … the covenants, the receiving of the law, the temple*

---

[599] Gidon Ariel, 'Surrounded by the Stabbing Intifada', *Root Source*, 13 October 2015, available at. <http://root-source.com/blog/special-report-surrounded-by-the-stabbing-intifada/> (25 October 2015).
[600] Glashouwer, *Why Israel?*, p. 25.
[601] Mark 4:37–38.
[602] Ibid, 4:38–39.

worship and the promises. Theirs are the Patriarchs, and from them is traced the human ancestry of the Messiah, who is God.'[603] Heavenly Father chose to birth a nation which would one day be the bearer of Good News for mankind. Israel never earned her God-chosen position. *'It is important to see that Israel does not deserve God's blessing and mercy. (Neither does the Church – let me emphasize that).'*[604] Without receiving forgiveness offered by the Messiah she, too, will *not* be allowed access into the Kingdom of God. Israel is not *yet* the 'team player' she was called to be. But do we have the right to judge?

PENALTIES

'And it came about that just as they hadn't listened when he called, so Adonai-Tzva'ot *said, "I won't listen when they call; but with the power of a whirlwind I will disperse them among all the nations ..." Thus the land was left desolate after them.'*[605] Not playing by the rules earns you penalties, which, although awarded by the referee, are inflicted by the rivals. As a nation, Israel has not chosen to stay under the protective covering of her heavenly Father, leaving her exposed to attack of all kinds.[606] God made an eternal covenant with the children of Israel to be their God and to give them a home as a permanent possession, even though He knew they would be sent off for foul play.

HALF-TIME

Perhaps now is the time to pause and reflect on key events that have enhanced the lustre of our Emerald Isle. Ireland's history with the Jews goes at least as far back as 1079 CE. Based on historic artefacts, some argue that St Patrick was Jewish.[607] If that

---

[603] Romans 9:3c–5; NIV.

[604] Prince, *End Times*, p. 152.

[605] Zechariah 7:13–14; CJB. 'Adonai-Tzva'ot' means Lord of (heaven's) armies.

[606] See the story of the Prodigal Son; Luke 15:11–32.

[607] Apparently Marcus Losack's book, *St Patrick and the Bloodline of the Grail*, makes a strong argument based on solid historical evidence.

were the case, how much more indebted would we be to the Jewish race?

IRISH SUPPORTERS

A few good men from the Ireland of yesteryear acted on behalf of the Jewish people. Irish philosopher, John Toland introduced the concept of Jewish emancipation to the British Isles. His 1714 publication (titled: *Reasons for Naturalizing the Jews in Great Britain and Ireland, On the Same Foot with All Other Nations. Containing also, a Defence of the Jews against all vulgar Prejudices in all Countries*) was instrumental in getting the dialogue started. With readmission into Britain after 350 years of exile, the returning Jews finally had an influential voice (and an Irish one!) to speak on their behalf. This led to the *Jew Bill of 1753*, which paved the way for rights previously denied to the minority group, such as land ownership and positions of authority.

The Jewish community of Daniel O'Connell's day had reason to hold 'the Liberator', in high esteem. When *De Judaismo* (Jewish dress law) was enforced in the British Isles in the eighteen hundreds, the barrister-cum-politician had the law repealed. Aware of the fraternal ties that bind Christendom to the Jewish nation, O'Connell once declared: *'Ireland has claims on your ancient race, it is the only country that I know of unsullied by any one act of persecution of the Jews.'*

FOUR COURTS

Note the comment of the late Raphael Siev, former curator of the Jewish Museum of Ireland: *'Where else would you see, not the Scales of Justice, but ... a statue of Moses holding the tablets containing the Ten Commandments, standing over the main entrance to the four courts in Dublin?'*[608]

Why does Moses, and not the usual symbol of justice, take 'centre

---

[608] Carol Sorgen, 'Tracing the History of Ireland's Jews', *Baltimore Jewish Times*.

stage' in the High Court of Ireland? Could it possibly suggest affinity with the 'people of the Book'? Whatever the motive, it's clear from the design that that which Moses signifies was held in honour.

IRELAND ON THE LINE

It would be remiss of me to comb through the throbbing annals of Jewish history without recalling the time when our own little nation was brought to her knees. Ireland's life was *on the line* during the Great Famine, when a million poor souls died of starvation. Many landlords paid no heed to the suffering of their emaciated tenants, some of whom were heartlessly evicted. Meanwhile, numerous Jewish people made donations and sacrifices on behalf of our people.[609] The family of the Jewish Baron Lionel de Rothschild received a noteworthy acknowledgement in a Dublin newspaper in 1850, in which they are said to have: '*contributed during the Irish famine of 1847 ... a sum far beyond the joint contributions of the Devonshires, and Herefords, Lansdownes, Fitzwilliams and Herberts, who annually drew so many times that amount from their Irish estates.*'[610] It's comforting to know that the successful Baron[611], along with many not-so-wealthy members of the Irish Jewish community, were willing to give a helping hand when it was most needed.

LIMERICK BOYCOTT

Jewish people who found refuge in Ireland through the centuries were treated relatively well. Most anti-Semitism amounted to little more than name-calling. That may be cruel and is certainly unacceptable but at least, as a nation, we are not guilty of Jewish

---

[609] Fortunately for them, the Jews of Ireland were not farmers, but business and tradesmen. Hence, the potato blight didn't directly affect their livelihood.

[610] See Irish Jewish Community website.

[611] The Baron would later become the first Jewish member of Parliament in Westminster.

bloodshedding.[612] Nonetheless, a boycott, instigated by Fr John Creagh, took place in Limerick in 1904. It lasted two years and resulted in five of the thirty-one Jewish families of the city relocating.[613] Advocating pluralism, many Irish voices spoke out against the Limerick Boycott. Fr Creagh was reprimanded by his superiors for provoking his parishioners to persecute the Jewish people, and was moved out of the parish and eventually out of the country.

'OH CAPTAIN, MY CAPTAIN!'

Lt Col John Henry Patterson (1867–1947) was born in Co. Longford to a Catholic mother and Protestant father. To this Irishman, the Israeli Prime Minister Benjamin Netanyahu paid tribute in 2014, designating Patterson 'the godfather of the Israeli army'. This was due to his exemplary command, during World War I, of the Zion Mule Corps – which the Israeli Premier considered to be the first organised Jewish fighting force in almost two millennia. Before embarking on its mission to Gallipoli, Turkey, the Zion Mule Corps marched past the Synagogue of Alexandria, Egypt, where the Chief Rabbi described Patterson as: *'a second Moses leading the children of Israel from Egypt to the Promised Land'.*[614] Such was the impression he made that, the Irishman was invited to take command of the newly-birthed Jewish Legion of the Second World War (members of which were future Prime Minister David Ben Gurion and Revisionist Movement leader, Ze'ev Jabotinsky). Patterson honourably defended his Jewish troops from anti-Semitic attitudes prevalent in the British army at the time, costing him promotions in rank. Comrade Jabotinsky, had this to say

---

[612] That is not to say that individuals are blameless in this regard. There were two fatal shootings of Jewish persons in Dublin in 1923. One was murdered in Stephen's Green and the other in Portobello, which was then known as 'Little Jerusalem'. Incidentally, this nickname was used because there was a large concentration of Jewish refugees in the area, who had arrived at the end of the nineteenth century, after fleeing pogroms in Eastern Europe.

[613] Fortuitously, one family, found refuge in Cork – a city that would sometime later honour one of their sons, Gerald Goldberg, as their first Jewish Lord Mayor.

[614] Yanky Fachler, Jewish Historical Society of Ireland lecture, 18 March 2015.

about our Irish hero of the Jews: *'In all of Jewish history we have never had a Christian friend as understanding and devoted.'*[615]

IRELAND'S SCORE

As the 'second half' is about to commence, it would help to know where we stand. Alluding to the Holocaust, in the poem, 'The Dying Synagogue at South Terrace', Irish poet Thomas McCarthy captures two unhelpful attitudes of the Irish to the Jewish plight.[616] When we should have been outspoken we were indifferent; when support was needed we have been guilty of hypocrisy.

If the winds of change were once strong enough to generate the *French Revolution*, if they were powerful enough to tear down the *Iron Curtain* of communism, then surely passion for truth and justice can grip the heart of the Irishman once again. Could we turn our intrinsic Irish spirit of rebellion into a passion for precision? If sin is said to mean 'missing the mark', may we make every effort to strike the target.

STRIKE THE TARGET

We shall now begin to address the first of the two questions posed at the beginning of the chapter: What is required for a nation to cross the finish line of history? It's time to start targeting the true opponent. According to a white, anti-apartheid South African: *'The Arabs, in their determination to annihilate Israel, have missed one opportunity after another to get what they say they want today. They have rejected every peace offer by Israel and have used their fabulous oil wealth to manipulate world opinion into believing that Israel is the bad boy in the Middle East process.'*[617] Terrorists and their ringleaders should be the ones

---

[615] Lucy Jennings, *We salute you, John Henry Patterson*, ICEJ publication, January/February 2015 edition.
[616] Thomas McCarthy, 'The Dying Synagogue at South Terrace', in Keogh & Whelan (eds), *Goldberg: A Tribute*, p. 71.
[617] Hedding, *Understanding Israel*, p. 163.

who suffer the glare of the global jury and feel the pinch of economic sanctions. The United Nations Universal Declaration of Human Rights states that all people everywhere are entitled to a life of *freedom from fear*. Surely Israel is also entitled to that basic human need.

JUST DO IT

I have heard it said that trainee bank clerks learn to identify counterfeit notes by spending hours handling the authentic! We would be wise to undergo the same training – studying the true Word of God and not the biased, unfair reports that are too often presented by the Irish and UK media on the subject of Israel. Then we will almost instantly discern lies and detect fakes. 'Just do it' is the effective slogan of the Nike sports brand. Do what? Do the right thing.

In his visit to Ireland a half a century ago, the late John F. Kennedy ruffled some republican feathers by quoting British Prime Minister David Lloyd George, who once said that the world is indebted to the seemingly insignificant nations: *'All the world owes much to the little "five feet high" nations ... The heroic deeds that thrill humanity through generations were the deeds of little nations fighting for their freedom. And, oh yes, the salvation of mankind came through a little nation.'*[618] I wonder if it ever occurred to Lloyd George that through little Ireland's monks, monasteries and missionaries this same Gospel of salvation was carried to Europe and the nations ... I wonder if the Irish know that it is time to bring the Good News to the nations once again.

BACK IN PLAY

'God chose the Jews to provide us with the Bible and the messianic line leading to Jesus. He chose them to suffer, for His own reasons – we don't see people arguing with that fact. But He also chose

---

[618] *Sunday Independent*, 9 June 2013, Donal Lynch.

them to inherit the land of Israel, unconditionally and forever. We have to learn to accept that fact.'[619] Might we be guilty of selective hearing? Derek Prince highlights the hypocrisy of picking and choosing what we want to believe from the Bible: 'since the same prophets who promised restoration were the ones who uttered the indictments, I see no logic or consistency in endorsing the indictments and refusing the promises of restoration.'[620] God warned that He would punish His nation for rebellion and idolatry by banishing them from the land. Israel got the 'red card'. Yet, God Almighty repeatedly in those same scriptures promised to bring His people back to the land following two distinct periods of exile. True to His word, the nation returned after the prophesied seventy years in Babylon.[621] Their second exile, which began in the year AD 70 and scattered them all over the world (even to the farthermost points of Siberia), came to a conclusion in 1948. Indeed, Israel is back on the pitch and back in play.

THE GATHERING

'Say to the house of Israel, thus says the Lord God: ... the nations shall know that I am the Lord ... when through you, I vindicate My holiness before their eyes. For I will lead you from among the nations, gather you from all the countries, and bring you into your own land.'[622] The Lord reassures the children of Israel that at the end of the second exile He will call those who are not Jewish to help them make their way home. 'See I will beckon to the Gentiles, I will lift up My banner to the peoples; They will bring your sons in their arms and carry your daughters on their shoulders.'[623] Christian organisations have for the last few decades, been assisting the Jewish Diaspora to make aliyah.[624] These are in need

---

[619] Maltz, Many Names, pp. 152–153.

[620] Prince, Destiny of Israel, p. 50.

[621] Jeremiah 25:11–12 and 32:36–37. Regarding the second exile see Jeremiah 30:18–24 and 31:8–10.

[622] Ezekiel 36:22–24.

[623] Isaiah 49:22; NIV. See also 11:11–12; 14:1–2; 60:4, 9–10.

[624] For the Jewish people to make aliyah is for them to return to live in the land of their

of prayer as well as financial support for the vital mission. *'For if the Gentiles have shared in the Jews' spiritual blessings, they owe it to the Jews to share with them their material blessings.'*[625]

OPERATION EXODUS

In 1991, the organisation Operation Exodus was born. With a view to helping the Diaspora leave the former Soviet Union, Christian businessman Gustav Scheller arranged sponsored flights, followed by chartered sailings. Over time, the ministry expanded to aid the global ingathering. A staggering 150,000 Jews have been assisted by the charity organisation in their move to the land of their forefathers. The late Gustav Scheller saw his team as representing the *fishermen* from ancient prophecy. *'For I will bring them [the Jewish people] back into their own land that I gave to their fathers. Behold, I will send many fishers, says the Lord, and they shall catch them; and afterwards I will send many hunters, and they shall hunt them out of every mountain and high hill and cleft of the rocks.'*[626] Jeremiah foresaw two different seasons. The fishing season relates to the time when Gentiles would physically help the Jews to return to Israel. What follows thereafter is the hunting season, which refers to when enemies would pursue and persecute them.

HUNTING SEASON

Here is a report of the persecution already faced by Soviet Jews at the turn of the millennium: *'Ultra-nationalist groups are openly inciting against the Jews in Siberia. I have seen signs on walls in cities; I have seen newspapers where they call for the extinction of the Jews. I have a strong sense we are in a countdown ... many of our intercessors ... have picked up in the Spirit that we are heading*

---

forefathers.
[625] Romans 15:27; NIV.
[626] Jeremiah 16:15c–16.

for turbulent times.'[627] Having spent some months working with the above organisation in Siberia in 2011, I can honestly say that the social climate is increasingly hostile to Jews. I witnessed anti-Semitic graffiti and met a number of Russian Jewish professionals, who spoke of the maltreatment they had suffered.[628]

READ THE SCOREBOARD

It's hard to imagine Israel not being the underdog of global politics. Yet God's oft-reiterated plan to purify them is not easy to ignore. The Bible informs us that the nation of Israel will embrace the Lamb of God, who will cleanse them and fill them with His Holy Spirit[629]. At that time, in the not-so-distant future, the Jewish remnant will take a hold of the New Covenant; the global implications of which will be *'life from the dead'*[630]. Their day of glory is coming.

> *'The sons of your oppressors ... shall come to you; all those who once despised you ... shall call you, "The city of the Lord, Zion, the Holy One of Israel." Instead of you being forsaken and hated ... I will make you an everlasting majesty ... then you shall know that ... your Redeemer is the Mighty One of Jacob ... Your people, every one of them, shall be righteous, and they shall possess the land forever ... I, the Lord, will hasten it in its proper time.'*[631]

---

[627] Gustav Scheller, *Operation Exodus: Prophecy Being Fulfilled* (Bournemouth, 2011 edn), p. 125.

[628] These professionals included a lawyer and surgeons (one of whom was the mayor of a town).

[629] See Ezekiel 36:25–32.

[630] Romans 11:12, 15.

[631] Isaiah 60:14–16, 21.

THE FINAL COUNTDOWN

Let's take a stroll down memory lane one last time. The year was 1986 and the music charts was topped by *Europe* with the electrifying song, 'The Final Countdown'. How timely! *'From the sign of the return of Jerusalem to Jewish hands we can safely say that we are now living in the countdown days to the return of the Messiah and the establishment of His kingdom on earth.'*[632] A timer was set in motion from the moment the Jews historically regained their ancient capital. When the prophetic clock strikes midnight the world will witness the second coming of Jesus, Son of God.[633]

EVEN THE SCORE

Until that time, the *end of the age* will be marked by hardship, not just for the nations but also the children of Israel. Before they enter glory, they must first endure the time of *Jacob's trouble*.[634] In Derek Prince's own words: *'Far from predicting peace when Israel is restored to her territory, the Bible warns us there will be a time of tribulation and anguish without parallel in Jewish history. And considering Jewish history, that is a startling statement.'*[635] If you are wondering why perilous times await them, consider ancient Egypt. God encouraged Pharaoh's harsh hand to weigh heavily on the enslaved Hebrews. It would stir them out of their comfort zone, so that they would welcome God's escape plan. Thus, the persecution and pain was for a purpose.[636] That is not to say that those who are responsible for inflicting the pain will go unpunished. We shouldn't forget that Pharaoh's army and chariots were swallowed up in the sea of God's anger.

---

[632] O'Higgins, *In Israel Today*, pp. 22–23.

[633] See Luke 21:24, 27.

[634] See Jeremiah 30:4–7; Isaiah 17:4–6; Zechariah 13:8–9; Matthew 24:15–22; Mark 13:14–20.

[635] Prince, *End Times*, p. 39; see also Jeremiah 30:4–7.

[636] This is also true of Gentiles – whether we're Christians or not. Because of our rebellion, God allows hardships to come, in the hope that it will wake us up and save us from ultimate disaster.

Similarly, all contemporary enemies of Israel will be dealt with severely. *'God can and has punished Israel, but anyone else who tries will be shattered'*[637] In the fullness of time, when Israel is ominously surrounded by all the nations that shake the fist and gnash their teeth at her, the Lord God of Israel will deliver her. *'In that day the Lord shall defend the inhabitants of Jerusalem ... In that day I shall seek to exterminate all the nations that come up against Jerusalem.'*[638] God will even the score and take revenge on behalf of His people, Israel.

STRIKER OR DEFENDER?

The Cross speaks of mercy. Yet, equally it signifies God's justice and judgement. As surely as the Cross satisfied the requirements of Kingdom justice[639] so too it set in motion the timer for judgement. Thankfully, we are still living in the season of grace, when there is time to get off the wrong road. But Jesus will soon be moving from the Mercy Seat to the Judgement Seat; no longer seen to be the meek Lamb of God, but the majestic Lion of Judah.

People of Ireland, a question must be answered without delay: Are we pro- or anti-Zionism? Are we pro-Jewish or anti-Semitic? There's no such thing as neutral with regards to this subject. We're either forward strikers on the attack shooting at Israel, or we are positioned in defence of her reputation supporting her right to exist. Let's not forget the challenging words of the Israeli Arabs quoted in this study – Arabs who are genuine witnesses of life in Israel, not propaganda pushers like so many of their deceived brothers. Father Gabriel Naddaf boldly calls on all people everywhere to *'End (the) Witch Hunt'* of Israel and to *'end your witch hunt of the only free country in the region.'*[640]

---

[637] Sid Roth, *Time is Running Short* (Pennsylvania, 1991 edn), p. 11.

[638] Zechariah 12:8–9. See also 12:3; Deuteronomy 32:43; Isaiah 29:8; 49:25–26; Jeremiah 30:16; Joel 3:21.

[639] At the Cross, punishment was procured and the price was paid in full for the sin of mankind.

[640] JNN, 27 September 2014, alluding to *Times of Israel*.

ON THE STANDS

In March 2015, in the run-up to the emergency general election in Israel, Mohammed Zoabi made the following speech at a Likud rally in favour of the nation's Prime Minister, Benjamin Netanyahu: *'I'm a proud Israeli Arab Zionist. I came to support a leader of every single citizen of Israel. I came to support a leader who will never give up or concede; the time of the Jewish people giving up and conceding on Israel is over.'*[641] It's clear that this young Israeli Arab places no trust in a 'Land for Peace' deal. Mohammed is the nephew of pro-Hamas Member of Parliament, Hanin Zoabi. (If Israel were really not the democratic republic that it claims to be, why ever are pro-terror Arabs allowed to hold seats in government?) Here's a man who is evidently not afraid to stand for the truth. Along those lines, any Christian who doesn't personally stand for the God of Israel must ask himself if he stands for Jesus Christ, because Jesus is the God of Israel.

BIASED COMMENTATORS

Unjustifiably, the nations of the world draw a distinction between terror against non-Jews and terror against Jews. When ISIS wields their wicked weapons against civilians, the world is in uproar. And rightly so. Yet, when Jewish men, women, children and babies are burned or bombed, rammed or hacked, shot or slashed, it's hush-hush: the world does not want to know. This is because, for various reasons already outlined, people generally want to believe that, *'The Jew is not the attacked but the attacker'*. The person who expressed this statement apparently believed he was speaking on behalf of God, because he also said, *'by defending myself against the Jew, I am fighting for the work of the Lord.'* Would you agree with such a person? This is an important question to ask yourself. As righteous and justifiable as these statements may appear, the cruel truth of the matter is that they paved the path to genocide and can, in actuality, be found in the

---

[641] Ibid, 16 March 2015, alluding to *Arutz-7*.

bestselling book '*Mein Kampf*'.[642] How does that mindset and its ultimate end differ from what we see taking place today? Can the world afford to turn a blind eye to the 'Autofada' terror method (which began in November, 2014 and continues to this day), whereby, you will recall, Muslim Israelis are encouraged by their religious leaders to use their personal vehicles to ram into Jewish civilians queueing in public places? Adolf Hitler would certainly have been an advocate of such inhumane acts. In fact, tension is indeed mounting around the globe towards the Jews of the Diaspora, as the media-seduced, misinformed nations point the condemning finger. Be that as it may, the world's terrorists and their supporters will *not* have the last say as their plan to obliterate Israel will not be accomplished. In the words of the late David Pawson: '*They [Israel] may have been disciplined, but they have not been destroyed. God will never allow his people Israel to disappear ... Its continued existence is one of the proofs that God ... is real.*' [643] This same God is impartial, unbiased and true. Israel's life may indeed be *on the line*, but she will never be a *flat liner*.

COMPLETING THE CIRCUIT

Israel will cross the finish line. The salvation plan that was born (some four thousand years ago) in Israel will come full circle. Here's a New Testament verse quoting an ancient prophet: '*Even though the number of Israel's sons were as the sand of the sea, only a remnant will be saved, for He will finish the work and round it out in righteousness: for thoroughly and with dispatch the Lord will execute His decree on the earth.*'[644] That which began with the call of God-fearing Abraham will finish with the descendants of his bloodline – namely, the redeemed remnant with their returned Messiah King. Thankfully, there is good news also for the Gentiles:

---

[642] Extracts from *Mein Kampf* by Adolf Hitler.
https://www.yadvashem.org/docs/extracts-from-mein-kampf.html> (12 February 2021).
[643] Pawson, *Unlocking the Bible*, p. 633.
[644] Romans 9:27-8.

The redeemed of the nations will join them. This is why it is imperative, on an individual and national level, that we get with the programme. It's God's programme, not Israel's. The destiny of our little nation depends on our treatment of God's first nation. *'Nations determine their destiny by how they respond to the restoration of God's people.'*[645]

GAME OVER

Hey, Ireland! Israel's on the line, and she wants to know if we'll take the call. If we wait too long, the line may be cut off. In the years leading up to the Holocaust, Jabotinsky was one of the leading voices who pleaded with his people not to ignore the signs of the times. In his own prophetic words he warned: *'Time is running short!'* Tragically, too few heeded his voice. Then, time ran out. Before we know it, Ireland, it will all be finished ... time will run out.

> *Kick off ... excitement ... thrills ... foul play ... penalty ... Half-time ... Hope ... excitement ... suspense ... tension ...*
> *Game over.*

> *'No extra time.'*

---

[645] Prince, *End Times*, p. 157.

Appendices

Appendix 1

Broadsheet.ie article, 16 November 2011

'Ireland "Most Hostile Country in Europe" Towards Israel.'

Hatred of Israel reaches new levels in Ireland

An outrageous anti-Israel display was held over the weekend on Dublin's main pedestrian street, presenting IDF soldiers as Nazi troops.

As part of the display, sponsored by the Dublin City Council, a group of pro-Palestinian activists set up a model of the separation fence and an IDF roadblock.

The activists dressed up as soldiers and beat, humiliated and pointed their weapons at other activists dressed as Palestinians, in front of thousands of Irish citizens and tourists.

The display joins accusations voiced against Israel at the Irish parliament last week, on the backdrop of claims that Israel 'kidnapped', abused and undressed Irish nationals who took part in a Gaza-bound flotilla stopped by the Israeli army recently.

Israel has strongly denied the accusations.

But that's not all. A Facebook group launched about two months ago called for heavy rocks to be thrown at the Israeli Embassy building in Dublin. Anti-Israel elements recently vandalized a Dublin auditorium slated to host a concert by Israeli singer Izhar Ashdot.

The Facebook accounts of Israeli Embassy officials have been attacked by Irish hackers and, in addition, anti-Israel elements are attempting to disrupt an Israeli film festival organized by the embassy in Dublin next week.

'The Irish government is feeding its people with anti-Israel hatred,' an Israeli official argued. 'What we are seeing here is clear anti-Semitism.'

Foreign Ministry sources said Ireland had undoubtedly become the most hostile country to Israel in the European Union, 'pushing all of Europe's countries to a radical and uncompromising approach.'

BROADSHEET news online: www.broadsheet.ie

Appendix 2

Former Israeli ambassador Boaz Modai's op-ed in the *Irish Times*, 11 October 2012, in response to Justin Kilcullen's op-ed in which Trócaire called for an EU ban on goods from Jewish settlements in the West Bank

'Call to Ban Imports from Settlements is Misplaced.'

An NGO's request for an embargo on goods from Jews in the West Bank is mere gesture politics, writes BOAZ MODAI.

AS AN Israeli, coming from a country with a very strong tradition and ethos of aid to less-developed countries, I have great admiration and respect for the ideals and practical work of NGOs around the world.

Irish NGOs have an especially good reputation internationally. Trócaire is particularly distinguished, working in 28 countries across troubled regions of the world like Africa, Asia, Latin America and the Middle East.

However, I find highly objectionable the actions of Trócaire in recent days — calling for an EU ban on goods from Jewish communities in the West Bank — and the arguments set forth in the opinion piece by Trócaire's executive director Justin Kilcullen ('Impose ban on imports from Israeli settlements', October 4th).

As I'm sure Mr Kilcullen is well aware, there are many cases around the world of disputed territory, unresolved conflict etc, yet Trócaire sees fit to single out Israel, and Israel alone, in a call for sanctions. As Trócaire is an NGO, I believe it is improper for it to involve itself in a partisan international agenda against Israel — the only democracy in the Middle East and the only country in that troubled region where NGOs are free to work and say what they like.

I also doubt if all donors to Trócaire share the same one-sided political view expressed by Mr Kilcullen – I assume they do not.

Mr Kilcullen's opinion piece is full of inaccuracies and bereft of proper context. It is not correct that over '500,000' Israelis live in Judaea and Samaria. Their number is about 350,000. He states that 42 per cent of West Bank land is allocated to Jewish 'settlements'. In fact, Jewish towns and villages cover less than two per cent of this territory.

True, some other space is taken up by security zones, but people like Mr Kilcullen never like to say why such security is necessary. It is because Jews in Judaea and Samaria live in daily fear of assault, or worse, at the hands of Palestinian extremists.

By contrast, the fifth of Israel's population who are Muslims are subject to no such fears and insecurities within Israel. In the West Bank, Jewish towns and villages exist only in Area C, a largely barren area that incorporates a mere four per cent of the Palestinian population.

In other words, 96 per cent of the Palestinian population live in parts of Judaea and Samaria where there are no Jews living at all. Furthermore, there have been no new settlements since 1998; the only construction for Jews in this area since then is within the already existing ones.

People also need to take into account the damaging consequences of a ban on goods from Jewish communities in the West Bank. Currently, 15,000 Arab Palestinians are employed in these settlements (the number was much higher in the 1990s, before the tragic second Intifada, but fortunately the number has been increasing again in recent years because of the relative calm and growing prosperity in the West Bank).

The average wage earned by Arab Palestinians in agricultural and industrial centres is double the average West Bank Palestinian income. A ban on goods would have a negligible impact on the Israeli economy (Jewish settlers could easily move to Israel proper and re-invest there). But it would have a devastating impact on the Palestinian economy, such as higher unemployment and diminished purchasing power.

The last thing the West Bank needs is damage to its cohesion and stability. This is a classic example of pernicious 'gesture politics' that would only lead to suffering for people on the ground; maybe this explains why even the Palestinian Authority does not support this idea of a boycott.

The underlying message in Justin Kilcullen's argument is that the Jewish presence in the West Bank is the main obstacle to a final, comprehensive peace between Israel and the Palestinians. This is simply not true. There were no Jewish communities in the West Bank before 1967, yet that did not stop the wider Arab world constantly trying to destroy Israel, or the terrorism of Palestinians themselves (the PLO was founded in 1964, a time when there wasn't a Jew anywhere in Judaea and Samaria).

Israel has repeatedly traded land for peace: in 1979, after peace was signed with Egypt, Israel evacuated all its citizens who lived in the Sinai; in 2005, as a unilateral peace offering to Palestinians, it evacuated its citizens from Gaza – only to be met with more ferocious terrorism and rocket attacks from Gaza. The Israeli government has stated its willingness to negotiate more land swaps with the Palestinians if only they would agree to come to the negotiating table. But they do not.

Lastly, I condemn a disturbing, growing problem in recent years, namely the politicisation of charity, whereby NGOs such as Trócaire have become manipulated, within and without, by those with a radical left agenda which demonises Israel as the cause of the problems in the Middle East. As we have all seen over the past two years of the Arab Spring, with tens of thousands of Arabs slaughtered by other Arabs, this is clearly an absurdity.

(Boaz Modai is a former ambassador of Israel to Ireland.)

See: http://www.irishtimes.com/opinion/call-to-ban-imports-from-settlements-is-misplaced-1.550763

Appendix 3

Article published in the Sunday Independent by filmmaker Nicky Larkin, 11 March 2012

'Israel is a refuge, but a refuge under siege.'

Through making a film about the Israeli-Arab conflict, artist Nicky Larkin found his allegiances swaying.

I used to hate Israel. I used to think the Left was always right. Not anymore. Now I loathe Palestinian terrorists. Now I see why Israel has to be hard. Now I see the Left can be Right – as in right-wing. So why did I change my mind so completely?

Strangely, it began with my anger at Israel's incursion into Gaza in December 2008 which left over 1,200 Palestinians dead, compared to only 13 Israelis. I was so angered by this massacre I posed in the striped scarf of the Palestinian Liberation Organisation for an art show catalogue.

Shortly after posing in that PLO scarf, I applied for funding from the Irish Arts Council to make a film in Israel and Palestine. I wanted to talk to these soldiers, to challenge their actions – and challenge the Israeli citizens who supported them.

I spent seven weeks in the area, dividing my time evenly between Israel and the West Bank. I started in Israel. The locals were suspicious. We were Irish – from a country which is one of Israel's chief critics – and we were filmmakers. We were the enemy.

Then I crossed over into the West Bank. Suddenly, being Irish wasn't a problem. Provo graffiti adorned The Wall. Bethlehem was Las Vegas for Jesus-freaks – neon crucifixes punctuated by posters of martyrs.

These martyrs followed us throughout the West Bank. They

watched from lampposts and walls wherever we went. Like Jesus in the old Sacred Heart pictures.

But the more I felt the martyrs watching me, the more confused I became. After all, the Palestinian mantra was one of 'non-violent resistance'. It was their motto, repeated over and over like responses at a Catholic mass.

Yet when I interviewed Hind Khoury, a former Palestinian government member, she sat forward angrily in her chair as she refused to condemn the actions of the suicide bombers. She was all aggression.

This aggression continued in Hebron, where I witnessed swastikas on a wall. As I set up my camera, an Israeli soldier shouted down from his rooftop position. A few months previously I might have ignored him as my political enemy. But now I stopped to talk. He only talked about Taybeh, the local Palestinian beer.

Back in Tel Aviv in the summer of 2011, I began to listen more closely to the Israeli side. I remember one conversation in Shenkin Street – Tel Aviv's most fashionable quarter, a street where everybody looks as if they went to art college. I was outside a cafe interviewing a former soldier.

He talked slowly about his time in Gaza. He spoke about 20 Arab teenagers filled with ecstasy tablets and sent running towards the base he'd patrolled. Each strapped with a bomb and carrying a hand-held detonator.

The pills in their bloodstream meant they felt no pain. Only a headshot would take them down.

Conversations like this are normal in Tel Aviv. I began to experience the sense of isolation Israelis feel. An isolation that began in the ghettos of Europe and ended in Auschwitz.

Israel is a refuge – but a refuge under siege, a refuge where rockets rain death from the skies. And as I made the effort to empathise, to look at the world through their eyes. I began a new intellectual journey. One that would not be welcome back home.

The problem began when I resolved to come back with a film that showed both sides of the coin. Actually there are many more than two. Which is why my film is called *Forty Shades of Grey*. But only one side was wanted back in Dublin. My peers expected me to come back with an attack on Israel. No grey areas were acceptable.

An Irish artist is supposed to sign boycotts, wear a PLO scarf, and remonstrate loudly about The Occupation. But it's not just artists who are supposed to hate Israel. Being anti-Israel is supposed to be part of our Irish identity, the same way we are supposed to resent the English.

But hating Israel is not part of my personal national identity. Neither is hating the English. I hold an Irish passport, but nowhere upon this document does it say I am a republican, or a Palestinian.

My Irish passport says I was born in 1983 in Offaly. The Northern Troubles were something Anne Doyle talked to my parents about on the nine o'clock News. I just wanted to watch Father Ted.

So I was frustrated to see Provo graffiti on the wall in the West Bank. I felt the same frustration emerge when I noticed the missing 'E' in a 'Free Palestin' graffiti on a wall in Cork. I am also frustrated by the anti-Israel activists' attitude to freedom of speech.

Free speech must work both ways. But back in Dublin, whenever I speak up for Israel, the Fiachras and Fionas look at me aghast, as if I'd pissed on their paninis.

This one-way freedom of speech spurs false information. The Boycott Israel brigade is a prime example. They pressurised Irish supermarkets to remove all Israeli produce from their shelves – a move that directly affected the Palestinian farmers who produce most of their fruit and vegetables under the Israeli brand.

But worst of all, this boycott mentality is affecting artists. In August 2010, the Ireland-Palestine Solidarity Campaign got 216 Irish artists to sign a pledge undertaking to boycott the Israeli state. As an artist I have friends on this list – or at least I had.

I would like to challenge my friends about their support for this boycott. What do these armchair sermonisers know about Israel? Could they name three Israeli cities, or the main Israeli industries?

But I have more important questions for Irish artists. What happened to the notion of the artist as a free-thinking individual? Why have Irish artists surrendered to groupthink on Israel? Could it be due to something as crude as career-advancement?

Artistic leadership comes from the top. Aosdana, Ireland's State-sponsored affiliation of creative artists, has also signed the boycott. Aosdana is a big player. Its members populate Arts Council funding panels.

Some artists could assume that if their name is on the same boycott sheet as the people assessing their applications, it can hardly hurt their chances. No doubt Aosdana would dispute this assumption. But the perception of a preconceived position on Israel is hard to avoid.

Looking back now over all I have learnt, I wonder if the problem is a lot simpler.

Perhaps our problem is not with Israel, but with our own over-stretched sense of importance – a sense of moral superiority disproportional to the importance of our little country?

Any artist worth his or her salt should be ready to change their mind on receipt of fresh information. So I would urge every one of those 216 Irish artists who pledged to boycott the Israeli state to spend some time in Israel and Palestine. Maybe when you come home you will bin your scarf. I did.

www.facebook.com/fortyshades

http://www.independent.ie/opinion/analysis/nicky-larkin-israel-is-a-refuge-but-a-refuge-under-siege-3046227.html

Appendix 4

Former Labour Councillor Richard Humphreys' speech at a Dublin city pro-Israel rally, 2012

'Israel's Right to Defend itself must be Respected.'

'This is a day when we stand in solidarity, friendship and dialogue with Israel. Israel's right to exist must be acknowledged, as the only Jewish state in the world and the only liberal secular democracy in the Middle East.'

'Any state that has a right to exist must also have a right to defend itself. There is no country in the world that could tolerate hundreds of rocket attacks launched on its territory, bringing hardship, fear, disruption, injury and death to its people.'

'This rally for peace in Israel is also a moment of optimism. This first major rally for peace in Israel is a historic moment and a sign that the tide of opinion is turning. There are many signs that Irish society is becoming more balanced and realistic in addressing issues relating to the Middle East. Anti-Semitic attitudes are increasingly being challenged – and the most insidious form of anti-Semitism is the systematic attempt to impose a standard to judge Israel which is not used to judge any other country. Many Irish champions of human rights are surprisingly silent about the brutal outrages perpetrated by the terrorist Hamas regime against women, gay people, or political opponents, and about many vicious attacks on human rights in some of Israel's near neighbours. This double standard is now being challenged, which I find very encouraging.'

'The inherent fascism of the attempt to impose a cultural boycott on Israel is also being named and exposed. As a Labour Party councillor I especially welcome the presence of the Tánaiste and

Labour Party Leader Eamon Gilmore at the Israel Film Days, organised by the Embassy of Israel, in November 2011.'

'It is hard to talk about solidarity with Israel without also acknowledging the enormously positive contribution that the Jewish people have made to society, not just in Israel but in Ireland and across the world. On a personal note I come to this issue with an enormous sense of gratitude for the opportunity I had to work for Ireland's first Jewish Cabinet Minister, the Labour Party's Mervyn Taylor. I am also profoundly grateful for the insights that so many Jewish writers and thinkers have shared with the world. Intellectuals of Jewish heritage such as Jacob Bronowski, Viktor Frankl, Irvin Yalom, Carl Sagan, Alain de Botton and many others are among the most inspiring figures of modern civilization.'

'As well as solidarity and optimism, I think it is also important to emphasise the need for compassion. Each death or injury of an innocent civilian in Gaza is a tragedy which must primarily be lain at the door of Hamas, but which also calls for restraint and for the path of peace. It is essential to recognise that there is a Palestinian perspective and there is Palestinian suffering. Many Arab commentators have taken the lead in pointing out that a great deal of that suffering is self-inflicted but it is real nonetheless. A lasting peace must be founded on dialogue between enemies and on a historic effort to accommodate both sets of identities.'

'I congratulate Naomi Gibson and the others involved in organising this event and I hope it is another milestone on the road to a more balanced view of Israel in our society.'

(Mr Justice Richard Humphreys was appointed to the High Court in 2015.)

Appendix 5

Article in *Israel Today*, 15 June 2015

'Top World Generals: No Israeli War Crimes in Gaza.'

Authors: *Israel Today* Staff

Israel at the weekend published the findings of 10 of the world's top generals who concluded that, contrary to widespread allegations, the Jewish state had not committed war crimes during last summer's Gaza war.

The delegation, headed by Chairman of the NATO Military Committee General Klaus Naumann said in a statement that its 'mission to Israel was unprecedented. We were the first such multi-national group of senior officers to visit the country. We were granted a level of access to the Israeli government and Defence Force that has not been afforded to any other group...'

After vigorously investigating the Israeli army's conduct during the war, the group found that, 'Israeli forces acted proportionately as required by the laws of armed conflict and often went beyond the required legal principles of proportionality, necessity and discrimination.'

In fact, the foreign generals noted that on many occasions, 'the measures taken were often far in excess of the requirements of the Geneva Conventions.' For instance, Israel repeatedly put off a major military response despite escalating terrorist rocket fire. And once war had begun, the IDF routinely paused military action to spare civilians, even though doing so allowed Hamas and its allies to re-group and replenish.

Addressing the high number of Palestinian civilian casualties, the generals said this was the sad, but inevitable reality of conducting war from such a densely populated area.

'We recognize that some of these deaths were caused by error and misjudgement ... But we also recognize that the majority of deaths were the tragic inevitability of defending against an enemy that deliberately carries out attacks from within the civilian population,' read the findings.

Earlier this year, Israel invited two leading American legal experts, Michael Schmitt and John Merriam, to likewise probe its conduct during the 50-day conflict that devastated much of Gaza.

Both Schmitt and Merriam lecture on the law of armed conflict at the US Naval War College, and Schmitt also advises on the topic at NATO, Harvard and Exeter.

Their survey took a sympathetic, if not uncritical, look at Israel's 'siege mentality' and the various other factors that create the, 'specific operational and strategic environment in which the IDF must fight.'

And while Israel's aggressiveness in some scenarios and the resulting collateral damage might be viewed by some as excessive and contentious, the authors determined that Israeli military policy and practice fell within legally acceptable boundaries.

'While there are certainly Israeli legal positions that may be contentious, we found that their approach to targeting is consistent with the law and, in many cases, worthy of emulation,' read the survey's concluding sentence.

BIBLIOGRAPHY

Boyne, John, *The Boy in the Striped Pyjamas*, David Fickling Books, 2010 edition (2006)

Crown Tamir, Hela, *Israel, History in a Nutshell: Highlighting the War and Military History*, TsurTsina Publications, 2011

Delap, Sean & McCormack, Paul, *Uncovering History*, Folens, 2007

Fachler, Yanky, *God's Little Errand Boys*, The History Publisher (an imprint of the Universal Publishing Group), 2011

Facius, Johannes, *As in the Days of Noah*, Sovereign World, 1997

Facius, Johannes, *Hastening the Coming of the Messiah*, Sovereign World, 2001

Finto, Don, *Your People Shall be My People*, Regal Publications, 2001

Gibson, Richard, *The Unusual Suspects*, Christian Focus Publications, 2008

Glashouwer, Rev Willem J.J., *Why Israel?*, Christians for Israel, 2001

Goldstein, Don, *I Have a Friend Who's Jewish Do You?* Shivat Tzion Ministries, 1986

Gray, Sr Ena, *Healing the Past: Catholic Anti-Semitism*, Veritas, 2010 edition (2009)

Hedding, Malcolm, *Understanding Israel*, Zion's Gate International, 2002 edition (1990)

Keogh, Dermot & Whelan, Diarmuid, *Gerald Goldberg: A Tribute*, Mercier Press, 2008

Maltz, Steve, *The Land of Many Names*, Authentic Lifestyle, 2003

O'Donovan, Edel & Kirwan, Fiona, *Take the Plunge*, Folens, 2005

O'Higgins, Paul & Nuala, *Christianity without Religion: The Message that's Changing the World*, Reconciliation Outreach, 2003

O'Higgins, Paul & Nuala, *Have You Received the Holy Spirit?: Receiving*

The Double Gift of the Holy Spirit, Reconciliation Library, 2013 edition (2000)

O'Higgins, Paul & Nuala, *In Israel Today with Yeshua: A Believer's Guide to Israel*, Reconciliation Outreach, 2004 edition (1987)

O'Higgins, Paul & Nuala, *New Testament Believers & the Law*, Reconciliation Outreach, 2003

O'Siadhail, Michael, *The Gossamer Wall*, Bloodaxe Books, 1982

Pawson, David, *Unlocking the Bible*, Collins (a division of HarperCollins Publishers), 2007 edition (1999)

Prince, Derek, *Prophetic Guide to the End Times: Facing the Future without Fear*, Chosen Books (a division of Baker Publishing Group), 2008

Prince, Derek, *The Destiny of Israel and the Church*, DPM, 1999 edition (Word UK, 1992)

Rivlin, Ray, *Jewish Ireland: A Social History*, The History Press Ireland, 2011 (an updated version of *Shalom Ireland*, published in 2003)

Roth, Sid, *Time is Running Short*, Destiny Image Publishers, 1991 edition (1990)

Scheller, Gustav, *Operation Exodus: Prophecy being Fulfilled*, Ebenezer Emergency Fund, 2011 edition (1998)

Silver, David, *A Slow Train Coming: God's Redemption Plan for Israel and the Church*, Lulu Enterprises, 2007

Taylor, Marilyn, *17 Martin Street*, O'Brien Press, 2011 edition (2008)

Uris, Leon, *Exodus*, Corgi Books (published by Transworld Publishers Ltd), 1992 edition (1958)

Yemini, Ben-Dror, *Industry of Lies: Media, Academia and the Israeli-Arab Conflict*, ISGAP, 2017 edition (2014)

PLAGIARISM STATEMENT

Quotations from published and unpublished sources are indicated in the footnotes and acknowledgements where appropriate. The source or statistic is also indicated as is the source, published or unpublished, of any material drawn from multimedia sources in researching the events reported on.

This book has not been created to be specific to any individual's or organizations' situation or needs. Every effort has been made to make this book as accurate as possible. This book should serve only as a general guide and not as the ultimate source of subject information. This book contains information that might be dated and is intended only to educate and entertain. The author shall have no liability or responsibility to any person or entity regarding any loss or damage incurred, or alleged to have incurred, directly or indirectly, by the information contained in this book.

ABOUT THE AUTHOR

Audrey lives with her husband Tom in southern Ireland.

Withdrawn from

South Dublin Libraries
www.southdublinlibraries.ie

9 781739 909802